STARBUCKED

STARBUCKED

A DOUBLE TALL TALE

OF

CAFFEINE, COMMERCE,

AND CULTURE

Taylor Clark

LITTLE, BROWN AND COMPANY
New York   Boston   London

To Gina,
my little sis,
a great lover of coffee —
even if she drowns it
in vanilla syrup

Little, Brown and Company
Hachette Book Group USA
237 Park Avenue, New York, NY 10017
Visit our Web site at www.HachetteBookGroupUSA.com

First Edition: November 2007

Library of Congress Cataloging-in-Publication Data

Clark, Taylor,
    Starbucked : a double tall tale of caffeine, commerce, and culture / Taylor Clark.
        p.   cm.
    Includes index.
    ISBN-10: 0-316-01348-X
    ISBN-13: 978-0-316-01348-2
    1. Starbucks Coffee Company.   2. Coffee industry—History.
3. Coffee—Social aspects.   4. Coffee shops—Social aspects.   5. Corporate culture—Case studies.   6. International business enterprises—United States—Case studies.   I. Title.   II. Title: Caffeine, commerce, and culture.
    HD9199.U52S733   2007
    338'17373 — dc22   2007013074

10 9 8 7 6 5 4 3 2 1

Q-FF

Book design by Brooke Koven

Printed in the United States of America

CONTENTS

STARBUCKED

INTRODUCTION

The Experiment

Depending on your ideological tilt — and, really, on how much you like coffee — it was either an assault on decency itself or the most brilliant decision Howard Schultz ever made.

In early 1991, just a few years after he had scraped together the money to buy a fledgling Seattle coffee company called Starbucks, Schultz's most profitable café sat on a bustling intersection in the chic Robson Street shopping district of Vancouver, British Columbia. Aesthetically speaking, this coffeehouse was unimpressive; it occupied a dilapidated, musty old space, and it had next to no room for patrons to sit down. Yet the store was a living testament to the world's sudden, intense, and puzzling thirst for expensive coffee drinks. In an age when concoctions like the latte still seemed exotic and obscure, this tiny Starbucks served ten thousand people *each week* — and those were just the ones who could get in. The café was so busy, its lines so endless, that the store's employees were certain they were turning away hundreds of potential customers every day.

Which didn't sit well with Schultz. A young and ambitious former housewares salesman who grew up broke in Brooklyn's housing projects, Schultz had been racing to snare customers and expand his chain since the day he bought it. When he acquired Starbucks in 1987, the company's store count stood at eleven; barely three years later, he had increased its size nearly eightfold, to eighty-five cafés. So Schultz was not one to take lost customers lightly. For years, he had been pressing his Vancouver Realtor to find another space in the neighborhood, but nothing suitable turned up. And to make matters worse, Schultz learned that the landlord of his Robson Street store was planning to close down and gut the building within a few years, which would leave Starbucks without its main cash cow for as long as it took to complete renovations. For a company still struggling to break even selling coffee drinks that many considered as faddish as fondue or fanny packs, this was distressing news. In 1989 alone, Starbucks had lost $1.2 million; it couldn't afford to lose much more.

But as unwelcome as this information was, it gave Schultz an excuse to try an idea he'd been mulling over privately for quite a while — something that, as far as anyone could remember, had never been attempted before; something any sensible businessman would have called outright crazy. One day, while talking to his real estate agent about options for locations nearby, Schultz revealed the proposal.

"What about the restaurant across the street?" he asked.

"What are you talking about?" the Realtor said.

"The one kitty-corner from us. I've been in there, and it's dead."

"I don't think they're going to make it, and I doubt you could afford the rent," the shocked Realtor replied, "but are you saying you'd open another one across the street?"

"I would."

With that, Schultz set in motion a peculiar experiment: what would happen if he put a Starbucks literally within spitting distance of another Starbucks? (Their addresses were 1099 Robson Street and 1100 Robson Street — they were that close.) Schultz justified his plan to skeptical employees and investors in two ways. First, he explained that the move was guaranteed to generate dozens of news stories about the coffee chain that was insane enough to put two cafés across the street from each other, which would amount to free advertising for their cash-strapped company. Second, he argued that the twin Starbucks stores could develop completely separate clienteles if they looked different enough — essentially, if the company minimized the impression that someone had placed a giant mirror in the middle of the intersection. To this end, Schultz gave the new location a darker, more subdued design, with tones of black cherry, deep green, and white, which was at least marginally dissimilar to the first café's touches of chrome and its emphasis on the loud colors of the Italian flag. On March 2, 1991, the dual-Starbucks intersection opened for business.

That a Starbucks could open across the street from another Starbucks at all is strange enough, but the truly mind-boggling part of the story is this: instead of laughing Starbucks out of town for doing something so presumptuous, customers flocked to the new café as if the nearest alternative were out in the wilds of the Yukon. Schultz expected the two stores to eat away at each other's sales, but nothing of the sort happened. As he'd hoped, they attracted mostly different crowds; the new café lured the well-heeled business set, while the original drew a hipper, more relaxed clientele. And both groups turned up in droves. Schultz's gamble had hit the jackpot — amazingly, his two Robson Street coffeehouses soon became the best- and second-best-performing stores in the chain. The bizarreness of this point begs to be reemphasized: Starbucks's top two stores were *fifteen yards* away from each other.

On that street in Vancouver, Schultz saw what no one else saw. He saw that each corner of the intersection had its own unique traffic flow. ("It wasn't a different neighborhood, but it had a different vibe," he later told *Newsweek* — referring, incredibly, to the other side of Robson

Street.) He saw that he could snag thousands of new customers just by making his store a few steps more convenient. But most important, he saw the sheer magnitude of society's thirst for gourmet coffee drinks. As Art Wahl, an early real estate broker for Starbucks, put it to me, "After that, we said to ourselves, 'Oh my god . . . We can put these things closer together than we ever imagined.'"

Today, of course, the multi-Starbucks nexus is a common sight. For instance, in Portland, Oregon, when people wander through the Pioneer Place mall and see the Starbucks on the first floor and another hovering directly above it on the third floor, the spectacle doesn't even merit a double take — despite the fact that a mere twelve feet of space separates them. If you stand in the right spot on Manhattan's Astor Place, you can make out *three* Starbucks: one by the subway entrance, another across the square, and a third in the bordering Barnes and Noble. We're now so accustomed to the chain's ubiquity that its café cluster bombs have become more a source of comedy than concern. Take the movie *Best in Show* (2000) in which two characters playing a married couple explain how they first met at Starbucks: "Not the same Starbucks," the husband clarifies. "We were at different Starbucks across the street from each other." This could actually happen. It probably *has* happened.

So again, depending on your particular worldview, you could see any number of things in Schultz's Robson Street gambit. Some view it as a victory for gourmet coffee or even as a welcome convenience. Others consider it a stroke of entrepreneurial genius, a monument to one of the great business stories of the past half century. And then there are those, like the comedian Lewis Black, who believe it foretells something far more dire.

"Things went fuzzy for a moment," Black wrote of his first double-Starbucks sighting, in Houston, "but when my head cleared, it felt as if God had reached down and bestowed upon me all the knowledge ever gathered since the beginning of time. I was indeed looking at the much-sought-after end of the universe."

Introduction

The Call of the Siren

Some things people need. Even the most Spartan lifestyle requires food, water, shelter, clothing, and so forth. No one in the history of humanity has ever needed a latte — much less a double tall vanilla soy latte, no foam, extra hot — yet the world's thirst for them appears unquenchable. Twenty years ago, you couldn't fill a high school gym with the number of Americans who knew what a macchiato was, but good luck finding a convenience store or gas station minimart that doesn't offer espresso drinks today. Modern society accepts a level of coffee micromanagement that would have appalled our forebears. When we see someone giving more attention to the precise, scientific application of Splenda to their morning cappuccino than they seem to bestow on their own personal hygiene, do we even bother to raise an eyebrow anymore?

Ours is a caffeinated nation. We buy more coffee than any other country in the world — almost a third of the planet's supply — and consume somewhere around 110 billion cups of it per year. There's no shortage of impressive-sounding statistics that demonstrate the little brown bean's dominance over our lives: coffee is the second-most-traded physical commodity in the world, after petroleum; four out of every five American adults drink the beverage regularly.

But these are just factoids. A better illustration of the pervasiveness of coffee in American life is currently floating around in Boston Harbor. In 1998, two researchers from the University of Massachusetts Boston performed a comprehensive chemical analysis of the harbor, and they learned something surprising in the process: its waters contain a significant amount of caffeine. The concentration was low — not even enough to give the fish a buzz — but its very presence was puzzling. Caffeine forms in only a few land-dwelling plants, so how did it get into Boston Harbor? The polite answer: human waste. Every day, the Boston metropolitan area ingests one thousand pounds of pure caffeine, a substance so potent in its crystallized form that one must don a

7

hazmat suit before handling it. Human bodies absorb only 95 percent of this, which means that a huge dose of caffeine enters the waste stream and trickles into Boston Harbor every day. The net effect of this is comparable to dumping around a million cups of coffee into the harbor each week. In fact, caffeine shows up in hundreds of the nation's rivers, lakes, and bays — as well as in treated drinking water. Edward Furlong, a U.S. Geological Survey researcher, even has a nickname for this phenomenon: "the Starbucks effect."

Starbucks didn't invent coffee, of course; it just did something with it that no one thought possible. The company took a commodity that Americans could get for a quarter at carts and diners, reshaped it into a luxury product, convinced customers to buy it at hugely inflated prices, and built stores only a few blocks apart in every major city, yet patrons continue to line up in ever-greater numbers to fork over their money. Indeed, Starbucks has grown so popular with consumers that it even has the power to turn them from sinners into churchgoers. When one Southern Baptist pastor in Cooper City, Florida, set out to boost attendance at his church's 2006 Easter service, he decided to send out a mailer promising a ten-dollar Starbucks gift card to every new parishioner. As the *Miami Herald* reported, the bait was devastatingly effective. On Easter Sunday, eighty-five hundred people — almost double the church's typical Easter attendance — showed up for the service; the church's staff actually had to turn people away at the parking lot. In the twenty-first century, apparently, the path to salvation includes pit stops for Frappuccinos.

Fueled by this cultlike popularity, Starbucks now owns its market like few other companies in recent memory. Here's a challenge: try to name the number two coffeehouse chain in America. Any ideas? The question is especially tough to answer because the company's closest competitor, the Minnesota-based Caribou Coffee, is just one twenty-fifth the size of Starbucks. In fact, if you merged all of its rivals (that is, chains with more than three stores) into one patchwork coffee goliath, it *still* wouldn't be even half the size of Starbucks. "It's like McDonald's with no Burger King or Wendy's or Subway," said Kevin Knox, a long-time Starbucks roasting expert who is now an industry consultant. "It's total domination."

With $7.8 billion in annual revenues, forty million customers a week, and more than thirteen thousand stores, Starbucks is no fondue-esque fad. It's a new American institution.

Actually, given the chain's breakneck international expansion and its ability to reshape coffee-drinking habits the world over, Starbucks is more like a global institution. Hyperbolically titled books abound these days, telling us How Velcro Shaped History and Why Paprika Matters, but with Starbucks, it's no stretch to say that the company has changed the dynamics of the modern world. It influences automotive traffic patterns, affects the welfare of some twenty-five million coffee farmers, and sways the cultural customs of entire nations toward espresso consumption. It has inserted itself into the American urban landscape more quickly and craftily than any other retail company in history, and it has forever changed the way Western companies market themselves to consumers. Former Starbucks CEO Orin Smith, speaking to *Fortune* magazine, stated all of this even more boldly: "We changed the way people live their lives, what they do when they get up in the morning, how they reward themselves, and where they meet."

When you think about it, this whole phenomenon is baffling. How could a simple coffee company attain such wide-ranging influence on society, with its luxury-priced products becoming a fixture in daily life virtually overnight? In 1989, the United States could claim a grand total of 585 coffeehouses, according to statistics from the Specialty Coffee Association of America, and most people considered the idea of a business dedicated to selling coffee by the cup to be absolute lunacy. For years, business pundits thundered predictions of the coffeehouse's impending demise; yet today, America boasts twenty-four thousand of them and counting. After decades of exponential growth, the industry is still expanding faster than ever. This sustained café explosion has been an incredible moneymaker, but it's far more than that: it's a legitimate social movement. All around the globe — both in countries with their own centuries-old café culture and in those where coffee drinking was virtually nonexistent twenty years ago — the coffeehouse template pioneered by Starbucks is becoming dominant and pervasive. Millions of people the world over have integrated cafés into the fabric of their lives, making them into second homes. So surely, there must be some astonishing secret behind the coffeehouse's raw, bewitching magnetism.

Luckily, we have the British government to help us figure these things out. In 2002, Britain's Economic and Social Research Council gave two Glasgow University professors a $250,000 grant to investigate the social factors driving the rise of café society in England. The researchers, Eric Laurier and Chris Philo, conducted an exhaustive three-year campaign into the very heart of human behavior; they became "regulars" at a coffeehouse, videotaped customers in their native environment, took extensive field notes, trained as baristas, conducted interviews with patrons and staff, and plumbed library archives for historical and literary context. The project's staggering conclusion? Coffeehouses are comfortable, welcoming places where people can enjoy time alone or with others. Among Laurier and Philo's crucial findings is the insight that the music played changes throughout the day (at night, "There is more funk. It is a hearable thing") and that a café visit is "a sequential object with a beginning, ordering, seat selecting, occupying the table, and leaving."

From this, we can draw a couple of conclusions: first, that the British government evidently plays it fast and loose with grant money; and second, that coffeehouses appeal to us on a deeper level than it might appear. Laurier and Philo's results feel underwhelming not only because they're painfully obvious and simplistic, but also because they fail to address exactly what it is about coffeehouses that makes them so enthralling to consumers. After all, cafés aren't the only warm and convivial places in Britain — so are pubs. What's more, the findings don't speak to why coffeehouses have such strong allure all over the planet, even in countries that have long avoided coffee altogether, like China and, well, England. Starbucks has certainly had a lot to do with glamorizing and popularizing the coffeehouse in America and abroad, but could it all be thanks to the company's Midas touch? Why would the concept work just as well in Shanghai as it does in Seattle?

Perhaps more important, do people *want* Starbucks to work just as well in Shanghai as it does in Seattle? For many, the answer is a resounding no. Starbucks likes to envision itself as a global good Samaritan, sprinkling community spirit and glee hither and thither like pixie dust, but the company has also kicked up a sandstorm of conflict. Foremost among the complaints are those about the chain's ubiquity; Starbucks often tests the boundaries of what consumers will accept. To illustrate, consider this question:

> *Which of the following places does* not *have a Starbucks?*
>   A. Guantanamo Bay Naval Base in Cuba
>   B. A Christian church in Munster, Indiana
>   C. Beirut, Lebanon
>   D. The town of Starbuck, Washington
>   E. The Great Wall of China

The correct answer, which was probably obvious since it doesn't seem likely to enrage anyone, is D. The tiny eastern Washington town of Starbuck lies forty long miles from the nearest Starbucks, though hundreds of tourists pop in each year and are shocked to learn that Starbuck is not the company's ancestral home. If Starbucks appears inescapable now, just wait. Howard Schultz likes to say that his company is only in "the second inning of a nine-inning game," and his goal of forty thousand stores worldwide would make Starbucks the biggest chain on the planet.

But it's not just Starbucks's ubiquity that riles tempers. To some, the company embodies all that is reprehensible about major corporations. Various critics have accused Starbucks of pillaging the environment, mistreating employees, fleecing Third World coffee growers, crushing independently owned cafés, sucking local economies dry, peddling a harmful product, and homogenizing the world. These are only the greatest hits. Not even the chain's *cups* have escaped controversy; the thought-provoking quotations Starbucks prints on its signature white paper cups have twice drawn protests, once from conservatives over a line by gay author Augusten Burroughs and once from liberals over evangelical pastor Rick Warren's statement that "You are not an accident. Your parents may not have planned you, but God did." Just about the only part of Starbucks that is *not* contentious is the bathrooms, which noncustomers in a state of extreme duress are generally free to use.*

All of these things — the Starbucks neighboring a Starbucks, the caffeinated harbor, the inquiry into the coffeehouse's seductive appeal, the heated ethical debate over the actions of Starbucks — are signs of one company's subtle impact on an entire planet. That essentially sums up the purpose of this book: to tell the story of how a major corporation, peddling a simple, age-old commodity, influences the daily life and culture of the world.

And Starbucks is a more important company than you might think. Throughout history, all civilized societies have had places where people could get together and socialize, share gossip, discuss ideas, or just unwind. These public gathering places are vital to a culture's health, and they have always reflected the unique national character of their patrons: London had its boisterous pubs, Paris its relaxed sidewalk cafés, Beijing its formal and proper teahouses, 1950s America its wholesome soda fountains and malt shops. Today, we have the cozy, indulgent coffeehouse as our social hub, and Starbucks is the first company ever to have taken this kind of communal place, standardized it,

---

*Although a Canadian man did once sue Starbucks after a faulty toilet seat smashed his penis against the bowl (don't ask — it's complicated), which, according to the *Toronto Star*, left his genitals "bruised, crushed, and rendered ineffective."

branded it, and sold it to the world at large. In effect, it's turning America's living room into the *planet's* living room. That customers across the globe have seized onto the chain and made it such an entrenched part of their lives says something significant about us all. It says that the things Starbucks provides — feelings of extravagance and invigoration, of social connection, of safe refuge — are things people desperately want. But as Starbucks spreads this American-born social institution around the world, a host of uncertainties follow. It still remains to be seen whether the company's ever-growing influence is for better or for worse.

Starbucked is divided into two sections. In part one, we investigate the mystery of why Starbucks and coffee culture gripped America so tightly and so suddenly, and we examine some related curiosities along the way. Why did Seattle become the planet's coffee epicenter? Why did Starbucks pay a firm to hypnotize its customers? Why doesn't Starbucks have any noteworthy competitors? Part two explores the ethical issues that swirl around the company as it pursues its goal of global coffee domination. Does Starbucks prey on independent cafés, as critics claim? Should we feel complicit in the plight of impoverished coffee farmers each time we buy a vanilla latte?

With every passing week, Starbucks looks more and more like a permanent fixture in the global landscape, thanks in no small part to the six new stores it opens daily. To some, this ubiquity is the height of convenience. To others, it's a sign of the impending apocalypse.

For those in the latter group, there is some consolation. If this truly is the end of the universe, at least there's comfortable seating.

PART ONE

The Rise of
the Mermaid

—1—

Life Before Lattes

Nearly a century ago, mankind discovered the secrets of the perfect cup of coffee.

These eternal truths revealed themselves not through ghostly messages in the steam of a Wisconsin secretary's cup of Yuban, but instead through a modern-day prophet of foodstuffs: Samuel Cate Prescott, a Massachusetts Institute of Technology professor who, in the first decades of the twentieth century, was one of the world's top food scientists. Prescott liked to imagine a future in which scientific analysis would make foods not just safer but ideal. A contemporary *Boston Daily Advertiser* story on him even predicted that one day, thanks to his efforts, the "application of growth-producing rays will bring forth cows the size of brontosauri, roosters the size of pterodactyls."

In 1920, Prescott's talents attracted the attention of the National Coffee Roasters Association, a group that had long been searching for a novel way to boost sluggish coffee sales. After bankrolling a string of ineffective publicity campaigns, the roasters decided it was time for a shift in tactics; coffee, they concluded, needed "a college education." Thus inspired, they issued Prescott a challenge: their group would build and staff a state-of-the-art coffee research laboratory for him at MIT if he would devote himself to uncovering the scientifically exact principles for creating the ultimate coffee elixir. Prescott accepted the mission. Armed with the very latest in beaker and Bunsen burner technology, he set out to bring coffee's Platonic ideal down to earth.

So how exactly does one go about perfecting a beverage? Prescott's answer to this was simple: you prepare it in every way you can possibly imagine and then have taste testers judge the results. At the lab, he and his staff played with all of the conceivable variables in the coffee-making process. They brewed it in pots made of copper, aluminum, nickel, glass, and many other materials; they dripped it, pressed it, and percolated it; they toyed endlessly with temperatures, grinds, and steeping times. Almost every day, Prescott would appear in MIT's main cafeteria bearing a tray loaded with cream, sugar, and two beakers of experimental coffee to try out on his crack "tasting squad" — fifteen people with expert, discriminating palates (that is, women from around campus). For three years, he watched them take their thoughtful sips, tallied their preferences, and adjusted his brewing accordingly.

By 1923, Prescott had zeroed in on perfection; his virtuosic coffee-making skills, he believed, simply could not be improved. That year, he announced his findings, a set of rules as unbendable as the laws of physics:

1. *Use one tablespoon of freshly ground coffee for every eight ounces of water.*
2. *Force these grounds through water that is a few degrees short of boiling, inside a glass or earthenware container.*
3. *Never, ever boil or reheat coffee, and never reuse the grounds.*

That was it, the culmination of years of painstaking research. Brewing the coffee of the gods was almost as easy as making toast. Anyone could do it. The elated roasters rushed to publicize the results in hundreds of newspapers and magazines, while the triumphant Prescott went on to try his hand at creating the optimal banana, ice cream, candy, milk, and cow. His guidelines for "the ideal cup of coffee" reached nearly forty million readers — and, incidentally, the formula still holds true today.

So it's not like we didn't know how to make coffee. We knew. And thus, it's truly a testament to the indomitable American spirit that we managed to violate every shred of Prescott's advice for the next fifty years.

We boiled countless pots of coffee into oblivion on stove-top percolators. We sat idly by as diner waitresses in hairnets poured us cups of mysterious brown sludge that could easily have been used as industrial paint thinner. Grim-faced, we downed concoctions that made us want to scour our tongues with sandpaper, having resigned ourselves to a fate of acrid and generally awful coffee. By the 1960s, the only true devotees of the brew left standing were truck drivers, traveling salesmen, and, well, *old* people. With this crowd representing the bleeding edge of coffee connoisseurship, it was no surprise that the American coffee habit soon plummeted to a historic nadir.

"I was born in 1945, and none of my buddies drank coffee," said Donald Schoenholt, who runs the Brooklyn-based Gillies Coffee Company, America's oldest roaster. "My friends would grab a Coke and have a cigarette in the morning because coffee tasted terrible! People would just run the tap water as hot as it could go, put a teaspoon of instant coffee in the cup, and shake it up." The situation grew so dire in the sixties that Schoenholt's father even tried to convince his seventeen-year-old son not to go into the family business — then in its 122nd year of operation — because he feared the avalanche of terrible coffee would utterly destroy the public's taste for decent beans. For many bitter years, coffee languished in beverage purgatory.

The brew's decline was particularly tragic because coffee has long been the quintessential American drink, a position it arrived at through one of the greatest public relations coups in history. In December 1773, fifty Bostonians dressed as Mohawk Indians registered their frustration with British rule by raiding three English ships and pitching the cargo, 342 crates of tea, into the harbor. The event is commonly known as the Boston Tea Party, but all of the rejoicing and merrymaking really took place in the homes of coffee importers. Suddenly, coffee drinking became a patriotic act; loyal Americans now had to resist the fondness for tea they had inherited from the British. "Tea must be universally renounced," proclaimed the revolutionary and future president John Adams — to which he added in a letter to his wife, Abigail, "I myself must be weaned, and the sooner the better."

Spurred on by this anti-tea imperative, Americans took to coffee in dramatic and decisive fashion. Boston's Green Dragon coffeehouse soon grew so popular that Daniel Webster dubbed it the "headquarters of the revolution." Almost immediately, the new national coffee habit blossomed into full-blown addiction, complete with uncontrollable cravings. In a July 1777 letter to her husband, for example, Abigail Adams told of how a group of Boston women dealt with a merchant who was rumored to be hoarding coffee beans:

> A number of females — some say a hundred, some say more — assembled with a cart and trunk, marched down to the warehouse and demanded the keys [from the merchant].
>
> Upon his finding no quarter, he delivered the keys, and they then opened the warehouse, hoisted out the coffee themselves, put it into a trunk, and drove off. A large concourse of men stood amazed, silent spectators of the whole transaction.

Coffee, a drink that symbolized productivity and vigor, soon became fused with the American way. Try to visualize the following scene: a group of grizzled cowboys gathered around a prairie campfire at nightfall, rifles leaning against their knees, talking in low voices as they brew a nice pot of tea. It seems absurd, doesn't it? Coffee is a vital part of that picture, just as it is a vital part of our national identity. The drink helped define us as a nation — industrious, energetic, and efficient — and provided the fuel of American ascendance. By the turn of the twentieth century, we were drinking half of the world's supply.

But if the coffee bean was so crucial to our lives, how did we let it decline in quality to the point where Starbucks's offering of a decent brew could spark a nationwide cultural revolution? More than anything else, the advent of gourmet coffee purveyors like Starbucks was a protest against the decrepit state of the once-proud American cup, carried out by a small band of amateur epicures who still remembered that coffee could taste good. These scattered and slightly batty men, tinkering in their spare time with beans and brews, knew nothing about coffee except that they wanted it to taste better than battery acid. Yet their experiments sparked a modern phenomenon.

To fully understand the dramatic redemption of coffee, the saga of Starbucks, and the ascendance of café culture, though, we must first travel back in time to the period when the whole caffeinated shebang began.

A Brief History of Coffee

Coffee is so pervasive in our lives and so simple to prepare — you just roast some beans, steep them in water, and drink — that the beverage seems to have been almost historically inevitable. Many of us shudder at the very idea of a world without coffee, our daily savior from the merciless ravages of fatigue. But considering all that the coffee bean had to go through in its centuries-long journey to reach the American "World's Greatest Dad" mug, we're actually lucky we ever got the drink at all.

First, there was the problem of finding it. *Coffea arabica*, the stout, leafy tree that generates all of the planet's palatable coffee, hails from the remote highlands of Ethiopia, which wasn't much of a high-traffic region in days of yore. According to one legend, humanity's first experience with coffee occurred sometime around the sixth century, when a young goatherd named Kaldi noticed that his normally placid goats were suddenly dancing jigs and turning pirouettes; they'd been nipping at the coffee trees. Kaldi popped a few berries in his mouth, found himself energized — as well as strangely inclined to talk about politics and write bad poetry — and thus the world discovered the coffee bean.

So now that we had a hard, bland seed that made goats hyper, what were we supposed to do with it? The Ethiopian natives tried fermenting the beans into a cold wine, making them into a porridge, and mashing them into dense pancakes that they sautéed in butter. Members of the Galla tribe would grind the coffee berries into pulp and blend them with animal fat, then roll this mixture into billiard ball–sized orbs that they would store in leather bags and take with them on war parties. Galla warriors claimed that one of these pulp-lard delicacies could fend off hunger for an entire day. It took seven centuries of culinary experimentation before the Yemeni mystic Ali Ibn Umar al-Shadhili found the perfect use for the beans, in about AD 1200: steeping them in water. The drink, he found, helped him stay awake during prayers, and thus coffee brought him closer to God.

Coffee soon voyaged east to the greater Arab world, where it swiftly established its supremacy over every other liquid in the land. Sixteenth-century visitors to the Middle East, mystified at the rage for this bitter brown drink, nicknamed coffee the "wine of Islam"; since Muslims weren't allowed to drink *real* wine, a caffeine buzz was the best they could hope for. No less a personage than the prophet Muhammad purportedly claimed that after a dose of coffee, he felt he could "unhorse forty men and possess forty women." Wealthy Arabs often constructed sumptuous rooms dedicated to the beverage in their homes, but it was the Turkish who truly set the standard for opulent coffee consumption. Ottoman sultans liked to lounge on cushions as a slave brought a gilded, diamond-encrusted demitasse of coffee — perched on a bejeweled saucer called a *zarf* — to their lips. The men of Constantinople would gather in plush dens to drink coffee brewed in huge cauldrons and seasoned with cardamom, saffron, or opium; the venti java chip Frappuccinos of today look positively austere by comparison. This Turkish coffee addiction was not to be toyed with. Sultan Selim I once punished two doctors who claimed coffee should be banned by ordering that they be sliced in half at the waist. Failure to provide one's wife with coffee was even considered sufficient legal grounds for a divorce.

The Turkish enthusiasm for the drink eventually kindled the two most famous and ornate coffee cultures on the planet, the Parisian and the Viennese — in the former through inspiration and in the latter through invasion. In 1669, the Turkish ambassador Suleiman Aga journeyed to Paris to deliver an important message from his sultan to Louis XIV, the enormously powerful and extravagantly vain monarch known as the Sun King. (When he received the Turk at court, for instance, Louis appeared in a new multimillion-franc robe, covered in diamonds, that had been commissioned specifically for the occasion.) Besides being vain, Louis was also a bit impetuous; after receiving the sultan's letter, Louis told his guest he'd get to reading it whenever he felt like it, which meant the Turkish emissary had no choice but to wait around for the imperial whim to strike. During his stay, Suleiman Aga turned his charm on the Parisian society women, inviting them to his lavish quarters for elaborate, dimly lit coffee ceremonies, complete with Oriental rugs and exotically dressed Nubian servants. These get-togethers became the most prized invitations in town, which stoked the fashion-conscious Parisians into a frenzy for over-the-top imitations of his coffee service. In salons all over the city, Frenchwomen donned turbans and ornamental robes, taking their coffee "à la Turque." A couple of decades later, after they had lived down the embarrassment somewhat, the Parisians opened their first proper café.

The ambassador wasn't just entertaining for fun, however; he was also collecting intelligence from the loose-lipped aristocrats, trying to discover if Louis intended to support his sultan's secret plans to invade Vienna. Louis didn't. The Turks invaded anyway. In July 1683, three hundred thousand Turkish troops descended on Vienna and surrounded the city with tents, intending to starve the Austrians into submission. Vienna's population shrank, its rulers fled, and the Viennese were left with only one hope: a small band of Polish soldiers who had come to their fellow Christians' aid. But with a force of only fifty thousand troops, the Poles needed to know the perfect time to strike or the Turks would crush them. Enter Franz Kolschitzky, the seventeenth-century Slavic James Bond. A Polish journeyman living in Vienna, Kolschitzky had served as a translator in Ottoman lands and knew how to pass for a Turk. Disguised in a Turkish uniform and fez, the spy sweet-talked his way through the enemy camp, quickly finding out the date the Turks planned to attack — information he soon slipped to the hidden Polish forces. As the invaders began storming the city on September 8, the vastly outnumbered Poles set off fireworks overhead and attacked the Turks' unguarded rear, sending them into such a panic that the mighty Ottoman forces fled the scene without collecting their belongings.

Among the odd effects the Turks left behind — including guns, gold, and thousands of camels — were many sacks of pale green beans, which the Austrians assumed to be camel food. The only one who recognized it as unroasted coffee was Kolschitzky. When the grateful Viennese asked the hero to name his reward, he baffled everyone by asking for the beans, later using them to open Vienna's first café, the Blue Bottle. So goes the legend, this battle also gave coffee its most stalwart pastry companion. Seeking to remind customers of his own valiant role in the war, one Viennese baker began making rolls shaped like the crescent on the Turkish flag, and thus the croissant was born.

This newfound taste for coffee represented an enormous improvement over what Europeans were sipping with breakfast before: beer. In fact, since their drinking water was so often contaminated, most Europeans downed beer with pretty much everything. The average Elizabethan-era Briton — children included — drank more than six pints of beer every day. Even Queen Elizabeth I knocked back a few each morning with her meat stew. But if you worry that you've missed out on the merriment of an ages-long frat party, ponder this recipe for a typical breakfast dish of the time:

Beer Soup

Heat beer in saucepan.
Add a hunk of butter.
Add cold beer.
Pour mixture into a bowl of raw eggs.
Add salt, and whisk to prevent curdling.
Pour mixture over scraps of bread.
Serve with beer.

Given this continuous bender, Europeans generally lurched through their daily existence in a state of mild intoxication. Drunkenness was *normal.* So one can imagine the great sensation coffee ignited; this was a drink that could revolutionize your life. For the first time in history, humans could easily regulate their waking and working hours — all it took to lift oneself out of the fog of grogginess was a life-giving cup of coffee. Sleep, long a cruel and domineering mistress, fell under our control. As any modern cubicle dweller can confirm, coffee almost single-handedly made office work possible. And centuries later, the brew would fuel the industrial revolution, especially once factory managers learned that filling workers with free coffee boosted productivity. Coffee made people feel smarter, helped them do better work, and enabled them to punch in at a consistent time every morning.

Some refused to accept this caffeinated future. "Everybody is using coffee," grumbled Germany's Frederick the Great in 1777. "If possible, this must be prevented. My people must drink beer." But the resistance quickly crumbled. Strangely enough, some of coffee's biggest early boosters were religious conservatives. Many members of the clergy clamored for widespread coffee use because they were annoyed that so many parishioners fell asleep during their sermons. The Puritans in particular campaigned for coffee as a great soberer and as a promoter of the mental effort necessary to understand the Bible's teachings. (As a bonus, they also thought it killed the libido.)

Horrible fates befell those who spurned coffee. Consider the following trend. What happened to Napoleon's army once the diminutive emperor insisted that his people substitute chicory (which grew in France) for coffee (which they imported)? Defeat. During the Civil War, how did the Confederates fare after the Union blockade deprived them of their morning cup? Poorly. Nazi-occupied territories in World War II were so starved for coffee that, according to the coffee historian Mark Pendergrast, British Royal Air Force planes sometimes scattered tiny bags of it over towns to remind the locals just how awful life under Hitler was. Need we ask why the Germans *really* lost?

Once the thinkers of the Enlightenment caught on to the bean's powers, the Western world's rich tradition of tweaking on coffee began in earnest. Artists, writers, and intellectuals came to see the drink as the key to their success, and they treated it with a corresponding level of obsession. Every day, Beethoven counted out exactly sixty beans for his ideal cup. Voltaire threw mugs of it back by the dozen, and the French novelist Honoré de Balzac reputedly drank as many as sixty cups daily — a claim that sounds absurd until one reads his acid-trip account of coffee's effect on his mental faculties: "Ideas quick-march into motion like battalions of a grand army to its legendary fighting ground, and the battle rages. . . . Forms and shapes and characters rear up; the paper is spread with ink — for the nightly labor begins and ends with torrents of this black water."

These trembling, caffeine-addled thinkers needed a place to unleash the lightning bolts darting around their minds, and they found it in the coffeehouse culture of eighteenth-century London. Here, coffeehouses reached their pre-Starbucks pinnacle. In 1652, London harbored one solitary coffeehouse, but by 1700, the city claimed more than two thousand of them; they grew so popular that patrons often used a favorite coffeehouse as their mailing address. London's coffeehouses were more than just places for heffed-up citizens to claw at the wallpaper and babble incoherently, however. This was *important* babble. The vibrant coffeehouse gossip industry ultimately spawned the world's first modern newspapers — the *Tatler* and the *Spectator*, two compendiums of the juiciest hearsay. One coffeehouse birthed the first ballot box, which allowed patrons to air their views anonymously, without fear of the government spies who prowled the premises in search of traitors.

For their frenetic intellectual activity and egalitarian atmosphere, these establishments were called "Penny Universities," because for the price of a cup of coffee, patrons could hear the latest news, participate in debate, or witness, say, Adam Smith writing his "Wealth of Nations." If a Londoner was in the mood for science, he could wander over to a place like the Grecian Coffee House, where Isaac Newton, the astronomer Edmond Halley, and the physician Hans Sloane once dissected a dolphin that had wandered into the Thames river. Edification came free with every purchase.

Historians disagree about why the Brits switched so abruptly to tea, terminating the London coffeehouse phenomenon, but one possible cause is this: the coffee tasted repulsive.* Since the government taxed coffee by the gallon, proprietors had to make it in advance — first roasting the beans in frying pans over a fire, which left them half scorched and half raw — and then reheat the brew later. Thus, the gastronomes of the day dubbed the beverage "syrup of soot" and "essence of old shoes" and called its flavor reminiscent of "Dog or Cats turd." A few hundred years later, displeased Americans started making the same kinds of complaints.

Salami Slicing

At least every visit to a London coffeehouse included an invigorating element of chance: the coffee could taste repulsive in a variety of

---

*Actually, it was probably because the state-owned East India Company held a monopoly on tea, which gave the Crown a financial incentive to quash coffee consumption. But humor me.

unique and shocking ways. But postwar America faced the opposite problem. All of the coffee was the exact same kind of awful.

By the 1950s, coffee had become a standardized product, just like spark plugs or paper clips. Over the past fifty-odd years, a diverse cornucopia of regional coffee roasters had merged into a handful of conglomerates, and the differences between their brands were slim; the only effective way to tell one coffee from another was by looking at the can it came in. Each brand used mediocre Brazilian beans, roasted them in massive batches, with consistent flavor (not quality) as the goal, and vacuum-sealed them in steel cans that were sturdy enough to withstand a tank assault — yet they couldn't keep the coffee from going stale as it sat on shelves for months. "Coffee was terrible back then," Jim Stewart, the founder of Seattle's Best Coffee, told me. "It was all the same thing with different names: Folgers, Maxwell House, Hills Brothers — just disgusting. It was the fact that it was so disgusting that gave rise to the specialty-coffee business."

Which brings us back to a question from the beginning of this chapter: why did decent, coffee-loving Americans let their national beverage slide so far into ignominy? Odd as it may seem, they likely had no idea anything bad was happening. Consumers thought science and mass production were giving them *better* coffee, while in reality the major brands were methodically slicing it apart and saving themselves millions. The coffee giants had discovered that as long as Americans were boiling their coffee to death in percolators, cuts in quality went virtually unnoticed — if they made them slowly enough. And to help carry out the systematic task of corrupting our coffee, nature gave the corporations a tool: *Coffea canephora*, also known as *Coffea robusta*, the Styrofoam peanut of the coffee world. Unlike its pleasant-tasting and expensive cousin, arabica, robusta is a high-yield, low-maintenance crop that produces coffee so bad that companies have to steam out the flavor before using it. To cut costs, the major roasters began adding robusta to their blends as filler in ever-greater amounts. The race to produce the cheapest can of coffee had begun.

In keeping with the great American custom of total corporate honesty, the conglomerates publicly denied using robusta; yet in private, they boasted of their prowess at bilking the consumer. At one 1980s coffee industry conference in Costa Rica, the gourmet coffee pioneer George Howell listened with astonishment as a marketing agent from a major brand frankly discussed his employer's approach. "He said the large companies were salami slicing — said it outright," Howell recalled. "They'd cut quality five percent and nobody noticed, so they'd cut quality another five percent and *still* nobody noticed."

To be fair, the major coffee companies slaughtered their product partly at the behest of others. Supermarkets and restaurants put relentless pressure on the roasters to sell for less, because they were both using the promise of ultra-cheap coffee to lure in customers, often selling it below their own cost. Grocery stores promoted low-priced coffee as a loss leader, since they knew it was one of the few products every household used daily. In diners, the bottomless five-cent cup of coffee was a nonnegotiable requirement for business; customers went into revolt if you tried to raise the price even a cent or two. But endless free refills threatened profits, prompting diner owners to dilute the product and demand the cheapest coffee possible from manufacturers. Over time, the country built up a tolerance for what amounted to acrid, coffee-flavored water, stewed from mulchlike beans and tortured for hours upon hours on hot plates.

And that was the *real* coffee. After the hardships of the war, Americans thirsted for technological marvels that would fill their lives with low-cost comforts, and what could fulfill this promise better than instant coffee? Here was the truly modern way to make a cup: from tiny granules that looked like asteroids under a microscope, dense with potent "flavor crystals." The victorious Allied troops practically lived on instant, and many of them returned to the States with a taste for it. Why would any right-minded person put up with the fuss of percolators and ground coffee when he could just heap a spoonful of patriotic minimeteors into hot water and stir?

Well, because instant coffee was pretty revolting stuff. Most soluble coffee is produced through the "spray-dry" process, a method that would have given Samuel Prescott nightmares. In spray-drying, companies brew superconcentrated batches of coffee in vats, squeeze every last bitter particle of flavor from the grounds, and then flash-heat the liquid with air so scorching hot that the coffee immediately turns into brown dust. Next comes the most insidious step of all. Just before sealing the powdered coffee in the cans, manufacturers inject a simulated coffee aroma, so when consumers open the container, they get a whiff of fresh coffee, which, because it's entirely fake, instantly vanishes. This being the age of Tang, when the idea of condensing real oranges into an enhanced superdrink seemed magnificent and credible, consumers vacuumed up instant coffee despite the awful taste. One contemporary review from a 1950 issue of the *Consumers' Research Bulletin* even declared that instant coffee was "hot and wet and looked like coffee" but "any resemblance to coffee is purely coincidental."

When it came to shoppers deciding between brands, though, the stuff inside the can didn't much matter — it was what was on the outside that counted. With all of the brands deadlocked in price and quality (or lack thereof), people bought based on which advertising campaign they liked best. As coffee became ever worse, consumers encountered a flurry of ads claiming it had never been better. Companies boasted that technological advances had made their blend more potent than that of the competition; some went so far as to claim that a pound of their coffee could make eighty or a hundred cups. And when they weren't trumpeting Incredible New Discoveries, midcentury coffee ads played havoc with the anxieties of housewives. In the Folgers television commercials of the 1960s, for example, husbands taunted their wives for making bad coffee: they withheld good-bye kisses, claimed the "girls at the office" made it better, and all but said the dreadful brew was destroying their lives. One TV husband is so brutalized by the coffee his wife hands him that he flings it into the garden and screams, "Oh, this coffee is criminal!" — to which his horrified wife responds, "Honey, you killed the petunias!" The only way to halt this senseless floral massacre is to rush to Papa Eddie's grocery store or Mrs. Olsen's kitchen and discover the marriage-healing power of "mountain-grown" Folgers.

The ads were remarkably effective, but they wouldn't work forever. As the quality-cutting derby thundered on, consumers — not being nearly as stupid as the coffee giants assumed — made a wise decision: they stopped drinking coffee. "So the consumer was faced with coffee that was tasting worse and worse, that was more expensive because of advertising, and plus, he had fewer choices because the smaller roasters were going out of business," said Gillies Coffee's Don Schoenholt, who is a sort of folk historian of the gourmet coffee movement. "We were falling into a deep pit, which people only realized in 1963. In one industry survey, which was based on 1962 data, per capita coffee consumption went down for the first time in U.S. history."

By the time the major roasters noticed something was amiss, it was too late. Their degraded, mass-produced beans had forced consumers to look elsewhere for a jolt. America found a replacement in soda, which offered a shot of caffeine in a liquid that, unlike bitter coffee, wasn't an acquired taste; it was drinkable sugar. Soon, soft drinks passed coffee as the nation's number one beverage. Rather than fight to stop the downward slide, coffee brands chose to cut more product costs and spend more on advertising, which, of course, led to more people losing patience with their morning brew. And so went the cycle.

What we might call the dramatic climax in the story of the decline and fall of coffee took place in 1975, in a courtroom in Long Island, New York. One night that April, a traffic court judge named William Perry asked his deputy to pick up a couple of coffees from the vending truck parked outside the courthouse. When the deputy returned with the provisions, Perry found the coffee so infuriatingly "putrid" that he demanded that the deputy and two plainclothes policemen bring the vendor, Thomas Zarcone, "in front of me in cuffs." According to court records, Perry "tongue-lashed" the handcuffed Zarcone for twenty minutes in front of the officers and a court reporter; the judge "threaten[ed] him with legal action and the loss of his livelihood," admitted the coffee cups as evidence in the pseudotrial, and forced Zarcone to apologize for the ghastly coffee. "Mister," Perry growled before releasing him, "you're going to be sorrier before I get through with you." An hour later, Perry was still so angry that he had Zarcone hauled in again.

Something had to be done about America's coffee.

Going Dutch

Right around the dawning of the Age of Aquarius, help for the beleaguered coffee market began to appear. It came first in the form of Alfred Peet, the headstrong son of a Dutch coffee roaster, who had immigrated to America in 1955 in search of his fortune. Peet had reasonably assumed that in such a modern and prosperous nation, he would find others who shared his obsession with coffee quality. But when he took a job with a San Francisco coffee importer, Peet quickly grew disgusted with the morbid state of the American brew. "After a couple of years, I said to one of the tasters there, 'Harvey, I came to one of the richest countries in the world, and they drink the lousiest coffee,'" Peet told me in his unusual brogue, which sounds equal parts Dutch and Scottish. Now eighty-six and still possessed of a fiery temperament that tolerates no flattery or glad-handing, Peet takes bad coffee personally. During World War II, he watched from a Nazi labor camp as the Germans pilfered all of Holland's decent coffee, leaving the Dutch with chicory and spoiled old beans — "just the memory of good coffee," he said. The United States had endured no such adversity, yet the coffee was still awful. This was unacceptable.

Peet resolved to do his part for the cause by opening a small coffee market and offering the kind of gourmet beans his father had roasted;

he even imported a European-made roaster, since he considered American coffee know-how so shaky. Taking the advice of a woman he knew from his Scottish dancing club, Peet chose the counter-culture enclave of Berkeley, California, as his business's home. On the morning of April Fool's Day, 1966, Peet's Coffee and Tea — a business that would one day serve as the inspiration for a vast coffee kingdom — opened its doors on the corner of Berkeley's Vine and Walnut Streets to zero fanfare. "The only advertising I ever did came out of my chimney," Peet said. "When I was roasting, people would come in and ask, 'What smells so good?' They didn't even know coffee could taste like that. I always let the coffee speak for itself."

Though the store had a few stools and customers could buy sample cups of coffee, Peet's was no coffeehouse; Alfred Peet's mission was to sell whole-bean, fresh-roasted, *good* coffee to the masses for at-home preparation. A notoriously difficult man, Peet berated customers who used percolators and informed any who violated his edicts that there were two kinds of coffee in the world: the kind made his way and the bad kind. Since no one else could possibly carry out his exacting standards without fail, Peet put in an endless string of fifteen-hour, micromanagement-filled work days. His daily shouting matches with his employees made many of them quit in frustration.

In the few scattered cafés of the midsixties, such behavior would have killed many a buzz. At the time, Starbucks-style coffeehouse culture — lattes, velour couches, and the like — simply didn't exist; America's handful of pioneering espresso bars were known not as providers of gourmet coffee, but as havens of art and rebellion. Coffeehouses like Café Wha? in Greenwich Village played host to defiant literary types and young folk luminaries, including a fresh-faced Bob Dylan. And as the beatniks merged into the hippies, coffeehouses increasingly became the haunts of scruffy hipsters who smoked pot, tried to pick up girls, and declaimed amateur poetry — often inspired by their patron saint, Allen Ginsberg, who was a constant, voluble presence at Caffe Trieste on San Francisco's North Beach.

Consequently, many of Peet's early devotees were of the unshaven, patchouli-scented persuasion, a fact that sometimes bothered the stern Dutch proprietor. "Some of those guys, my god, they were unkempt!" Peet told me, a touch of shock still in his voice almost forty years later. "I'd think, 'You better go to the Laundromat next door, and then I'll give you some coffee.' But the funny thing was, they understood what I was doing. It was big business they were fighting, and they appreciated that I had a good product at modest prices. So spiritually, I was one of them." Even Peet had to laugh at this thought, coming as it did from a man who once removed his store's stools in an effort to keep his more free-thinking patrons from hanging around. (They sat on the floor instead.) But the Dutchman's theories on coffee roasting actually resided on a deep, far-out astral plane the hippies would have appreciated. "The coffee talks to me," he explained. "So I ask it, 'How do you want to be roasted?'"

As it turned out, the coffee wanted to be roasted darker. Because of their focus on the bottom line, the major brands chronically under-roasted their product; more weight equals more profit, and shorter roasting times meant less of the beans' mass burned off and floated out the chimney. Peet corrected this by letting his beans roast longer and lose more moisture in exchange for a bolder, fuller flavor. The result was far from an overnight success. Most patrons winced when they first tried Peet's industrial-strength brew, but almost against their will — legs striding involuntarily toward Vine and Walnut, arms flailing cupward — their bodies demanded more. Lines slowly swelled, then twisted around the block. Loyal customers (who called themselves "Peetniks") scoffed at those who drank inferior coffee, and they structured their lives so they'd never have to go without.

Alfred Peet wasn't the only person in America trying to roast good beans, but he was the first to attract the kind of cultlike devotion to coffee that later boosted Starbucks, among others, to prominence. In effect, Peet made coffee a religion. "Coffee wasn't new, but it was very much a rebirth of something old," explained Schoenholt. "The birth

34

of specialty coffee was much more like a cat giving birth to a litter than a mother to a child, in that there were multiple births all over the place, with lots of screaming."

Beset by processed foods and homogeneous coffee blends, Americans craved something different, something robust and aromatic and genuine that master roasters scooped out of huge burlap sacks before their very eyes. For years, we deemed foods *gourmet* not if they were high in quality but if they were *exotic* — things like chocolate-covered butterfly wings and roasted kangaroo tails. Eating a pickled rooster comb was no doubt a fascinating culinary adventure, at least insofar as it can be fascinating to look at a bearded lady or the world's largest petrified cow pie, yet one didn't exactly feel compelled to repeat the experience on a regular basis. After a decades-long hiatus, food that actually tasted good started making a comeback in the 1970s at stores like New York's Zabar's and Dean and DeLuca. Thanks to a key technological innovation, coffee shared in this gourmet boom. In 1972, the nation first met a gentleman called Mr. Coffee, an affordable home drip coffee brewer that rendered the percolator obsolete and let consumers actually taste the differences between coffees for the first time.

All over the country, small roasters started popping up, unified by two common bonds: they all wanted better coffee, and none of them had any idea what they were doing. They were, almost without exception, idealistic white men in their thirties who had liberal arts backgrounds and a disproportionate fondness for afros; Schoenholt termed them "Berkeley dressers," with all of the hemp clothing and Birkenstocks that phrase conjures. John Blackwell, a veteran espresso machine mechanic, explained the phenomenon to me: "We were just a bunch of old hippies trying to figure out which drug to sell, and coffee was the only legal thing we could come up with."

They started with little in the way of coffee knowledge, but since the veteran coffee men were busy sucking up the cheapest beans they could find, no one else was going to change things. Ed Kvetko, who founded Gloria Jean's Coffee Bean in Illinois, was a contractor. Martin Diedrich prowled around the jungles of Guatemala as an archaeologist before founding the Diedrich Coffee chain. Jim Stewart opened an ice-cream and coffee shop called the Wet Whisker — which later became Seattle's Best Coffee — after studying to be an optometrist. "Let's just say that when we started, this wasn't what we had in mind," Stewart said, referring to the enormity of the gourmet-coffee business today. "We were all so stupid, we didn't really know *what* we had in mind. We just didn't want to work for the phone company."

A series of amateur science experiments ensued. In 1969, for instance, a Bronx-raised social worker named Paul Katzeff loaded a woodstove, a waterbed, and a few belongings into the back of a Mack truck, took a hit of acid, and let the voices guide him to Aspen, Colorado. Surrounded by hippies drinking tea made from tree bark, he decided to roast his own coffee. "All I knew was that if you heated it, it turned brown," recalled Katzeff, who now runs Thanksgiving Coffee Company in Fort Bragg, California. "In Aspen, after I roasted my first batch of coffee for an hour, it just turned tan. It wouldn't roast. I racked my brain to figure out why, and it was because I was up at eight thousand feet — there wasn't enough oxygen! So I figured out a way to rig up a vacuum cleaner to provide extra air. Then, when the coffee started to snap, crackle, and pop, I thought the machine was broken and took the coffee out, but it was just a light roast."

Perhaps the most strident recruit to the cause was George Howell, a Yale-educated art dealer who specialized in works by Mexico's Huichol Indians. After sipping Peet's every morning for six years in Berkeley, Howell moved his family to Boston in 1974 in hopes of finding more lucrative work. Instead, he became outraged at the vile Bostonian coffee. "The coffee was infernal," he explained. "If you found any loose coffees at all, it was at old tea and spice shops in plastic bins — but they were really brown painted wooden pellets that they ground into sawdust. It was that bad." Recognizing that improving the coffee was an "aesthetic necessity," Howell opened the Coffee Connection in a tiny space he shared with an ice-cream vendor and a cheese shop in Harvard Square. He had just a few seats, and the ceiling overhead was a jumble of chicken wire and plywood, but for the first time customers could get fresh coffee, brewed to order in a plunger pot before their very eyes. Unlike Peet's, the Coffee Connection was an immediate hit. "We didn't know what to do with all of the people," Howell told me. "We didn't have enough coffee for everyone. We were potentially faced with bankruptcy due to overpopularity!"

But the first roaster to give coffee the kind of social cachet that would later propel Starbucks into the stratosphere was Southern California's Coffee Bean and Tea Leaf, founded in 1963 in the Brentwood district of Los Angeles. Owner Herb Hyman hoped to make his business fly by drawing wealthy socialites from nearby Beverly Hills, but he did even better; he snared celebrities. If Peet's was coffee's cathedral, Coffee Bean and Tea Leaf was its Hollywood red carpet. Johnny Carson had his own blend there. The actor Jason Robards ordered fifty pounds at a time to take with him during Broadway runs, and the oceanographer Jacques Cousteau arranged to have coffee care packages from Hyman meet him at ports around the world. Half of Hollywood had Hyman's home phone number in case of emergency coffee shortages. The *National Enquirer* even once offered Hyman $5,000 to divulge what the stars drank — "But we had a big 'fuck you' for them," Hyman told me.

"All of the celebrities came into our stores," he said. "We never put pictures of them on the wall, never made a big deal out of it or took advantage of them. They just enjoyed coming in. They were marvelous people. I enjoyed all of th — well, maybe there were one or two I didn't like. I don't want to mention any names, but some stars weren't as good about paying." Among Hyman's most scrupulous customers was Ronald Reagan, who occasionally dropped by with Nancy (a tea drinker) when he was governor of California and always insisted on paying right away with a personal check. Lee Marvin — the square-jawed, gray-haired leading man who played the commander of the "Dirty Dozen" — was devoted enough to Hyman's product that he often worked behind the counter just for fun.

The clique of coffee-mad Americans grew slowly at first, but a distant national catastrophe made it gain steam. In July 1975, Brazil endured a cold snap unlike anything seen in centuries — the so-called Black Frost, which killed over 1.5 billion coffee trees and destroyed more than half of that year's anticipated harvest. Coffee prices immediately skyrocketed. But while this was a tragedy for Brazilian farmers, it was a boon to gourmet roasters; suddenly, their product wasn't much more expensive than the canned stuff, enticing many dissatisfied coffee drinkers to give their beans a test brew. With even the most expensive coffees costing far less per cup than a can of soda, it was a luxury in which most could afford to indulge. "If you want a custom-made Bentley with leopard-skin seats, you're not getting it," Schoenholt explained. "If you want a custom-tailored shirt, it's three hundred dollars. So what can you get? You can get a custom-roasted, custom-ground pound of coffee for four bucks."

Bit by bit, the movement was taking shape. Stories began bouncing around about people making so much money selling bulk coffee that they had to stuff fistfuls of cash into their pockets because the till was already full. Anxious that the major brands would catch on and use their immense bank accounts to squash their fledgling businesses, the small roasters sought strength in numbers by founding the Specialty Coffee Association of America in 1982. (*Specialty* was the preferred term because the word *gourmet* had lost some of its prestige through misuse.) But even though members of the SCAA pooled their knowledge and financed campaigns to get Americans accustomed to better coffee, and even though the coffee giants were so busy scrapping among themselves that they ignored the SCAA entirely, none of these small roasters had the ability to vault gourmet coffee into the national consciousness. Out in the Pacific Northwest, however, a peculiar phenomenon had begun.

A Star Is Born

In the world of specialty coffee, every roaster acknowledges that he owes his livelihood to one ironclad law of human nature: once you get used to very good coffee, there's no going back. Those who had been content with Folgers for years would suddenly retch at the mention of the canned stuff. Soon, these ordinary-seeming people — who were once responsible, well-adjusted adults — found themselves going to heroic lengths to secure top-notch beans, undeterred by petty inconveniences like, say, international border crossings or global trade restrictions.

So it was with Gordon Bowker. Once a month, Bowker would leave his home in Seattle and drive to the nearest place he could get decent coffee. This being 1970, that place was 140 miles north: a roaster called Murchie's, in Vancouver, British Columbia. "I was a writer," Bowker later told the *Seattle Times*, explaining his motive. "I had just gotten a job and I had a paycheck and I thought, *now that I have money, what do I want to buy?* What I wanted was, I didn't want to drink any more bad coffee." As his friends learned there was a bean courier in their midst, Bowker began carting ever-larger payloads of coffee back to Seattle, to the point where customs officials on the Canadian border had to give him a gentle lesson on the strict legal definition of smuggling. A brooding idea man who sometimes became so lost in thought that he'd stare right through acquaintances on the street, Bowker hit upon a solution to his coffee dilemma on one drive back and promptly shared it with his friends. They thought he was insane.

"I was driving in Gordon's car one day and I smelled a ton of coffee," recalled Terry Heckler, a designer who worked with Bowker. "I said, 'Jesus, Gordon, what's with all of this coffee?' He said he was just up in Vancouver for his monthly run and he was getting tired of this, so he was going to import coffee himself. I said, 'Are you kidding?' I thought it was a joke." Heckler paused. "I think that was the first time I really realized coffee came from beans."

Two of Bowker's friends thought his plan sounded like the perfect enterprise for them. Zev Siegl, the son of the Seattle Symphony's concertmaster, had trekked through Europe with Bowker a few years before and was now searching for any profession that didn't involve teaching history to teenagers. Jerry Baldwin, who knew Bowker from their college days at the University of San Francisco, was likewise trying to escape his cramped desk at Boeing. Baldwin and Siegl had come up with plenty of business ideas of their own — starting a classical radio station, shooting documentary films about indigenous peoples — but nothing seemed quite right until the day the three were relaxing on the lawn outside Siegl's house on Magnolia Bluff, and Bowker uncorked his idea to open a coffee shop. "I'm willing to concede that it was Gordon's idea," Baldwin said with a laugh. "Zev and I just wanted to find something to do."

The three, who fancied themselves quite the urbane young sophisticates, had a lot to learn about gourmet foodstuffs. "I remember Gordon and I having an argument once," Baldwin recalled. "We had this roommate who was convinced that canned vegetables were better than frozen vegetables. I mean, no one thought to mention fresh ones. It wasn't pretty back then."

Bowker and Baldwin soon dispatched Siegl to San Francisco to do reconnaissance on the coffee roasters they'd heard whispers about. In the Bay Area, Siegl scouted shops like Capricorn Coffee, and Freed, Teller, and Freed, but the one place that made his heart thump wildly in his chest was a little storefront in Berkeley: Peet's Coffee and Tea. After Siegl sped home with his findings, the trio agreed they had found their sage. Said Baldwin, "I thought Alfred Peet invented coffee." Despite Peet's severe demeanor, he was always eager to instruct genuinely curious souls in the right way — *his* way — of roasting and handling the bean. Once the Seattleites had genuflected properly, Peet agreed to help them in their quest by advising them and supplying them with coffee, on the condition that they each work at his Berkeley shop for a week to learn the basics — or at least how not to mangle his product.

The three each invested $1,350, they borrowed $5,000 collectively from a bank, and the endeavor was on its way.

Of course, the bibliophiles still needed to settle the most important question of all: what would they name it? "Baldwin, Bowker, and Siegl" was an unappealing mouthful. All of them liked nautical imagery and the idea of high-seas adventure and importing from afar: "We wanted to have this sense of world trade, of things coming in from around the world," Baldwin told me. They considered, accepted, then vetoed "Cargo House" and "Customs House." Bowker was convinced that words beginning with *st* suggested confidence and power — think *strong, strapping, stellar, stupendous* — so they contemplated calling it "Steamer," which sounded perhaps a bit too much like a bathhouse. Zev and Jerry had named their hypothetical film company "Pequod," after the ship in *Moby Dick*, but their friend Terry Heckler torpedoed this idea by reminding them that "there's no way anyone's going to drink a cup of PEE-quod." They told Heckler that if he was such a naming genius, he should come up with something.*

"I looked at the names of ships and old maps from the Seattle area," Heckler recalled, "and on a map of old mining camps, I saw one called 'Starbo.' I imagined a can of coffee at the old Starbo Mine. That really sounded like coffee to me. When I told them the name, they all looked at each other, almost simultaneously, and said, 'Starbuck — the first mate in *Moby Dick!*'"† As corporate names go, Starbucks is outstanding. (They pluralized the name for aesthetic reasons.) It's easy to pronounce, and the explosive *k* sound at the end makes it pop; this also worked for Coke, Nike, and Kinko's. The word manages to evoke the vaguely mystical, hint at an antique tradition, and subtly remind customers what they're there to spend. The partners were pleased.

---

*Heckler later came up with the names for Cinnabon, the software company Visio, and Microsoft's Encarta encyclopedia.
†Twenty-five years later, Howard Schultz would make the puzzling claim that Starbuck was the *Pequod*'s "coffee-loving first mate," though Herman Melville never mentions Starbuck's views on coffee drinking.

Going along with the freewheeling spirit of the time, Heckler added to the name's allure by designing Starbucks's first logo around a naked woman spreading her legs. Well, technically they were fins, and you wouldn't exactly want to call her a woman, since any mythology buff could tell you she was a split-tailed baubo siren — but there she was, clad only in a crown, hair cascading down her back, bare-chested and smirking as she held the tips of her two fin-legs at shoulder height. Heckler replicated the design from a fifteenth-century Norse woodcut; after removing some unsightly stomach bulging and making the image slightly less scandalous, he placed her in the middle of a chocolate-brown, cigar-band-style logo, encircled by the words *Starbucks* and *Coffee* • *Tea* • *Spices* in white. "I like the idea of the siren calling to the sailors for a cup of coffee," Heckler explained.

Since Starbucks was still many years from becoming a corporate goliath, the fact that sirens were said to be spiritless beings who sang to lure sailors into disaster and then feed on their souls wouldn't have given anyone pause. This was a much different company from the Starbucks of today; Baldwin, Bowker, and Siegl were in it for the ad-venture more than the money. "We wanted to be as far away as possible from the business world," Baldwin said. "We never thought about brand-ing or touching a nerve with people." For the first Starbucks store, in the dilapidated Harbor Heights building just off Pike Place Market, they landed a bargain space for $137 a month in rent; Bowker recalls carting out enough debris to fill a dozen Dumpsters. "To give you an idea of how undercapitalized we were, I built the fixtures for our first store by hand in my parents' basement," said Siegl, who was the com-pany's only paid employee at first. With advice from Peet and copious manual labor, they scraped together a rustic storefront and opened for business on March 29, 1971.

Today, the Pike Place Starbucks — a seatless, wood-paneled space the size of a stretched-out one-car garage — is one of Seattle's main tourist attractions. One sunny winter day not long ago, chattering cus-tomers jostled around inside, snapping pictures of each other in front of the giant original Starbucks logo and listening to the black gospel quartet that often performs outside. Steam wands hissed, and grinders rumbled. To the bafflement of many visitors, the air overhead was thick with flying paper cups. (There's no room for them by the espresso machine, so the cashier has to toss the cups diagonally across the room to the barista.) The employees were unfazed by the constant bustle; they're used to the spotlight. "Only the pretty people get to work here," a brunette barista with an orthodontically flawless smile told me — to which she hastened to add that she was kidding.

Particularly perceptive visitors to this Starbucks might notice two peculiar things. First, the place looks and feels nothing like a Starbucks. The dark wood floors and counters are dimpled and well-weathered; rows of cream-colored industrial lamps hang from the unfinished ceiling; clean light flows in off Puget Sound through plate-glass windows; and, crucially, Kenny G is nowhere to be heard. The shop seethes with old-world authenticity, and there's a good reason why: the first Starbucks was more or less a Peet's. With the Dutchman's blessing, Baldwin and company closely emulated the Peet's store design. Just like their Berkeley-based forebear, the original Starbucks stores offered sample cups of the thirty-odd whole-bean coffees on offer, but their true purpose was to sell coffee by the pound for home brewing.

The second oddity about the shop is this: despite the abundant signage declaring this the original Starbucks, including a waist-high commemorative brass post that reads "First Starbucks Store, Established 1971," this actually isn't the first Starbucks. As the framed newspaper clips on the walls show, that store had a different address. The rundown building that housed the first store was knocked down in 1974, so they built a new one a couple of blocks away, right across from the public market. But in the meantime, the three founders had opened new stores near the University of Washington and on Capitol Hill in 1972 and 1973 — making what's now called the "original" the fourth store by chronology.

Like with Peet's, business was slow at first as customers got used to the dark-roasted beans, but as the three friends learned their individual roles, Starbucks matured into a local coffee force. "Each one contributed something very different," explained Jean Mach, an early Starbucks employee who is now an English professor in the Bay Area. "Gordon was the advertising mind. I think Gordon would have characterized himself — to himself, mind you, not to others — as the most sophisticated. Jerry was the business brain and the electrician — literally. We built the stores ourselves at first and Jerry wired them. Zev was the people person. With customers in the stores, he was always chatty and funny."

Baldwin soon became the roasting expert as well. After Starbucks began moving far more coffee than anyone had anticipated, the exasperated Peet told the partners he couldn't keep up; they'd have to learn to do it on their own. With only a manual in German to guide them, the three put together a used roaster in a building by Fisherman's Terminal and began experimenting with even darker Full City and French roasts, creations that eventually inspired the company's infamous nickname, "Charbucks." "The thing about French roast is it's roasted about as dark as you can get it without it actually catching on fire," said Gary Talboy, a former competitor in nearby Portland. (He's not exaggerating; if they're roasted a minute too long, the superheated beans can ignite when they fall into the cooling tray and hit oxygen.) The dark roast was an acquired taste, but Starbucks didn't care to make concessions to its critics. "People's heads would snap back and they'd say, 'God, this is really strong,'" Baldwin recalled. "It was absolutely a revelation for people." Alfred Peet offered to give the trio roasting lessons, but the curmudgeonly Dutchman later distanced himself from the company and its ultra-dark beans. "Baldwin never learned anything from me," Peet grumbled. "What is he, an English major?"

For most businesses, an unwillingness to adapt to customer feedback equals financial suicide, but in Starbucks's case, the attitude only made their coffee seem more desirable. People were *proud* to drink Starbucks coffee; the cultivated, uncompromising demeanor of the proprietors gave customers a feeling of validation and refinement. Other roasters in the Pacific Northwest saw the Starbucks trio as snooty and cocksure. "Starbucks has always been successful by saying, 'You're lucky if we allow you to buy our coffee,'" said Talboy.

But maybe they were just jealous; Seattle was getting addicted to Starbucks coffee. On Saturdays in the 1970s, a Starbucks store might have six people behind the counter frantically shoveling beans. Terry Heckler, the designer, drank sixteen cups a day. "All of us were drinking that much," Heckler told me. "Driving home at night, I would see deer and dogs and stuff crossing the road. I'd think I was going to hit them, but nothing was there." The company was profitable every year, and it established a reputation for beyond-the-call-of-duty customer service; when the partners ran out of coffee at the height of the Christmas rush in 1972 because a Peet's shipment hadn't arrived, they pledged to hand-deliver every order as soon as the beans came in. They even caved in to social norms and gave the siren back her public dignity. "When it came time to put the logo on a truck, I had to redraw her hair down," Heckler said. "It was too much even for us to handle."

The employees were just as devoted as the customers. Something about Starbucks made people believe they were serving the greater good by selling decent coffee, and they were willing to work for pennies. "There was this sense that we were doing something very different, that we were pioneers," said Mach. "It felt like a *worthy* cause, with these three guys embarking on this great adventure, just making it up as they went along." When Starbucks first opened in 1971, Seattle was stuck in an economic quagmire known as the Boeing Bust; after the aerospace company failed in its quest to build a supersonic passenger jet, the city lost more than a hundred thousand jobs, and so many people moved away that a local sign company erected a billboard asking, "Will the last person to leave Seattle please turn out the lights?" But by 1982 Seattle was back on the ascent, establishing a reputation as a high-tech mecca and a livable city. With its five thriving gourmet stores, Starbucks epitomized Seattle's promising future.

As far as the original partners were concerned, those five stores were plenty. Gourmet coffee was still a niche business, limited to a few lefty cities, and the three considered themselves lucky for their modest success. Rumors floated around town that the local coffee cart operators who sold a concentrated coffee drink called espresso were earning six-figure incomes, but Baldwin and his friends preferred to focus on home brewing and stay out of a field as volatile as the foodservice business. And so it would have stayed, if a driven young vice president at a New York housewares corporation hadn't noticed that some small Northwest coffee company was selling a phenomenal number of his drip coffeemakers. When Howard Schultz flew out to Seattle to investigate, everything changed.

~2~

A Caffeinated Craze

On a wintry Wednesday morning in downtown Seattle, a capacity crowd of several thousand waited inside McCaw Hall, the city's elegant new glass-fronted auditorium, not knowing exactly what to expect. When the twinkling scarlet curtain lifted, the hum of the audience gave way to a collective gasp: onstage, a full choir stood bathed in purple light, bellowing the fiery opening bars of "O Fortuna," from Carl Orff's tempestuous *Carmina Burana*. Timpani drums thundered. A grand piano surged and crashed. With this maelstrom roaring before them, the spectators exchanged bemused, astonished glances; this was, after all, a legally mandated meeting of shareholders.

While some corporations just hold their annual public meetings in the lunchroom at headquarters, Starbucks — a company whose business model relies on creating hysterical enthusiasm about something that amounts to roasted beans steeped in water — has always approached the task with flair. Every February, Starbucks rents out a Seattle auditorium and stages a hugely popular three-hour-long ode to itself, complete with staged antics and surprise celebrity cameos. For this, the 2006 meeting, McCaw Hall's twenty-nine hundred seats proved insufficient to accommodate the five thousand shareholders who came from all over the country to take in both the spectacle and the free Starbucks swag. (A pair of elderly women on the scene declared this year's loot woefully inadequate, however: "It's just bags of coffee . . . that's it!") Not many corporate meetings are enticing and entertaining enough to require huge swaths of overflow seating, but this one is; anticipation about which star will appear leaves the crowd rapt. Just like Starbucks itself, it's coffee theater.

As the singers chanted their way through Orff's rousing piece, slides of Starbucks-related scenes flashed faster and faster on a giant screen behind them. Even the sign language interpreter at stage right gesticulated with ever-increasing ferocity. And as the stirring final notes resounded to jubilant applause, out walked Howard Schultz.

This was an oddly theatrical introduction for someone who has long maintained the image of a selfless public servant, even while building a globe-straddling, multibillion-dollar coffee goliath. A tall, exceptionally poised man with wavy chestnut hair and an impeccable wardrobe, Schultz possesses a gift for making people see in him exactly what he wants them to see. Today, striding coolly across the stage in a dark gray pinstripe suit, he projected a balance of relaxed confidence and embarrassment at the ovations being heaped on him. In his college days, Schultz was a student of communications and public speaking; this was his element.

"As I was coming out, I was handed a note that with our stock price at its all-time high —" he began, but cheers from the audience quickly drowned him out. The promise of celebrity sightings and free coffee makes for effective bait, but the spectators also came to celebrate the profits they had reaped from their investment in Starbucks — in just the last two years, the company's shares had doubled in value, and they were soaring again even as Schultz spoke. One might think that after fifteen years of the company's explosive growth, the onlookers would be a bit bored with their double-digit capital gains. But no; when

Schultz reminded everyone that a $10,000 investment in Starbucks in 1992 would be worth nearly $650,000 that day, the audience stoked itself into a sort of financial rapture.

Given this euphoric response, Schultz could have just lobbed some more figures at the crowd and relied on the mystery guest to provide the pizzazz. But because of his charisma and his unique, touchy-feely management style — not to mention the astronomical success of his company — the Starbucks chief is now something of a star in his own right. In 2000, Schultz traded in his CEO title for the loftier "Chief Global Strategist" tag, so imparting his "vision" is now his primary job; "inspiration" is his stock in trade. To Schultz, Starbucks is more than a mere money-making enterprise. Instead of talking about financial targets and cold numbers, he spoke earnestly of Starbucks as a balm for our "secular existence" and told the crowd how honored he felt to be able to "share with you the dreams and aspirations we have for the future." He even mentioned the human condition. (The company's investors are happy to indulge the New Age–speak as long as Schultz's most important vision, the one of a forty-thousand-store coffee megalith, keeps inching closer to reality.) Schultz sometimes looks vaguely smug in photos, but in person he seems the model of the self-effacing, nonthreatening leader striving to be genuine — the kind of guy you might like to chat with over a venti chai latte.

The day was no soul-searching retreat, however; the people were there for a show, and Schultz gamely led the festivities. On the giant screen behind him, a recent *Late Show with David Letterman* stunt began playing: from a spigot at the desk in Letterman's Manhattan studio, the show's staff had strung 550 feet of clear plastic tubing all the way to a Starbucks down the street. The attending barista, Brad, hit the switch on a pump, and a jet of decaf Sumatra shot down Broadway, arriving ice-cold in the host's mug. When Letterman declared that "One day, every house in America will have their own private plumbing to Starbucks," the shareholders roared. Schultz promised a "Seattle-style" interpretation of the feat, and everyone cheered as they watched coffee spiral down the nearby Space Needle and into McCaw Hall, culminating with Schultz raising a triumphant mug to the audience. For those who hadn't yet grasped the message that this company was God's crowning commercial achievement on earth, a slew of pro-Starbucks television clips played next — including one of Oprah Winfrey exclaiming, seemingly at random, "Yay, Starbucks!" And later, on came the special guest at last: Tony Bennett, who sang a few standards and told the crowd they were beautiful.

Before the festivities began, though, Schultz presented his yearly reminder that the success of Starbucks didn't come easily — indeed, on a number of occasions the company nearly failed altogether. "Not only was it not an overnight success, but I laugh sometimes when I hear Starbucks partners [aka employees] talk about the good old days, the glory days," he said. "I gotta tell ya, they weren't that good." In a sense, Starbucks never *should* have worked. Twenty years ago, a national chain of stylish cafés selling coffee at unheard-of prices seemed as likely to succeed as a designer corn-on-the-cob vendor or a luxury thumbtack company — and Schultz knows this as well as anyone. This is the mystique of Starbucks. "People weren't drinking coffee," he explained to Larry King in 1997. "So the question is, how could a company create retail stores where coffee was not previously sold, . . . charge three times more for it than the local doughnut shop, put Italian names on it that no one can pronounce, and then have six million customers a week coming through the stores?"

Actually, that weekly customer number was at forty million and counting as of 2006, making Starbucks one of the most-trafficked retail companies in the world. But the question remains: How did this niche phenomenon take hold on such a massive scale? And why would urban epicures and blue-collar mainstreamers alike form a fierce daily need for decadent, expensive, European coffee drinks? Common sense expected Schultz's multithousand-store fantasy to fail, but the mood in McCaw Hall — the sheer intensity of the crowd's ardor for a company that isn't selling anything *that* innovative — gives us a clue about why the opposite happened. Without doubt, coffee itself was (and still is) a certifiable craze. It tastes good, it boosts energy, and in a pinch, you can even use it to exterminate frogs.* Yet how excited can people really get about coffee and milk? Starbucks's worldwide explosion was about more than coffee; it was about the way the company was selling it. As we'll see, coffeehouses provided something society needed: a place to just *be*. But no one had any idea how badly we needed it.

The Idea Strikes

Setting foot in Milan for the first time, one is tempted to characterize the city as being "functional" or "culturally robust" in the same way that a tactful person might describe a female friend as having a "good personality" — that is, they're each exceptional in their own right, but you wouldn't quite want to hang a picture of either one on the wall. This is no city of sunlit piazzas and elegantly dilapidated terraces; with its vaunted high-fashion industry and its legendary opera house, La Scala, Milan is cosmopolitan and culturally vital, but homely. As Italy's commercial and industrial hub, the city exudes efficient sturdiness and overwhelming gray.

There is one way in which the Milanese live a more beautiful life than their compatriots to the south, however. Take a stroll through the heart of the city, and every twenty yards — virtually without fail — you will pass a bustling espresso bar. In fact, Milan's 1.3 million citizens have their pick of more than fifteen hundred of them, a figure that puts Seattle's measly 650-odd coffeehouses to shame.

Enter a busy one, and a blur of activity soon engulfs you. From wall to wall, a mass of business-suited, cigarette-smoking humanity waits to be served, as Top 40 radio competes with the buzz of conversation and hundreds of clattering dishes for auditory supremacy. Behind the

---

*Seriously — caffeine is incredibly toxic to them.

marble bar, baristas — typically male and clad in navy slacks, matching vest, and collared white shirt — greet each customer with a "Prego." The standard order is a simple espresso shot; almost no one requests a milk drink, and if they do, it's a small cappuccino. Preparing the same order every fifteen seconds has made each barista into a kind of coffee ninja. In a whirl of lightning-quick motions, he grinds and tamps down the coffee, locks in the portafilter, and slams a demitasse down below. Within seconds, he sets a white porcelain cup and saucer in front of the customer, along with a tiny spoon. (He'd sooner hand the customer an old shoe than serve the drink in a paper to-go cup.) Since there are no seats, everyone stands and sips at the bar, chatting with others for a moment before paying the tab and moving on. The entire experience takes less than five minutes.

When Howard Schultz first witnessed this spectacle in the spring of 1983, the experience literally made him tremble with excitement — not because he loved the feel of the viscous espresso trickling over his tongue, but because he immediately knew he had found the idea that would make him rich. At the time, Schultz was in the opening months of his new job as Starbucks's director of marketing, and the company had sent him to Milan to attend a housewares exhibition. One morning, while walking from his hotel to the convention center, Schultz happened to duck into a coffee bar; soon, he was visiting them all over Milan, his heart aflutter. Here was an entirely different take on coffee: whereas Starbucks offered it by the pound in retail stores, these places were social hubs, like all-day cocktail parties. And instead of coming in once a week for beans, the Italians visited espresso bars *several times a day*. According to his 1997 autobiography, *Pour Your Heart into It* — which has more than three hundred thousand copies in print — these insights sparked an epiphany for Schultz.

"It was so immediate and physical that I was shaking," he wrote. "It seemed so obvious. . . . If we could re-create in America the authentic Italian coffee bar culture, it might resonate with other Americans the way it did with me." At that moment, Schultz became the true believer, an espresso evangelist determined to bring his vision of a chain of Italian-style coffee bars to life. In hindsight, this scheme sounds both brilliant and financially prudent. But at the time, even the eager Schultz knew the idea he was pushing was a huge, potentially disastrous gamble. "Howard will always say he knew this would work, but he's full of shit," Howard Behar, a member of Starbucks's board of directors who was Schultz's right-hand man for many years, told me. "We didn't know how it would turn out."

Gourmet coffee was, in every regard, a strange career path for Schultz. Born in 1952 to working-class parents, Schultz spent his childhood in Brooklyn's federally subsidized Bayview Projects. He was a mediocre student but a gifted athlete and an obsessive Yankees fan; for years, he drew Mickey Mantle's uniform number, seven, on all of his belongings. Growing up, Schultz believed his athleticism would carry him out of the projects, and he budgeted his time accordingly. Every spare moment went to pickup baseball, basketball, and football games in the P.S. 272 schoolyard, where your team had to win to stay on the field. At Canarsie High, a 5,700-student school too cash-strapped to pay for even a home football field, Schultz was the star quarterback. "He wasn't really a great football talent, but he was a really hard worker," one of his teammates, Mike Camardese, told a BBC television crew in 2002. "The team back then wasn't that good, so he was always getting banged around. But he always came back."

More than anything, Schultz wanted to avoid turning out like his father. Fred Schultz worked a string of low-paying, blue-collar jobs, from delivering diapers to driving a cab, which left his homemaker wife and three children with no savings to fall back on if he were unable to work. Howard thought his father had no dignity, and he resented his family's poverty deeply; once, the young Schultz refused to return to a summer camp after discovering that it was for children from needy families. It wasn't until after Fred Schultz's death in 1988, from lung cancer, that Howard forgave his failure to provide better for the family. (His father also expressed doubt that people would ever pay as much for coffee as his son was charging, while his mother, Bobbie, drank instant coffee and never developed a taste for Starbucks's roast — a source of constant frustration for her son.)

In the end, Schultz's prediction proved correct: sports broke him out of Canarsie. By chance, a Northern Michigan University football scout saw him play and offered him a scholarship. Since it was the only offer Schultz received, the following autumn his parents drove him out to frigid Marquette, Michigan, to become an NMU Wildcat. His college football career lasted less than a week. In one of Schultz's first practices, a linebacker hit him from his blind side, shattering his jaw and bringing his playing days to a sudden halt. The injury was severe enough that twenty years later, Schultz had to have his jaw rebroken on both sides and his teeth moved because of recurrent dizziness and headaches. Consequently, when Starbucks was spreading across America in the early nineties, its leader wore braces. They made Schultz so self-conscious around reporters that some early profiles called him "timid," with an "apologetic manner"; a *New York Times* story from 1994 said of him, "He looks like a well-meaning camp counselor."

Schultz floated through school without distinguishing himself, and after he graduated in 1975 he found himself adrift. An intense fear of failure made him ambitious, but he had little idea what he wanted to do with himself. At one point, he even considered acting school. Back in New York, he took an unglamorous sales job with Xerox, for $800 a month. From this experience came two lessons that would serve him well in later years at Starbucks: first, that after making fifty cold sales calls a day, often encountering outright hostility, he could handle rejection; and second, that he was a very good salesman. Schultz parlayed his Xerox job into better and better sales posts, finally landing a vice president position with Hammarplast, a Swedish housewares company, which paid him $75,000 a year, as well as providing a company car and an expense account. He and his soon-to-be wife, an interior designer named Sheri Kersch, bought an apartment on the Upper East Side and settled into a comfortable life, spending weekends in the

Hamptons. Yet the twenty-eight-year-old Schultz couldn't muster much passion for kitchen utensils and bird feeders.

In early 1981, Schultz spotted something strange about one Hammarplast account: a tiny Seattle company called Starbucks Coffee, Tea, and Spices was placing more orders for a certain kind of drip coffeemaker than Macy's. This being well before the meteoric rise of Microsoft and Amazon.com, most East Coasters envisioned Seattle as a remote and rustic place, like Alaska — especially New Yorkers, many of whom still seemed to think that the preferred mode of transportation in the Northwest was the covered wagon. Curious about this accounting oddity, Schultz decided to fly out to investigate.

The specialty-coffee industry may be packed with misanthropic ex-hippies, but they still enjoy their gossip, and one particularly pervasive rumor about Schultz alleges that he arrived in Seattle with an embarrassing gift for Jerry Baldwin: a can of supermarket coffee. Baldwin claims it didn't happen. Still, the Howard Schultz who stepped off the plane that spring day knew next to nothing about coffee; he'd never had much interest in it. That would soon change. After checking into his hotel, Schultz headed for the Pike Place Market Starbucks to try the product, and his recounting of his first fateful sip is a remarkable piece of advertising in itself. The store, he says in his book, "looked like a temple for the worship of coffee." When a Starbucks employee bestowed a cup upon him,

> The steam and the aroma seemed to envelop my entire face. There was no question of adding milk or sugar. I took a small, tentative sip. *Whoa.* I threw my head back, and my eyes shot wide open. Even from a single sip, I could tell it was stronger than any coffee I had ever tasted. Seeing my reaction, the Starbucks people laughed. "Is it too much for you?" I grinned and shook my head. Then I took another sip. This time I could taste more of the full flavors as they slipped over my tongue. By the third sip, I was hooked. I felt as though I had discovered a whole new continent.

Chalk up another epiphany: Schultz was smitten. Before long, the slick sales shark was imploring Baldwin, the erudite Berkeley liberal who had organized Starbucks as an anticapitalist enterprise, to invent a marketing position for him. (Zev Siegl had sold out of the business in 1980, and Gordon Bowker was busy founding other ventures — like Redhook Ale Brewery and the newspaper *Seattle Weekly* — which left Baldwin in charge of things.)

Baldwin was skeptical. He realized it was time for his company to bring in professional business expertise, but Schultz's sudden fervor spooked the Starbucks clan. Baldwin still wanted to keep things small, yet Schultz insisted the company could be a national megahit. Schultz was persistent, finding several excuses over the course of the next year to fly back to Seattle and woo Baldwin. Over dinners and phone calls, he employed characteristically lofty selling pitches, telling Baldwin and company that if they would only expand, "You could enrich so many lives." Baldwin tried to tell him no; Schultz redoubled his efforts. He spoke of Starbucks's destiny and the need for courage. After more than a year of this, Baldwin finally caved. Schultz had the job, but they couldn't pay him much, and there was no guarantee they'd actually listen to his suggestions. But Schultz was not a man who argued with his epiphanies. In August 1982, he and his wife loaded their belongings and their golden retriever, Jonas, into their Audi 5000 and made the transcontinental drive to Washington.

Despite the yawning chasm between their personalities, Baldwin and Schultz got on well — Schultz, wife, and dog even lived at Baldwin's home for a few weeks after they arrived. Schultz also won over his coworkers quickly. "We all liked Howard," Jim Reynolds, an Einstein-haired former Starbucks roaster, told me. "He did create some shockwaves because of his personality, and maybe I didn't always agree with his business decisions, but Jerry liked him and I liked him a lot." His pull over the younger employees was especially strong. "We all looked up to Howard," said Roger Scheumann, Baldwin's stepson, who worked at Starbucks as a teenager. "He was incredibly charismatic and unbelievably motivating. You wanted to be around him and do right by him." By all accounts, Schultz enjoyed donning the apron and selling customers on the virtues of Sumatran beans.

But after his trip to Milan in 1983, Schultz grew increasingly frustrated. He had sacrificed a high-paying job and posh lifestyle in Manhattan for Starbucks, yet Baldwin wasn't buying into his espresso-bar idea. As Baldwin explained it, "We just had no interest in selling cups of coffee. We were focused on quality and brewing at home, so the idea of expanding into foodservice wasn't appealing at all." Schultz couldn't stand it. "Howard came back from Milan and he was just insane," said Dawn Pinaud, an early Starbucks employee. "He kept saying, 'This is where the money is — we *have* to do beverages. We're crazy if we don't do this.' And when Howard wants to do something, nothing can stop him."

Opera and Bow Ties

Judging him solely by his autobiography and his various public statements over the years, one can reach but a single conclusion about Howard Schultz: that he is the nicest, most warmhearted guy on the planet. In the book, Schultz relentlessly adorns his memories with inspirational platitudes; for instance, one chapter is titled, "Act Your Dreams with Open Eyes." He wants his company to "lead with its heart and nurture its soul" and asks, "Who wants a dream that's near-fetched?" His worst vice, he implies, is his overwhelming passion for coffee. (In today's business culture, of course, feeling "passion" for a product or service is roughly akin to having saintlike nobility of spirit.) Flipping through the pages, one almost starts believing that the whole Middle Eastern conflict could be cleared up in an hour if the leaders of Israel and Palestine would just grab a couple hazelnut lattes at the nearest Starbucks and share their feelings.

The sappiness is hardly surprising — CEOs today aren't exactly renowned for their soul-baring candor — but the sentimental bromides don't tell us much about how one actually builds a global coffee juggernaut. If you really want to get to know Schultz, try engaging in a friendly sporting contest with him. How about volleyball?

"Howard was so competitive," said Dawn Pinaud. "I remember once we played volleyball at a company picnic and I missed the ball. Howard was so furious. I asked him, 'Are you going to fire me because I missed the volleyball?' He wouldn't play again for two years because everybody made such a big deal out of how competitive he was. I'm surprised he hasn't had a heart attack by now. He just loses it."

Okay, maybe basketball?

"I formed an intracompany basketball team with Jim Reynolds, me, Gordon, Jerry, Howard, all of those guys, in some little gym on Capitol Hill," recalled Chris Calkins, who managed Starbucks's restaurant accounts. "Howard's a hell of a guy, but he is the most aggressive guy I've ever played basketball with. I mean, he really showed his colors."

Put simply, Schultz despises losing. In a drawer of his old mahogany desk at home, he keeps dozens of newspaper and magazine clippings by those who have doubted Starbucks; he once told *Fortune* magazine, "Not a week goes by when I don't look at those pieces." Schultz has been known to call reporters at home and berate them after reading stories he disliked, and according to Dori Jones Yang, the coauthor of his autobiography, he even named his first child, Jordan, after one of the most fiercely competitive athletes who ever lived: Michael Jordan. This drive to succeed made Schultz stick out in the tranquil Pacific Northwest. "I didn't know what to make of Howard back then, to be honest," said Joe Monaghan, a Seattle coffee industry veteran. "He was aggressive, not at all like the typical person I was used to dealing with in the coffee industry — laid-back people who thought one or two stores would be plenty. Howard was always thinking bigger than that."

Given his distaste for defeat, Schultz refused to let his Italian espresso idea die, and when Baldwin decided to open a sixth Starbucks in the spring of 1984, Schultz finally convinced him to devote a small corner of the space to an espresso bar. With the help of Bowker, who was always game for making a scheme work, Schultz threw himself into the preparations, practicing steaming milk and pulling the levers on the new chrome espresso machine. The three decided not to advertise the experiment; they'd just let customers find it on their own.

Everyone agrees that Starbucks served its first espresso on a cold, damp morning that April, on the corner of 4th and Spring in Seattle. Everyone also agrees that the store was crowded with espresso customers that opening day, though not necessarily because of popularity. "Yes, it was gangbusters with the coffee bar," Baldwin recalled. "Gordon and Howard said there was a line out the door from the first moment — but that may have been because we were moving so slow. It's not like they knew how to handle it yet." By Schultz's reckoning, four hundred customers visited the store that day, 150 more than usual. Two months later, it was serving twice that number. The experiment was a success, and it was mostly thanks to one drink: the caffe latte, a cup of warm milk with a shot of espresso dropped in.

Here's where things get contentious: Schultz claims that he personally discovered the latte in the Italian town of Verona, and that he served the first one in American history on that April morning. Many disagree with this assertion. "He said *what?*" Baldwin howled when I put the proposition to him. "There's no way that could be true. Italians were bringing espresso machines into New York in the 1950s. He couldn't have served the first latte." Indeed, at the time, a few embryonic Seattle coffeehouses — The Last Exit, Raison d'Etre, Cause Celebre — were already serving "what we'd now be embarrassed to call espresso," as Monaghan put it. The city's first espresso cart, opened in 1980 and dubbed Monorail Espresso, was said to pull in more cash than some successful lawyers; another early cart, Ambrosia Espresso, was forged from spare Boeing avionics parts. Certainly, no one obtained a notarized court document showing the exact time they served their first latte, but by 1984, espresso-and-milk drinks like the cappuccino did already exist in Seattle, making Schultz's claim sound dubious.

Nobody disputes that the latte was a hit, however. "Caffe latte right out of the blocks was the most popular drink, and as they get bigger and bigger, people like them more," Baldwin told me. "I had no idea how much Americans liked milk." Years later, in the midst of the great coffee-house deluge, media stories would trumpet a national espresso obsession. But Americans didn't drink espresso; they drank lattes. "Espresso never caught on here," said Corby Kummer, author of *The Joy of Coffee*. "It was always milk drinks. They're easier to drink, and it was also a logical transition for someone going from a big tall cup of drip coffee. People think they like espresso. They don't." In the land of Big Macs and supersizing, a dainty one-ounce serving of espresso could never appeal to consumers accustomed to getting something with a little heft for their money, but the latte satisfied this requirement admirably. With each one sold, Schultz gained confidence that this was an idea worth billions.

So his anguish was even more acute when Baldwin told him that he still wasn't interested in opening more espresso bars, in part because a strangely oedipal acquisition had left the company's finances tight. In 1983, Starbucks bought Peet's; the upstart kid was succeeding its grizzled mentor. After many years of nonstop toil, Alfred Peet had burned out and sold his beloved business to a Peetnik named Sal Bonavita, who soon burned out as well. When Bonavita told Baldwin over lunch one day that he wanted to sell, Baldwin became so excited that he had to walk to the men's room to calm down. He immediately called Bowker to tell him they were buying Peet's, end of discussion. "We didn't have any money, though, so I don't know where I got my confidence about it," Baldwin said. But the thrill was short lived; burnout seemed to come with the job at Peet's. Under the strain of running two companies in two cities eight hundred miles apart, Baldwin too was growing exhausted, and he didn't care to increase his stress by gambling on Schultz's espresso-bar concept.

Schultz's frustration boiled over: in 1985, he decided to leave Starbucks and strike out on his own. Perhaps out of relief that he'd never have to spar with Schultz again, Baldwin volunteered to invest $150,000 from Starbucks's depleted bankroll, provide Schultz's new venture with coffee, and even let him keep his office. Bowker likewise offered to help, both by making a research trip to Italy with Schultz to visit local espresso bars and by giving the new business its name. Seeking to lend the enterprise an air of European class, he thought up the moniker "Il Giornale," which literally means "The Newspaper," though the intention was to suggest something one consumed daily. For an emblem, Schultz picked a Starbucksesque green circle, with an etching of the Roman messenger god Mercury's head inside.

From the outset, Schultz had grand plans for Il Giornale; a 1986 *Seattle Weekly* story reported, quite prophetically, that Schultz "envisions Il Giornale packing them in on opposite sides of the same street." He intended to open fifty stores at a rapid clip, which meant he needed to raise about $1.7 million from investors. But even coming out of the mouth of a talented salesman like Schultz, the espresso-chain pitch sounded a bit harebrained. Of the first 242 potential investors Schultz talked to, only twenty-five bit. "We raised money from what is called 'sophisticated individual investors' in the early stage," Schultz later told CNN, "and basically, anyone who would write us a check fit that criteria." To give an idea of how wide a net he cast, one of Schultz's initial investors was an up-and-coming jazz saxophonist on a mission to create the easiest-listening music humankind had ever known: Kenny G. (Schultz knew his uncle.)

Eventually, Schultz scraped together enough to start. He immediately hired Dawn Pinaud and joined forces with Dave Olsen, an army-man-turned-coffeehouse-owner who had been peddling cappuccinos out of a former mortuary garage in Seattle's University District since 1975. Olsen was another sandal-sporting, frizzy-haired Peet's devotee, and his Café Allegro was pure counterculture. But crucially, Olsen knew how to run a profitable coffeehouse — a concept that shocked some of his customers. "They would ask, 'How do you *really* make your living?'" he told me. "And when I said, 'With this,' they'd be astonished." Olsen was even willing to work for cheap: only $12,000 a year. "The synergy was too good to be true," Schultz wrote of the partnership.

The café the three put together was an over-the-top Italian experience. Where Starbucks and Peet's were antique and warm, Il Giornale was stark and sleek. Schultz wanted the venture to ooze sophistication. The gleaming espresso machine was front and center, manned by baristas in white dress shirts and bow ties. Nonstop opera blared from the speakers, and newspapers on sticks hung from the walls. Nary a chair nor a stool was in sight. In April 1986, in the ground-floor lobby of a downtown office building, Il Giornale opened for business. Schultz worked like a man possessed to make it click with Seattleites. "He'd go up to customers and ask very seriously, 'How do you like the coffee?'" Pinaud recalled, "and I'd say, 'Howard, don't be so serious! Quit furrowing your brow! Smile!' But he was studying." When customers complained about the opera, he axed it for lighter fare; the bow ties went as well, after his baristas grumbled about the hassle of tying them. Chairs appeared. Schultz personally approved every detail of the business, and even caused a minor controversy when he got a beloved popcorn vendor kicked out of the building because the buttery scent from his wares was wafting into the hypercontrolled environment of Il Giornale.

He soon opened another store in Seattle, then another in Vancouver, despite the fact that these expansions left him perilously close to not making payroll several times. Schultz himself had never taken a salary, making his pregnant wife the family breadwinner. Once, when her family came out from Ohio for a visit, Schultz's father-in-law took him on a walk to try to convince him to get a real job and provide for his family; Schultz was only able to pacify him by having one of his investors give his word that he'd personally pull the plug if things got any worse. But Schultz's vigilance soon paid off: within six months, Il

Giornale was drawing a thousand addicted customers per day. By the summer of 1987, there were five Il Giornales. Then one day, thanks to a world-shaking twist of fate, the number leaped to eleven.

The original Starbucks partners wanted out — Bowker to pursue his other projects, and Baldwin to move to Berkeley full-time. To the puzzlement of friends, Baldwin planned to sell off Starbucks and manage Peet's. When Alfred Peet heard the news, he tracked down Baldwin at a Berkeley hotel early one morning and demanded in his firm brogue, "Let me get this straight: you're selling your company and keeping mine?" For Schultz, there was never any question that he would acquire Starbucks, the gem that lured him west. Just eighteen months after struggling to fund Il Giornale, Schultz made the rounds once more, this time seeking almost $4 million. Though Il Giornale was still losing money and he had little experience actually running a company, he got it. In the process, Schultz weathered a coup attempt by one of his investors, the local business titan Sam Stroum, whose verbal assault in one meeting was harsh enough to leave Schultz in tears in the lobby afterward. Nevertheless, his other backers stuck with him.

In June 1987, the succession was complete. Baldwin departed for Berkeley to maintain the legacy of Peet's, leaving his creation to the young man he'd hired and tutored in the ways of the coffee bean five years before. Soon, Baldwin and Schultz's friendship would fracture irrevocably. But for the time being, Schultz finally had the freedom and the cash to carry out his vision. No one was holding Starbucks back. Since Starbucks was a snappy name with local cachet — while no one could even pronounce Il Giornale — Schultz christened the entire enterprise Starbucks Corporation.* He had Terry Heckler combine the logos, so that a stylized version of the siren hovered inside a green circle, and he charged ahead with his mission of bringing lattes to the

---

*For those keeping score at home, this means that Peet's is actually Starbucks, and Starbucks — which started out as an imitation of Peet's — is really Il Giornale.

masses. He aimed at what most everybody considered a very optimistic goal of 125 stores within five years. But even Schultz couldn't have predicted how strongly the nation would react.

Pandemonium

If you need proof that something about espresso-flavored milk turns otherwise normal people deranged and obsessive, look no further than the nearest specialty-coffee industry trade show, where any element of the coffee experience that can be tweaked, enhanced, or accessorized becomes the subject of intense, almost theological debate.

A few minutes before noon on an overcast October day, several hundred people jammed the entrance to the exhibition hall inside Seattle's Washington State Convention and Trade Center, waiting for a bank of metal doors to swing open and reveal the caffeinated circus known as Coffee Fest. The room echoed with excited chatter, which fell into two main categories: (1) spirited discussions about the best cup of coffee you've ever had, and (2) spirited discussions about how awesome that night's performance by the convention's special guest, KC and the Sunshine Band, was going to be. The diversity of the crowd gave living proof of gourmet coffee's wide appeal: tattooed hipster baristas, businessmen with cell-phone holsters, puffily permed mom-and-pop café owners, aging flower children, and giddy teens all mingled excitedly. With a total attendance of around six thousand, Coffee Fest isn't the biggest of the industry's conventions, but it truly excels in the eccentricity department. This was the coffee craze made tangible.

When the doors opened, the mob flooded into the cavernous exhibition hall to hunt among the hundreds of booths for the Next Big Thing in coffee. Free espresso shots and samples of strange new drinks, like the unappetizingly named "Yoguccino," beckoned from every direction. The room overflowed with coffee-related tchotchkes. For example, there was the "Quff," from a company called Qumfort

Qreations, which was a reusable thermal sleeve for paper cups. (Available designs included "U.S. Army," "Purrty Kitty," and "Elephant Party.") Another booth offered "Cruzin Caps": colorful stickers used to plug the hole in to-go lids, thereby preventing spillage on the go. Neither would be necessary, of course, if you were using the sealable TimeMug — advertised as "The world's only dishwasher safe time-telling mug" — which even came in a rhinestone-encrusted version. Also on offer: a mint-flavored postcoffee mouthwash called "Brite Shots"; jewelry made out of coffee beans; "eXtreme Barista" training videos; Joe Bag, "the ultimate new concept in coffee transportation" (basically, a bag that held four coffee cups); tickets for coffee-themed ocean cruises; and "hypercaffeinated" coffee beans, samples of which were handed out by a provocatively dressed woman in front of a bright yellow Humvee. Demand for these trinkets, and many more, was brisk. Among the convention-goers, optimism about the future of the coffee-house business ran sky-high.

And just in case anyone forgot who was responsible for sparking this frenzy, a prominent reminder stood just down the hall from the exhibition area: a Starbucks, one of the company's nearly three hundred stores in the Seattle area. The store sat mostly empty that day (only a fool would *pay* for coffee at a coffee trade show — a bit of wisdom that came to me while paying for coffee at this particular Starbucks right before this particular trade show), yet many attendees took note of its symbolic presence. Some looked away in silent protest, others offered a mock respectful bow of the head, and a few just shrugged their shoulders. Regardless of their feelings about the company, however, they all had to acknowledge this: the coffee mania that made their livelihoods possible took root in this very soil, under Howard Schultz's guidance.

In the late eighties, as the Schultz-run Starbucks was taking its first toddling steps, management started noticing small, peculiar signs that the espresso-bar idea was catching on. When they spotted people toting around their distinctive white cups, they'd sometimes observe that the logo faced conspicuously outward, broadcasting the customers' refined tastes to all passersby. Proprietors of breakfast cafés saw patrons show up with their own cups of Starbucks coffee already in hand. At the first Portland, Oregon, Starbucks, employees noted that customers were hovering around outside at six a.m.; the store didn't open until seven. Some fanatics even adopted a new in-crowd ordering lingo that went well beyond the cute terms Schultz, Pinaud, and a few others invented one day in a conference room (that is, the "tall," "grande," "venti" phenomenon, about which more later). If you requested a "short wet harmless cap," you received a small decaf cappuccino with no foam — assuming the barista had brushed up on espressoese and didn't think you'd just escaped from the asylum. A "cake in a cup" order got you double cream and sugar. And if you asked for a "schizo unleaded speed ball on a leash," well, maybe you really *did* need professional help.*

Needless to say, Starbucks wasn't the only coffeehouse in town — it was just the most prominent, the popularizer of the trend. Coffee-crazed Seattle could claim a slew of roasters and coffeehouses before most Americans had even heard the word *espresso*, and each one had its disciples. Choosing a bean provider was like becoming a Chevy man or a Ford man in the 1950s; you were either a Starbucks person or a Seattle's Best person or a Torrefazione Italia person, and this preference spoke volumes about you as an individual. In Seattle, coffee was the new alpha beverage, and the race was on to profit from the citywide addiction.

Which leads us to a question: why, out of the nation's many chic culinary hubs, should America's frenzy for espresso drinks have first taken shape in this specific Pacific Northwest city?† Schultz's ambition surely influenced the fad, but Seattle also had several inherent advantages going for it. First, there was the damp and gloomy weather; going

---

*For the record, this order translates to a decaf coffee to go, with one shot of decaf espresso and one shot of regular espresso added in.
†I should point out, however, that the American city with the most coffeehouses per capita today isn't Seattle — it's Anchorage, Alaska.

a month without any sight of the sun would make anyone want to huddle around something warm. Then there was the city's water, which had the perfect hardness for brewing espresso. And coffee had another secret weapon in Seattle as well: in the early 1900s, droves of Scandinavians immigrated to the city to work in the fishing industry, and Northern Europeans drink more coffee than anyone else on the planet. Years later, their cultural predilection for coffee hadn't faded. Add young tech workers with disposable income to the mix, and it becomes obvious why Seattleites took so strongly to the brew.

As customer devotion soared to cultish heights, casual observers had to wonder: was this level of fanaticism about a beverage healthy or even rational? Starbucks had always radiated a hint of exclusivity, but this seemed like something else entirely — almost like a religion. The intensity of customer need stunned Dave Olsen, for one. "I sometimes feel like I'm operating a public utility," he told *Seattle Weekly* in 1989. "If we're ever closed, people can't understand how we could do that to them." According to Robert Thompson, a professor of popular culture at Syracuse University, the Starbucks cult of the time occupied a privileged spot in the geek pantheon. "Starbucks fans were once nearly as passionate as *Star Trek* fans," he explained. "They couldn't imagine life without Starbucks. They'd get on the mountaintop and evangelize about it. People used to say to each other, 'How can you live there? That's not a Starbucks town.'"

While the public showed impressive enthusiasm about Starbucks, the people behind the counter put them to shame; the first employees to don the green apron lived and breathed the Starbucks ethos. As Dawn Pinaud told me, "Our blood was brown." Part of their zeal sprang from the coffee itself: the product is, technically speaking, a powerful, mood-boosting psychotropic drug. But an equal share of this dedication to the company was due to its charismatic leader. Shortly after he took control of Starbucks, Schultz decided to give all employees who worked more than twenty hours a week both health insurance and stock options, an unheard-of scheme in a time when few full-time retail employees, let alone part-timers, enjoyed any benefits at all. Schultz made plenty of public relations hay with the plan, and the company's employees (or "partners," as Starbucks now called them) responded so favorably that annual turnover fell to 60 percent, compared to an industry average of 200 percent. But it wasn't just the financial incentives that enthralled employees; it was Schultz himself. His workforce considered him the quintessential benevolent boss. At one early town hall–style company meeting, an employee from the roasting plant stood up and yelled, "Howard, for you, we'd put a store on the moon!"

Not that it was a total lovefest for Starbucks in the early days. Many found the company's coffee bitter and overroasted, and some customers chafed at the haughty attitude they got from baristas. (Schultz himself even boasted in a 1993 *Seattle Times* story, "We do have a bit of arrogance. We feel we deserve it.") Starbucks also got a tiny, comical taste of the controversy that would dog it in later years. When the company unveiled a print ad featuring a picture of a schoolteacher, it drew complaints from *actual* schoolteachers, who grumbled that the woman in the photo looked "too schoolmarmish." And thanks to protests from angry mothers, the logo's siren had to go under the knife once more. As Terry Heckler explained, she was still hardly the image of chastity: "She was kind of split in the middle, holding her fins up. The feminists called up and said, 'My kids asked me why her legs were spread. I refuse to buy your coffee until you fix this.' Howard was sick of it." In 1991, Heckler redrew the logo once and for all, rendering it in its current inoffensive form. "I don't even know if anyone knows it's a mermaid anymore," he said, exasperated. "It looks more like a queen for a day with baking mittens on."

These were nothing more than speed bumps on the highway to hegemony, however. Everyone wanted in on Starbucks. "The first thing out of a client's mouth was, 'Can I get a sign?' — 'Proudly Featuring Starbucks Coffee,'" recalled Jana Oppenheimer, who worked in restaurant and wholesale accounts at Starbucks. "They'd ask, 'Do you have any cups I can use?' People wanted a piece of the action." The exponential growth commenced: Schultz added eleven stores in 1988, twenty in 1989, thirty in 1990, thirty-two in 1991. Everything was going according to plan.

But the chaos of Starbucks's expansion did take its toll, even putting the company briefly on the brink of ruin. In 1987, the ever-ambitious Schultz had decided to prove that Starbucks would work outside the Northwest. Because of its thriving downtown and cold climate, which he supposed would drive customers in for hot lattes, Schultz targeted Chicago. The move was a catastrophe from the outset. The first Windy City Starbucks opened on October 19, 1987 — also known as Black Monday, the date of the second-largest one-day stock market drop in U.S. history. Despite the ill omen, Schultz quickly plowed ahead with more stores. Knowing little about Chicago, he picked sites with entrances fronting the street, when they should have been in lobbies; people didn't want to brave the bitter cold just to get coffee. And when they did drink it, many spat the ultradark brew out. "I remember in Chicago, one coffee roaster said to me, 'You guys are the most arrogant sons of bitches — your coffee tastes here just like it does in Seattle, and these people are used to Folgers,'" said Kevin Knox, an early Starbucks roaster. "No one there had ever tasted coffee that strong." What's more, Schultz had far higher rents and labor costs to pay. The company was losing money, and investors were losing faith. It was a disaster.

"No question, Chicago was the closest Starbucks came to failure," said Harry Roberts, a Starbucks marketing ace who had known Schultz since his Hammarplast days. "We were really tanking. It was expensive to do everything; there was the time zone difference to manage, and Chicago didn't even like the coffee." To turn things around, the company needed a savior.

In the history of Starbucks, there is only one man who can rival Schultz in the cult of personality department: Howard Behar. A bearded and bespectacled retail expert with the lewd vocabulary of a dockworker, Behar was something of an oddity at Starbucks. He had no college degree, he was a decade older than most of the other employees, and he had some peculiar tendencies: for some time, he would wear only black clothing, and he was such a fount of nervous energy that he'd often tear pieces of paper into little strips during conversations. But Behar was a wizard with people. Employees adored him for gestures like sending personally signed birthday cards to everyone in the company, even when they numbered in the tens of thousands. He was also fiercely loyal. "What used to piss me off was when they'd say 'Charbucks,'" Behar told me. "That's like walking into a gallery and saying, 'Your art is shitty.'" (Incidentally, he also matches Schultz in output of sanctimonious catchphrases; for example, "We're not filling bellies; we're filling souls.") Behar made it his mission to eliminate the storied Starbucks haughtiness. When Schultz dispatched him to Chicago in 1990, Behar infused the local stores with rambunctious friendliness, and they soon turned profitable.

Back in Seattle, though, Starbucks was locked in a constant state of disorder; the company was nearly doubling in size every year, and no one knew how to cope with it. Consider Brooke McCurdy, a designer and architect who joined the company in 1990. When she reported for duty at Starbucks's brand-new headquarters on Airport Way — which Schultz had figured would be large enough to last a decade — there was no room for her or for the other store designers. So they worked in the lobby. "Every time the door opened, our papers would go flying in the air," McCurdy told me. Then there were the fire drills. "We were on one side of the building and the roasters were on the other," she recalled. "The chaff from the coffee accumulates, and at some point it combusts. So every time it caught fire, we'd all have to run out of the building. French roast was the longest roast, so French roast day — Friday — was always exciting. You never knew what would happen on Fridays." Before long, McCurdy and the designers claimed a space next to the cupping room, where Dave Olsen sampled coffees; thus, their meetings were often punctuated by thunderous slurping sounds from the other side of the wall. But the comforts of the new space were short lived. "I'd say every six months we had to move," McCurdy said.

Even Schultz found himself lost in the chaos on occasion. He still approved every decision personally and monitored each store's sales daily — calling the managers to praise or berate them accordingly — but no one could keep track of the pandemonium at headquarters. Recalled Roberts, "Howard would come up and ask me very quietly, 'Who are all of these people? What do they do on this floor?' I'd say, 'Why are you asking me? I have no idea.'" Stores were opening so quickly that Schultz and Roberts would sketch out designs for them on napkins and scraps of paper and hand them off to McCurdy's department. This was the kind of chaos Schultz craved, the kind that came from popularity. And it was only the beginning.

Going Hollywood

For all of the company's heady growth under Schultz — it octupled in size in just three years — Starbucks was still confined to the Pacific Northwest and Chicago at the dawn of 1991. Schultz intended to establish a strong foothold in every city Starbucks entered before moving on; competitors like Gloria Jean's Coffee Bean had expanded far too hastily and left themselves dangling just above the abyss of insolvency. With Starbucks dominating its main markets, Schultz next took aim at Los Angeles, a proposition that seemed even more foolish than going into Chicago. Sweltering, smog-choked days didn't quite make a person crave hot coffee, the thinking went. But the common wisdom underestimated one thing: the trend sensitivity of Angelenos. Seattle may have birthed the espresso revolution, but Hollywood got it ready for its close-up.

Unlike in Chicago, the company's success in Los Angeles was never in doubt. Just before Starbucks opened its first store there, in

Santa Monica, the *Los Angeles Times* proclaimed its coffee the best in America. The result was a torrent of humanity at California's earliest Starbucks. "When we opened that store in Santa Monica, it just blew up" said Behar. "We absolutely could not handle the volume. The tile on the floor right in front of the counter wore out completely within a few months. That's when I knew we had a tiger by the tail — or it had us." Starbucks kept rolling out cafés, yet the demand kept rising. "Every store we opened in L.A. was a million-dollar store within the first year — *Boom! Boom! Boom!*" Pinaud recalled. L.A.'s sudden infatuation with Starbucks shocked everyone. Seattle, Lattetown USA itself, had taken years to develop a similar fervor.

But Seattle didn't have movie stars, who apparently require greater quantities of coffee than the little people in order to survive. Celebrities had long delighted in expensive beans (recall Coffee Bean and Tea Leaf, in chapter 1), but they had yet to discover well-prepared, stylishly presented espresso, which, being Italian, was naturally a far more glamorous product. Complicated espresso drinks took off so quickly among the Hollywood elite that Steve Martin was already making fun of them within the year in his movie *L.A. Story.* In a joke that ranks as one of the first mainstream media acknowledgments of the coffee trend, Martin's character asks a waiter at the café L'Idiot for a "half double decaffeinated half-caf, with a twist of lemon," which, aside from being impossible, hardly even seems a fussy order today.

As Hollywood soon discovered, designer coffee was a product born for the diva treatment. There are only so many ways to order, say, a steak, but at Starbucks, you have literally fifty-five *thousand* drink combinations to choose from, thus ensuring that you can express your individuality through an order so convoluted it can't be finished in one breath. Technically, a "venti wet cappuccino extra hot" and a "tall double 190-degree no foam latte" are more or less the same drink, but that wasn't the point. At Starbucks, being finicky was celebrated; this was a place that actually glorified and indulged our neurotic tendencies. Hence, Hollywood — a town with finickiness to spare — helped launch the vogue for coffee fussiness. The trend continues unabated today. For instance, take Joel Madden, the prolifically tattooed lead singer of the punk-pop band Good Charlotte and a man who insists on beverage perfection. "Joel gets a soy nonfat sugar-free vanilla latte," his assistant told *Teen People*. "If I send someone else to get it, they'll come back with not enough Splenda or something. You might as well not even hand him that."

Even today, years after the company lost its patina of exclusive cool, celebrities are still inseparable from their Starbucks cups. A glance through any gossip magazine yields at least a few photos of stars wearing their public camouflage gear — sunglasses — and holding the familiar white cup with the green logo. Britney Spears and Madonna seem to have Starbucks cups surgically attached to their hands, and the actors Ben Affleck and Jennifer Garner were photographed with the cups so often in 2005 that the *New York Daily News* claimed the couple had signed a "seven-figure" contract with Starbucks to be seen holding the product. (Both parties denied this.) A few Web sites even track stars' coffee preferences, which often reflect on their personalities: Katie Holmes takes a half-caf grande soy latte; Elijah Wood favors a quad espresso over ice; and Hulk Hogan likes the venti caramel Frappuccino.

The upshot of this celebrity enthusiasm was millions of dollars in free advertising each year for Starbucks, and the company never hesitated to cash in. By the end of 1991, Schultz had cranked his enterprise up above 115 stores, and the espresso craze was just beginning to crack into the mainstream consciousness. To most, it appeared to be no more than a fad nearing the end of its fifteen minutes of fame. In a sense, espresso could have been like juice bars, just another concept that spawned cultlike zeal and grandiose plans before petering out.

But people don't get addicted to juice. Those who were paying closer attention noticed a few telling clues that the coffeehouse wasn't a fad at all; it was an emerging American institution. Starbucks opened as many stores as it possibly could, yet almost none of them failed. Its customers didn't just pop in when they felt like it — they needed their fix every day, sometimes multiple times. As Schultz showed in Vancouver, he could even put two stores across the street from one another and keep both full of customers. And it's not like coffee was a faddish product, since most of America drank it habitually. Maybe this idea had longevity.

When Starbucks went public on June 26, 1992, many thought it was a cute gesture from a niche company. Three months later, after its stock price on the Nasdaq index doubled to thirty-three dollars, they stopped laughing and started buying. The evening before the IPO, Schultz gathered Olsen, Behar, and several others in his office, which overlooked the roasting plant. Schultz recorded a congratulatory announcement that each employee would receive the next morning, then grinned from his chair for a moment before telling his colleagues, "Get ready for the ride of your life, because the lid is about to come off this thing."

The great mermaid had arrived.

Whither Starbucks?

America has been cruel to its food fads in recent years. Things always get off to a torrid start, with the nation pledging its undying love to the hot young victual — be it Krispy Kreme Doughnuts or frozen yogurt, wraps or low-carb bread. But the affair generally ends in tears, as the cold-hearted Lothario abruptly dumps the new foodstuff and returns to the old standbys, like an errant husband back to his meatloaf-baking wife.

Why should gourmet coffee have been any different? After all, the craze had many of the hallmarks of the soon-to-be-dumped fad: it was fashionable, grew suspiciously popular with astounding speed, and no one really *needed* the product. Sure, people needed coffee (or caffeine, at least) to survive the day, but not necessarily four-dollar pitchers of hot milk and espresso. Coffeehouses *did* provide something that frozen yogurt shops couldn't, however — a solution to a glaring problem in American society. Just as McDonald's filled a need for quick, cheap sustenance in a busy postwar culture obsessed with driving and convenience, the coffeehouse gave a harried and disjointed nation a place to hang out and recharge. This, every bit as much as the addictive and alluring main product, was what made Starbucks into a new cultural institution: we went there because we had nowhere else to go.

Let's take a closer look at the America of the 1990s. First, we notice that it's a richer and more productive nation than ever before. With the seventy-five million baby boomers in their peak earning years, incomes were soaring. Between 1980 and 1999, average income in constant 1999 dollars shot from $15,744 to $21,239, according to U.S. government statistics, a 35 percent increase in just two decades. And just as earnings were rising, discount superstores like Wal-Mart and Target were driving down the cost of living. So began the age of disposable income, when millions of Americans accustomed to penny-pinching could suddenly afford to participate in a new consumer universe of unnecessary crap.

Everyone should have been thrilled, right? Actually, no. Sociology researchers were finding that increases in wealth didn't add to the average person's level of happiness at all; instead, Americans were reporting ever-higher levels of stress. This was not entirely unexpected. In 1970, the Swedish economist Staffan Linder predicted that mounting levels of affluence would only increase social pressures to succeed, leading to what he called a "harried leisure class"; paradoxically, labor-saving innovations would make us work *more*, not less. Work became a national fetish, and America started doing more of it than any other country on earth. On average, we now work 160 hours per year more than we did thirty-five years ago. Consequently, we also get less sleep — 20 percent less per night than Americans of a century before.

We sought refuge from stress in opulent trinkets, spending our surplus cash on what some began calling "affordable luxuries." Ads encouraged us to "indulge" in self-pampering products like chocolates and lotions as a balm for daily anxieties. In the book *Trading Up: The New American Luxury*, authors Michael Silverstein and Neil Fiske claim that the top benefit consumers look for in a product today is emotional satisfaction — they want to be coddled, to feel their all-consuming work has yielded something meaningful. Many of the people Silverstein and Fiske spoke to said that owning expensive, indulgent products made them feel more accomplished and satisfied with their lives. Thus, a new industry of luxury products aimed at the middle class arose, and no item was too basic for the treatment — in fact, the more basic, the better. A twenty-three-dollar bottle of liquid hand soap at Bath and Body Works, anyone? Maybe an eleven-dollar head of organic arugula at Whole Foods?

Or how about a dolled-up cup of coffee for $4.25 at Starbucks? Now we can fully understand the appeal of designer coffee as a product for the nineties and beyond: for frazzled, affluent worker bees looking to feel spoiled and get a kick of energy, nothing could beat a warm, custom-made espresso drink. Indeed, the advent of a constantly exhausted, hyperprosperous society in search of emotional soothing almost makes the rise of specialty coffee seem preordained. People had long felt sentimental bonds with the drink. "Keep in mind that coffee is a very personal thing," said Dave Olsen, Starbucks's longtime coffee expert. "It can be stimulating and soothing, often at the same time. It can be private and social. It has all of these opposites contained within it." Schultz seized on the emotional pull of his product quite early, relentlessly bringing up the "romance of coffee" in interviews. "There are very few things you start your day with, and brushing your teeth just isn't very romantic," he told *Brandweek* in 1999. "There is something romantic and comforting about coffee. . . . It is something you hold and you hold it every day."

Gourmet coffee was an ideal product for the time, but the pull of the coffeehouse as a *place* went deeper still. On top of the country's sense of nervous exhaustion and its need for emotional fulfillment, we also suffered from a long-standing social malady: an increasing feeling of disconnection from our fellow citizens. As the Harvard political science professor Robert Putnam outlines in his book *Bowling Alone*, civic engagement has been on the wane for decades in America. Putnam blames technology for this. Instead of participating in community activities, he says, people were staying home and staring at the television — and with the personal computer becoming an office necessity, many had to spend their working hours staring at a glowing screen as well. These technologies certainly thwarted a lot of daily socializing, but so did our housing choices. If you lived in the mushrooming suburbs, where neighbors seldom met and the idea of walking somewhere was laughable, your sense of belonging to a community was doubly foiled.

And even if we *did* want to make an effort, where could we have gone? In many cities, the only businesses that could legitimately claim to be community gathering places were bars, most of which were smoky, sleazy, and too loud for conversation. Plus, only goods that enhance productivity could curry favor under the new social regime; alcohol and tobacco were increasingly being seen as health-wrecking evils. "Smoking is now considered a worse sin than at least five of the ten commandments," the *New York Times* columnist David Brooks explains in his book *Bobos in Paradise*. "Coffee becomes the beverage of the age because it stimulates mental acuity, while booze is out of favor because it dulls the judgment."

The coffeehouse offered an antidote to these social deficiencies: a place to just hang out. As a comfortable and safe community nexus, free of drunks and secondhand smoke, the café eased the problem of disconnection while offering an item that people could come in for every day; it became America's version of the British pub. Of course, there was no pressure to actually *be* social (as the Austrian writer Alfred Polgar once quipped, the coffeehouse is "a place for people who want to be alone, but need company for it"), yet it was the feeling of unwinding among other humans that counted. Where else but a coffeehouse could you pay a couple dollars for a drink, then fritter away four hours splayed across a couch, reading a book? And how many other businesses would let lonesome telecommuters, whose ranks quadrupled in the nineties, use them as makeshift offices? Jim Romenesko, the webmaster of a prominent media industry news blog (as well as a lesser known one called Starbucks Gossip), works in four or five different Chicago-area Starbucks stores each day. "I can sit at a Starbucks for five hours with one coffee and no one gives me subtle hints to leave," he said. "No one hassles me." As something of a connoisseur of the Starbucks environment, Romenesko also knows how much some regulars rely on Starbucks for a sense of social connection. "I think there are some customers who think that these baristas are their real friends," he said.

The perfect catchphrase for the coffeehouse's vital social function happened to be languishing in disuse, just waiting for someone to seize on it. When Harry Roberts found himself struggling to put the communal appeal of Starbucks into words, he shared his trouble with his wife, who soon stumbled across the solution in a bookstore: an out-of-print book called *The Great Good Place*, by a sociology professor named Ray Oldenburg. In his book, Oldenburg describes America's need for the neutral, safe, public gathering spots that had gradually disappeared; he calls this nexus the "third place," with home and work being places one and two. His words were eerily prescient — he even pointed out that third places generally revolve around beverages, like with teahouses and pubs. As Schultz might have said, the synergy was too good to be true. The company now had its philanthropic rallying cry: it wasn't a coffee company, but a third place bringing people together through the social glue of coffee. And who could disagree?

Well, Ray Oldenburg, for one. Now retired, Oldenburg is grateful for the renewed attention that Starbucks brought to his third-place idea, but he remains displeased that the company co-opted his concept. "It was a little tacky of them not to consult me," he told me.* Oldenburg's

---

*Adding to the injury, Schultz has lately taken credit for the third-place concept himself, telling CNBC's *American Made* program in 2006, "I coined this phrase over the last ten, fifteen years about Starbucks being this third place between home and work."

idea of a third place was actually of a calmer, mom-and-pop establishment without Starbucks's high volume and fast turnover. He appreciates the headway against the civically disengaged suburbs, however. When I asked him what inspired the third-place idea, he replied, "Oh hell, I bought a house in a subdivision. That's what did it. Jesus! Nobody knows each other! I mean, it's like forming community is against the law in the suburbs." Still, when Oldenburg got a call recently from an advertising firm representing Starbucks and the caller asked if he would be willing to endorse the company, he declined.

But despite Oldenburg's disapproval, Starbucks soon spread the third place across America, and neither the company nor the country would be the same again. As Howard Behar put it, "When it became the third place, the dynamics changed completely."

Breve New World

Coffeehouses hit the mainstream so hard in the mid-1990s, one might have thought the nation was just emerging from a prolonged national shortage of overstuffed chairs and giant muffins. Designer coffee became more than just a chic thing to drink; with the third-place idea as its lodestar, Starbucks was making coffee into a way of life.

As with most things trendy, the first people to base their lives around coffeehouses were hip young urbanites. Here was a place with awesome potential for romance, an ideal environment in which to absentmindedly flaunt your battered copy of *Ulysses* while showing off your taste in the finer things. And if your sophisticated ways successfully lured in an attractive stranger, a coffeehouse made the perfect setting for a first date; it involved less pressure and expense than the standard dinner and a movie, and if things went poorly, you didn't have to wait for the check before hitting the emergency eject switch. Coffeehouse cool also got a boost from another cultural phenomenon back in Seattle: the city's grunge music scene. The members of

Nirvana, Pearl Jam, and Soundgarden never went so far as to wreck an espresso machine onstage with their guitars, but the relationship between grunge and coffeehouses featured prominently in the 1992 proto–Generation x film *Singles,* wherein the hipster Seattleite characters split time between grunge concerts, romantic meltdowns, and witty repartee at coffee shops.

If the kids were into it, the entertainment media couldn't be far behind. The most symbolic coffeehouse of the time was a fictional haunt called Café Nervosa, on the NBC sitcom *Frasier.* The show's neurotic psychiatrist star had been a regular at the iconic 1980s bar where everybody knew your name, Cheers, but when he went solo in 1993 and moved out to Seattle, he switched his allegiance to a coffeehouse. It was a cultural changing of the guard; out with the bars, in with the cafés. And another, more infamous example soon followed: Central Perk, a Starbucksesque Manhattan coffeehouse and second home of the sextet from *Friends.* Unlike the effete snobs of *Frasier* (whom one would *expect* to see drinking cappuccinos with pinkies raised), the attractive *Friends* cast inspired popular emulation — not just by the legions of women who wanted "Rachel hair," but by the millions of ordinary Americans suddenly itching to loaf around at coffeehouses. Budding coffee impresarios designed their cafés to look exactly like the *Friends* hangout, down to the orange velvet couch and the comically large mugs. Before long, everyone wanted to sell espresso, no matter how odd the circumstances. Even *Hustler's* sex superstore in West Hollywood added a coffee bar, so customers could enjoy a latte while perusing the merchandise.

All coffeehouses benefited from the national spotlight on the caffeinated lifestyle, but Starbucks was the only one with the funds and cachet necessary to flood the country with its stores. Between 1992 and 1995, Starbucks mounted full-scale assaults on Boston; New York; Washington, DC; Denver; San Diego; Minneapolis; Dallas; Atlanta; Las Vegas; Cincinnati; and Philadelphia, just to name a few. (The opening of the first Manhattan Starbucks was such a huge event that the company had to hire someone to do crowd control at the door.) In 1990, Schultz had brought in Orin Smith, an elder-statesman-like financial expert with a Harvard Business School pedigree, to help rein in the chaos, and the decision paid off. With Smith as the company's president, Schultz as its charismatic CEO, and Behar as its retail whiz — a management trio employees dubbed "H2O," for Howard, Howard, and Orin — Starbucks showed the first signs of becoming a disciplined, dominant profit machine. As one former executive explained it to me, "You had the visionary in Howard Schultz, the scrappy executioner who wouldn't let any bullshit get in his way in Behar, and Orin was the pillar." In July 1993, the month of his fortieth birthday, Schultz made his first appearance on the cover of *Fortune* magazine.

Competitors like Seattle's Best and Diedrich Coffee certainly couldn't match Starbucks's management or bankroll, but the company had one more weapon in its arsenal that truly secured mainstream domination: a glorified milkshake called the Frappuccino. "It just got so big so fast, and '95 was the turning point," the longtime barista Suzanne Foster told me. "The Frappuccino reinvented them."

Despite its explosive success, Starbucks hadn't added a single new drink to its menu since Schultz bought the company in 1987.* If Schultz had gotten his way, it never would have; the boss still believed Starbucks was bringing the authentic Italian espresso bar experience to Americans, and he flew into a rage whenever anyone suggested altering the drinks even slightly. After Howard Behar proposed that Starbucks cave to customer demand and offer nonfat milk — a painfully obvious choice today — Schultz grew so livid that Behar thought he would be fired. (Schultz and the rest of the company's ultraconservative faction finally gave in to skim milk after a day and a half of tense, combative meetings on the subject.) And when Harry Roberts suggested

---

*Although it did take some things off. According to a 1989 *Seattle Weekly* story, the company decided to jettison its selection of spices after a couple of unfortunate felines overdosed on Starbucks-bought catnip and spasmed out of lofty windows.

that Starbucks carry a few syrups to add to the drinks, Schultz sent him in front of an employee firing squad at a charged town hall meeting, where Roberts had to defend the idea under withering questioning. The spirit of innovation wasn't exactly roaming free.

So try to imagine how Schultz responded when some proposed that the company introduce a cold blended drink that would require a noisy blender and a radical departure from the Italian aesthetic — you can't get much less Italian than a milkshake. "I remember Howard telling me, 'We'll never have that product in our stores,'" Behar recalled. "So we just did it behind his back." There's plenty of dispute over who can include themselves in that "we," however; at least half a dozen different people told me they "invented the Frappuccino." Many have legitimate claims, but all roads lead back to Santa Monica.

At the time, the Southern California Starbucks stores were deserted in the afternoons. Customers would overwhelm them in the mornings, when the weather was relatively cool, but once the Californian heat started cranking, few people had any interest in hot coffee. In the early nineties, various Starbucks teams had tried to formulate a recipe for a powder-based granita — a milky, sugary coffee slush — but Schultz inevitably hated the chalky-tasting results. By May 1994, the project had fallen all the way to Anne Ewing and Greg Rogers, the two managers of a Starbucks on the Third Street Promenade in Santa Monica. Since the two had worked together previously at a smoothie bar called Humphrey Yogart, they knew the intricacies of blended drinks. Rogers began experimenting, and before long he had something he liked. "It was just half and half, regular sugar, espresso, ice, vanilla powder, the chocolate powder we used for mochas — basically, all of the ingredients we happened to have in the back room," Rogers told me. "I didn't even go out and buy anything for it."

Once Behar tasted the new drink, he insisted on giving it a test run — much to the chagrin of the company's old guard, who considered it a blended abomination. "Then as soon as they saw our sales, they changed their tune," Rogers recalled. "By the end of that summer, it was thirty percent of sales." Starbucks refined the formula and gave the concoction a proprietary name it had acquired from George Howell's Coffee Connection earlier that year: the Frappuccino. When Starbucks debuted the drink on the national stage in April 1995, it was an instant hit. The bottled version, produced jointly with Pepsi, initially sold ten times faster than either company expected; Pepsi had to pull the product completely until it could build enough capacity to keep up with the demand. Today, the Frappuccino alone brings in well over a billion dollars a year.

In exchange for their gift to Starbucks, Rogers, Ewing, and their district manager, Dina Campion, each received a five-thousand-dollar bonus, a glass statue called the President's Award, and — after Rogers complained — a Rolex watch. ("They would laugh if someone asked if Starbucks is corporate and bureaucratic," Schultz wrote of the three in his book.) Rogers remained a manager at the Santa Monica store for a while but soon left, bitter that he hadn't even received a promotion within the company; customers at the time reported seeing an employee wearing a shirt that read, "I invented the Frappuccino, and all I got was this lousy T-shirt." He eventually came to terms with the resentment, but not the sad reality that he couldn't even use his creation as fodder for cocktail party conversation. "About a year after the Frappuccino came out in grocery stores, I was standing in line next to a girl," he said. "She asked me, 'Have you tried these? They're so delicious.' So I said, 'Well actually, I invented it,' and she just looked at me like I was the village idiot and turned away. I kind of eased up on telling people about it after that experience."

With the invention of the Frappuccino, the company's metamorphosis from small-time latte peddler to caffeine dynamo was finally complete. In the drink, Starbucks had more than a wildly successful product; it now had a draw for those who would've never fallen for bitter espresso drinks. The coffeehouse had once been a place to make a statement about one's political and artistic values, but Starbucks — with its perky employees, mainstream chic appeal, and coffee-flavored shakes — transformed it into a haven for moms and office workers. Anywhere Starbucks went, customers of all types flocked in.

No one was safe from the coffeehouse's charms. Lured in by the Frappuccino — what we might call a gateway drink — teenage girls latched on to coffee as a signal of maturity and celebrity-endorsed cool, and the vanilla latte became their beverage of choice. It was also a fashion accessory; one teen told the *Seattle Times*, "Carrying around a cup of coffee helps complete a look. A pair of capris, flip-flops, and a coffee — and it has to have that cardboard sleeve — is very trendy." Evangelical Christians took to it as well; some megachurches even put cup holders in the pews. As Monique Willett, a customer who coerced her family into driving to Starbucks whenever possible, explained it to the *Washington Post*, "We just have to stop at a Starbucks. . . . Sure, it's a little expensive. But we're Christian and don't have any other vices. Coffee is it." (In Utah — stronghold of the Mormon church, which forbids caffeine consumption — independent coffeehouses reportedly offered to serve customers drinks in opaque 7 Up cups to conceal their sinful habit from others.)

By the end of 1995, Starbucks was up to almost seven hundred stores, and coffeehouses were a certifiable phenomenon; when cappuccinos became available at Mobil stations, we had passed a point of no return. In the decade since Schultz had started Il Giornale, specialty coffee had developed from an afterthought inside the mass-market coffee trade into a vigorous $2.5 billion growth machine. Coffee-crazy Americans were buying up products like "Lipachino" caffeinated lipstick, "Shower Shock" caffeinated soap, and "Coffee Tights" caffeinated hosiery. (The caffeine was supposed to eliminate cellulite by revving up skin cells.) The gourmet coffee industry was doubling in size every four years, and Starbucks was doing that every *two* years. The national validation emboldened Schultz, fueling increasingly grandiose pronouncements. "If I look at the landscape of America, we have an opportunity to change the way people live," he declared to the *Seattle Times*. Whereas before Schultz had been awestruck that the

CEO of Pepsi wanted to fly him around in his private plane, now he was making public appearances with President Bill Clinton.

But even though America was responding so enthusiastically to its coffee and to the third-place concept, Starbucks was still a company with a major internal problem: Schultz wanted his company to be growing by thousands of stores a year, not just hundreds, yet the costs of designing and building each store individually were spiraling out of control. New competitors were popping up all the time. Meanwhile, Schultz himself was reaching the limits of what he could micromanage; he was still approving each decision personally and attending almost every store opening. "I can't do this. It's killing me — it'll keep me from being a good father," he confided to one coworker. What Starbucks needed was a system for opening dozens of stores a week without breaking a sweat, and a formula that would hook its customers permanently. The endearing coffee-fanatic ethos and anti-fast-food philosophy had to go. To get where it is today, Starbucks had to become a machine.

-3-

The Siren's Song

In the spring of 1999, keepers at the National Zoo in Washington, DC, noticed that their most famous resident, the giant panda Hsing-Hsing, had stopped eating his daily meal of bamboo and rice gruel. At the ripe old age of twenty-eight, Hsing-Hsing — who had arrived at the zoo in 1972 as a gift from Mao Tse-tung to mark President Richard Nixon's infamous China visit — was suffering from arthritis, which left him lethargic and uninterested in food. The worried keepers knew the only way to keep him comfortable was to get him to swallow anti-inflammatory pills, but Hsing-Hsing had no interest in swallowing anything at all. For years, they had been able to trick the panda into taking his medication by hiding it inside a sweet potato; now Hsing-Hsing eyed these with distaste. Zoo veterinarians knew better than to try to force pills down Hsing-Hsing's throat (pandas may look like teddy bears, but they're still *bears*), so they just kept trying different foods, hoping that something would stir his appetite again.

One day that June, a keeper named Brenda Morgan — a self-described "Starbucks addict" — was having her morning coffee and blueberry muffin near Hsing-Hsing's cage when the panda suddenly caught the

86

scent and became unusually animated. After Hsing-Hsing enthusiastically accepted Morgan's offering of muffin, the keepers were elated;
now they could embed the panda's medication in a blueberry muffin,
and he'd be feeling better in no time. But as they soon found, there
was one hitch to this plan: Hsing-Hsing wasn't interested in just any
muffin — in fact, he refused even to touch store-bought or frozen varieties. They had to be *Starbucks* blueberry muffins.

In other words, Hsing-Hsing was the ideal Starbucks customer. For
him, no other muffin experience would suffice, a sentiment Starbucks
has long endeavored to drill into its customers' brains. After all, Starbucks doesn't sell a patented, complex product like a microchip; the
bulk of its sales comes from two commodities you can buy anywhere,
coffee and milk. When your core product is something that basic and
easily copied (and you're charging an outrageous markup), you must
give people a reason to believe that no competitor is even worth considering. To become a globe-straddling colossus, you must create millions and millions of Hsing-Hsings.

Starbucks has an uncanny knack for this. Its ability to lure customers in, convert them into devotees of the Starbucks brand, and milk every penny out of them is virtually unequaled in the retail universe.
The average Starbucks customer comes in eighteen times a month, a
rate Howard Schultz claims makes the company "the most frequented
retailer in the world." Just how good is Starbucks at winning over the
hearts and wallets of its clientele? Consider the case of Tully's Coffee,
a midsize chain that has made a policy of locating each of its stores as
close to a Starbucks as possible, to capitalize on overflow customers
and Starbucks's savvy real estate machine (which we'll discuss in the
next chapter). "The theory is, Starbucks probably has more people in
its real estate department than we have total," explained Tom O'Keefe,
the head of Tully's. In effect, most every Tully's goes head-to-head with
a Starbucks. Tully's offers more or less the same drinks as its giant rival,
its stores look very similar, and its freshly baked pastries are vastly better than those at Starbucks — many of which are prepared at massive

bakeries in Texas and Pennsylvania, then shipped frozen all over North America. On the surface, Tully's seems an awful lot like Starbucks. Yet the average Tully's brings in revenues of about $400,000 a year; the average Starbucks has over *$1 million* in revenue.

So why would Starbucks stores demolish the competition by such a wide margin? Price couldn't have been a factor, since the chain generally charges more than its competitors. And it certainly isn't due to the company's advertising presence; between 1987 and 1997, Starbucks spent $10 million *total* on ads — an amount Coca-Cola blows through every two days. Maybe it was something about the coffee? Indeed, research by the *Wall Street Journal* revealed that Starbucks's drip coffee packs more of a caffeine wallop than any other major brand, which makes it easier to develop physical dependence on its product. But really, the caffeine gap is too slight to provide Starbucks with any actual advantage. In truth, the quality of the company's coffee has very little to do with its dominance, as many who have worked for the chain admit. "To be honest, you could train a monkey to pull a double shot," said Scott Bedbury, a former Starbucks marketing director who also guided Nike's legendary "Just Do It" campaign in the 1990s. "It's just not that hard. The coffee wasn't the hard part."

If it wasn't advertising, value, or even the main product that ensnared so many customers, then what was it? The secret behind Starbucks's magnetic pull on consumers lies in the extraordinary amount of control it exercises over its image. At Starbucks, nothing is accidental. Everything the customer interacts with, from the obsessively monitored store environment down to the white paper cups, is the product of deliberation and psychological research. The coffeehouse as we know it is a calculated creation, tweaked and refined in large part by Howard Schultz and his army of designers. In an age when homogenous ad campaigns cover every surface that can be bought, Starbucks chose a novel marketing approach: it transformed into an *ad for itself.* Its stores became billboards, its cups and bags mobile brand beacons. And the company made sure to keep people thrilled to help the cause.

No longer would consumers just grab coffee; now they would come for the "Starbucks Experience."

For its ability to create a new, brand-centered coffeehouse lifestyle, Starbucks has become a darling of the business world and an object of considerable emulation. Companies now want to turn themselves into "the Starbucks of the ham business" or "the Starbucks of fuel-injector makers." "Starbucks has moved coffee from being a commodity to an experience," said Kirk Kinsell, the CEO of the Hangars Cleaners chain, in *Inc.* magazine. "We are moving dry cleaning from being a chore for the customer to an experience." With the right amount of Starbucksian finesse, would customers even relish having a shirt pressed? Who knows? As the cultural critic Virginia Postrel explained in her book *The Substance of Style*, Starbucks's aesthetic focus in many ways rewrote the rules of American business: "With its carefully conceived mix of colors and textures, aromas and music, Starbucks . . . is to the age of aesthetics what McDonald's was to the age of convenience or Ford was to the age of mass production — the touchstone success story, the exemplar of all that is good and bad about the aesthetic imperative. Hotels, shopping malls, libraries, even churches seek to emulate Starbucks."

But imitating Starbucks's branding and design is no easy task; it's not just a matter of inventing some New Age iconography, jamming stores with plush furniture, then tripling prices and watching the cash flow in. At Starbucks, what you don't see can be more important than what you do see. As Eric Flamholtz, a business consultant who worked with Starbucks for many years, told me, "All of these things they were doing were invisible to their competitors. It's like the stealth bomber — if you can't see it, how can you copy it?"

Phase 1: Know the Target

One drizzly November morning in Portland, Oregon, I met Jerome Conlon for coffee at one of the city's two-hundred-plus Starbucks stores. Though one wouldn't guess it from his scowling, brooding demeanor, Conlon happens to be an established authority on the psychological nuances of this exact social activity: getting coffee. When I first shook his hand, Conlon wore a huge, dark trenchcoat and a facial expression that seemed to imply that his mind contained ideas no other human has ever conceived; later on, that look was in full bloom when he told me, "I know more about the social role of coffee than anyone alive."

Now in his late forties, Conlon has spent his career plumbing the depths of the consumer brain to uncover not only what people want to buy, but how they want to feel when they buy it. During much of Nike's growth spurt in the eighties and nineties, he was its one-man market research department, responsible for keeping marketers and designers aware of the consumer's mood toward the company. When teens began seeing Nike as soft and institutional in the early nineties, for example, Conlon raised the alarm, spurring the company to launch an edgy and controversial ad campaign that featured the basketball star Charles Barkley declaring "I am not a role model." In 1996, Conlon left Nike to join his former boss, Scott Bedbury, at Starbucks as the company's first head of "consumer insights." His assignment was to find out exactly what people want in a coffeehouse.

Starbucks badly needed the help. Despite the company's massive popularity and the burgeoning espresso craze, a significant obstacle endangered its future: a lack of knowledge about its customers' desires. By the midnineties, Starbucks had a solid lineup of drinks and a strong service reputation, but the company struggled with its image — specifically, in outfitting itself to attract its target customers: high-income urban professionals aged eighteen to forty-five. The company wanted to be an ideal haven, a quintessential "third place," yet its stores hardly encouraged lingering. Efficiency, not coziness, was the goal. Store walls often blared the loud colors of the Italian flag, and customers had to perch on a piece of furniture nicknamed the "eight-minute stool." "With the stool, there was no place to put your feet, so your legs dangled and your ass fell asleep after about eight minutes," Bedbury recalled. "Starbucks definitely wasn't going out of its way to make people comfortable. It was all about volume and capacity."

The solution was to find a uniform image around which Starbucks could shape itself, and it was Conlon's job to quiz consumers and provide the general parameters this image should take. Bedbury gave him broad instructions for this mission, which he christened the "Big Dig": go anywhere, talk to anyone, read anything — just find out what people consider the best interaction they can possibly have with coffee. Thus, Conlon embarked on a nine-month-long, multiphase investigation into the metaphysics of coffee. He scoured the literary landscape, from the writings of eighteenth-century London's coffeehouse denizens to the musings of the beats. He studied coffee's cameos in art, music, and film. Bedbury and Conlon interviewed hundreds of coffee drinkers, sorting their responses according to their "need states" and "lifestyle segments." (Or, as Bedbury later jargonized the process in his book, *A New Brand World*, "We probed the conflicted lexicon of the coffee category to ensure that we would be able to establish a clearer dialogue with coffee drinkers on all levels.")

They were struck immediately by the strong emotional pull the interviewees felt toward their daily jolt. "When these people locked into the focus groups and we told them they had to spend two hours talking about coffee, they all groaned," Bedbury told me. "Then at the end we had to kick them out of the room — they had so many associations and recollections about it that they just kept on talking." Conlon asked some of the participants to close their eyes and go into a "dream state," then describe what they would see, taste, hear, touch, and smell in the greatest coffee experience imaginable. "We did over a dozen focus groups, and all of them told us about the same place," Conlon said. "It was almost as if they'd all watched the same movie."

That movie must have been a chick flick, because — to the dismay of the company's coffee-focused hard-liners — the interviewees talked very little about the coffee itself, but quite a bit about *feelings* and *atmosphere.* Most consumers didn't really care about coffee minutiae like flavor profiles and acidity, as long as the product tasted decent; instead, they craved a sense of relaxation, warmth, and luxury, all within the safe coffeehouse social sphere. "The coffeehouse, when it's as good as it gets, is much like a public living room," Conlon explained. People wanted to have that coveted coffee *experience,* an idealized version of the much-loved "coffee break." And they were willing to pay for it.

To the Starbucks brass, this was shocking news. Company executives already knew that few customers wished to sit down in the stores (only two or three out of every ten), and even fewer said a word to anyone but the barista, so it was puzzling that people would crave a cozy social atmosphere above all else. But the reality was this: for those seeking a refuge from the world, the cup of coffee they bought was really just the price of admission to partake of the coffeehouse scene. As Conlon knew, café dwellers through the ages had endured absolute swill for the privilege of loitering in the right setting. The coffee wasn't the point — the place was. "The consumer is spending his money for a total experience," said Harry Roberts, the longtime Starbucks marketing executive. "They may not be able to articulate that, but it's the truth." Even momentary contact with a soothing environment was important to harried office workers taking a latte to go; it was relaxation by osmosis.

In later years, Starbucks took this kind of research on customer desires to new heights — it even paid one market research firm to hypnotize "hip young people" and find out the deep-rooted reasons why they so often derided the company as "corporate coffee" — but the overarching message was clear. Starbucks needed to concentrate on its customers' feelings. Soon, planning began on what the company dubbed the "Starbucks Experience," a phrase one sees in most every press release, pamphlet, and interview associated with the company today. In fact, if you read a comment by a Starbucks employee and he or she doesn't mention the "Starbucks Experience," the phrase "surprise and delight," or the company mission statement, something has gone horribly wrong. Because once Starbucks figured out what its customers wanted, it never went off-message again.

Phase 2: Salivating at the Dinner Bell

That Starbucks would seek to become — in the liberal social critic Naomi Klein's words — "the coffee shop that wants to stare deep into your eyes and 'connect'" was no surprise, given the tenor of the time. After the minor cataclysm known as "Marlboro Friday" sent Wall Street into a panic, every American company with a pulse scrambled to infuse itself with a lofty "purpose." On April 2, 1993, Philip Morris announced that, because of competition from generic brands, it was slashing the price of a pack of Marlboros by 20 percent, a previously unthinkable defeat. The rugged "Marlboro man" was one of the world's best-known advertising icons; he'd been chain-smoking his way through the American wilderness for forty years, thinking deep and manly thoughts while staring off into the distance. But despite the billions Philip Morris had poured into the ads, consumers were increasingly turning to bargain brands. One cigarette was as good as another, they reasoned, so why should they pay a premium to smoke Marlboros?

Hence the panic. If this happened to the once-mighty Marlboro, the same fate could befall Coke, Nabisco, Levi's, or any other name brand. (Those companies' stock prices did indeed dive, along with many others.) Terrified executives saw that they had a simple choice: convince consumers that your brand stands for Something Important — and thus that buying your merchandise is not just crass materialism, but something closer to an artistic statement — or fall into a price-cutting bloodbath with the generics. As David Brooks, the *New York Times* columnist, once explained it, "The people who thrive in this period are the ones who can turn ideas and emotions into products."

In so many words, Brooks just put Starbucks's astoundingly success-ful marketing apparatus in a nutshell. Through unwavering repetition of a basic theme — Starbucks coffee equals romance, relaxation, and luxury — the company made itself synonymous with those concepts, transforming a cheaply produced, age-old commodity into a "sophisti-cated coffee indulgence." Bedbury claims a strong brand should influ-ence consumers the same way Pavlov's bell affected his dogs: just as the dogs would salivate at the bell's ringing even when there was no food around, the briefest glimpse of a logo should stir up a cloud of pleasant associations in the consumer brain. Starbucks's record in this area has been phenomenal. Within a decade of its debut on the na-tional stage, the carefully sculpted Starbucks brand had become one of the most powerful in existence. In 2004, the consulting firm Inter-brand named Starbucks the fourth-most effective brand in the world, behind Apple, Google, and Ikea.

Schultz often insists that his company attained its current cachet almost by accident, just by being nice. "We never set out to build a brand," he wrote in *Pour Your Heart into It*. "Our goal was to build a great company, one that stood for something." In reality, however, Schultz had obsessed over the company's image since the beginning, supervising everything from the typefaces on coffee bags to the word-ing of phrases in company literature. "He signed off on everything — *everything*," Bedbury said. "Nothing went out without his approval." Using the "Big Dig" research, Bedbury and Conlon had formulated a short "mantra" through which Starbucks could filter its marketing efforts — "Rewarding Everyday Moments" — but the choices were still made according to the instincts of a committee of one: Howard Schultz. His inability to cede marketing decisions to those he hired to actually *make* those decisions has long been a source of amusement within the company; during one three-year period, Schultz sent four different marketing vice presidents packing. "That job was the death knell," one former executive told me. "It was because no one was better at marketing than Howard. He couldn't keep his hands out of it."

Schultz considers himself the guardian of the Starbucks brand, and as such, he's very careful about the ideas he associates with the company and its core product. For one, you'll never see Starbucks drinks discounted in any way; Schultz wants you to view his product as the epitome of opulence, and would you ever see a "buy one, get one free" deal at a Jaguar dealership? On national issues, the company stakes out its positions with brand enhancement in mind. Its print ads usually "thank" customers for helping Starbucks provide some humanitarian service like tsunami relief funds, thereby aligning itself with the righteous cause in the consumer's mind — in effect, making customers feel that buying a Starbucks latte is a form of global altruism. Another area Starbucks has monitored with particular vigilance is its movie and television cameos. The company received cartloads of Hollywood scripts in the nineties, and in order for one to get authorization to use the siren logo, it had to reflect especially well on the brand. So when the director David Fincher approached the company with the screenplay for the Brad Pitt vehicle *Fight Club* and asked for permission to destroy a Starbucks with a wrecking ball–sized metal globe, the request got a thumbs-down. But a suggested scene for TV's *Ally McBeal*, wherein the title character and a costar would slowly and sensually savor their first sip of the day — as Bedbury put it, "Ally and her friend basically had oral sex with a Starbucks cup" — won enthusiastic approval.

In the cafés, on the other hand, Schultz was far less stingy with the company emblem. "It was all about the brand," Harry Roberts told me. "We would put a dozen logos inside each store. They were everywhere." The more logo sightings, the merrier. (Unless the idea of failure was involved; on the few occasions when the company has had to shutter a location, every indication that the space had been a Starbucks was whisked away the same night the store closed.) The cups in particular were devised with brand exposure in mind; Starbucks intended them to be handheld ads. "Over the years, we've had a lot of arguments about the design of the cups," said Terry Heckler, who shaped the look of both the cups and the logo. "We agree now that the Starbucks cup is probably the most effective piece of media that Starbucks has. Lots of people have wanted to change the design, but Howard's taken a strong stance on it. I mean, forty million people a week — that's a lot of billboards."

Over this painstakingly planned company image, Schultz and his marketers spread a thick layer of noble-sounding sentiment. Starbucks is more than a fleet of brick-and-mortar coffeehouses, Schultz says — why, it was "built on the human spirit." In a video shown to incoming employees, a narrator claims, "At Starbucks, we are purveyors of coffee, and tea, and hope. And a little bit of sanity." Some passages in Schultz's book veer so far into the touchy-feely realm that they read almost like coffee erotica:

> I dipped my hands into the warm, fragrant beans and lifted out a handful, rubbing them slowly between my fingers. Touching the beans grounded me to what Starbucks was all about, and it became a daily tradition.

One has to wonder how he can deliver lines like these and keep a straight face. Does Schultz really expect us to believe that he, a billionaire businessman — from *Brooklyn*, no less — shivers with delight as he plunges his hands into any container of coffee beans left unattended? Probably not. But he pulls it off in part because of the emotionally charged nature of the business. His oft-mentioned "passion" makes for an effective selling tool, perhaps because customers wish they had more of it in their own lives. (As a 2002 *New York Times Magazine* profile insightfully put it, "Schultz is very good at getting what he wants by imagining what you want and then telling you that.") "The soul thing is a bit of a stretch, since not every tall nonfat latte will enrich your soul," Bedbury explained. "But I also don't think a lot of people go to Taco Bell or Wendy's just to chill."

Some are less lenient than Bedbury about Schultz's tendency to drone on about the human condition. A few critics have even called it a calculated scheme intended to deflect the ethical debates that surround the company (which we'll go into in part two of this book); one writer for London's *Guardian* characterized Schultz's public persona as "the most nauseatingly sanctimonious cloak for perfectly ordinary hard-nosed commercialism." Said Jerome Conlon, "That's Howard's shtick. If Starbucks is a nine-thousand-pound monster and Howard is a two-hundred-pound man who occasionally talks about heart, you have the right proportion." Occasionally, the shtick gets exposed as such. In 1996, a *Los Angeles Times* reporter sat in on a Starbucks marketing meeting and overheard an executive discussing the company's "passion" in unexpectedly callous terms: "My overall message is Starbucks coffee is a passion and an art, and the umbrella message is coffee is an art form and coffee is an inspiration. We're looking at a focus on the art of whole-bean coffee, the romance of espresso, artisans, and inspiration."

But disingenuous or not, Schultz's high-minded talk wasn't what truly set Starbucks apart. The company's signature innovation in the world of marketing was its invention of an entire proprietary language for its products. Before Starbucks came along, America lived in a state of ignorance, our cup-sizing lexicon limited to three archaic terms: small, medium, and large. Starbucks vanquished those dark ages, ushering in a world where customers had to keep detailed records of the various languages that stores required them to use before receiving goods and services. Want a double espresso at Starbucks? Order a *doppio*. And did you say you wanted a medium latte with orange syrup? You obviously meant to ask for a *grande Valencia* latte. Surprisingly, most of these words, now entrenched in the national vocabulary, were coined off-the-cuff in a single Il Giornale planning meeting. Today, though, some terms have acquired a sinister tint; when your smallest listed size is called "tall," people will inevitably feel a bit manipulated. Starbucks has even trademarked the name of its largest size, "venti," despite the fact that it is the Italian word for "twenty" (that is, a twenty- ounce cup).* "One day, I expect to pick up *La Repubblica* and learn that Starbucks has purchased the entire Italian language," said Bruce Milletto, a coffee consultant. "It's insanity."

Of course, not everyone is thrilled to have to use ridiculous-sounding made-up terms just to get a cup of coffee — some customers stick to "small," "medium," and "large" as a display of personal integrity — but Starbucks-speak works. Consider this: for which of the following options would you be willing to pay more, a "grande caffe misto" or a "medium coffee with milk"? The former reeks of European sophistication, while the latter sounds boringly American. But they both describe the exact same drink. In adopting proprietary language, Starbucks bet correctly that once customers learned the lingo, they would feel out of place at other coffeehouses; if your native coffee language was Starbucksese, then Peet's or Tully's might seem that much more foreign. Mostly, customers don't just tolerate the Starbucks vernacular — some actually go out of their way to get the phrasing of an "iced venti cinnamon nonfat mocha" order exactly right. The company accommodated them by publishing a twenty-two-page booklet called "Make It Your Drink," which explained the syntax and helped customers "build confidence in beverage ordering." It even included worksheets.

The success of the build-your-own-vocabulary tactic at Starbucks generated scores of imitators. At Seattle's Best, for example, to get a large coffee, one had to request a "Grande Supremo," an indignity that sent the humorist Dave Barry into a tirade. "Listen, people," Barry wrote. "You should never, ever have to utter the words 'Grande Supremo' unless you

---

*A quick explanatory note: There's actually a decent reason why the names of Starbucks's three basic sizes all connote the same idea of bigness. Originally, Il Giornale offered three cup options — the eight-ounce "short," the twelve-ounce "tall," and the sixteen-ounce "grande." In this context, "tall" actually makes sense. But when Starbucks added the "venti" cup to cater to America's supersizing tendency, "short" got bumped from the menu. The "short" cup is still available at Starbucks stores, as a sort of in-crowd secret.

are addressing a tribal warlord who is holding you captive and threatening to burn you at the stake." (That's not even the worst of it; at the Cold Stone Creamery ice-cream chain, the three size options are called "Like It," "Love It," and "Gotta Have It.") No one could capitalize on this linguistic fad like its creator, however, because the reward for learning the Starbucks dialect was so high. With consumers increasingly bent on expressing themselves through product consumption, mastering the lingo ensured that they could get *exactly* what they wanted: a beverage tailored to their unique needs by a Starbucks "customologist."

And it wasn't just the drinks that Starbucks adapted to the consumer's desires; the company also designed its stores with the customer's subconscious in mind. Howard Schultz might claim that Starbucks was "built on the human spirit," but it was really shaped after the human id.

Phase 3: *"Grow, Roast, Brew, Aroma"*

In 1994, the management consultant Eric Flamholtz sat in on a high-level meeting at Starbucks headquarters. The question under discussion was straightforward: "How can we become invulnerable?" Executives tossed in a variety of ideas for establishing the company as the planet's dominant coffee purveyor, but the conversation soon focused on one divisive proposal — that Starbucks should set a goal of opening two thousand stores by the year 2000. To many in the room, the idea seemed preposterous. At the time, Starbucks had only four hundred stores, so it would have to *quintuple* in size in just five years. Others saw it as a challenge, an achievement that would firmly entrench Starbucks as the industry giant. "It was like Kennedy putting a man on the moon by the end of the decade," Flamholtz recalled. "It was essentially a statement." Naturally, Schultz was game. Once the "two thousand by 2000" plan gained approval, many investors started betting that this bit of hubris would sink the company. "When I took the job at Starbucks,

I got a call from an institutional investor friend of mine who said, 'You fool! We're shorting that stock!'" Bedbury told me. "He gave me ten or fifteen reasons it would never work. People thought that after McDonald's, nobody could expand like that again."

In a sense, those people were right: if Starbucks had continued down the path it was taking in 1994, it would have gone bankrupt straight away. The company was still designing and constructing each new store from scratch, at enormous expense; the cost of building a store had climbed to an average of $350,000, up from $200,000 a few years before. If he wanted to open sixteen hundred stores in five years without going broke, Schultz had to find a design template that Starbucks could replicate inexpensively, while still providing the warm and cozy "experience" that was the key to satisfying customers' desires. In essence, Schultz needed a cheap look that didn't *seem* cheap. Plus, in contrast to the old "here's your coffee, now leave" system, the new design had to adhere to the third-place model and encourage people to hang out in the stores. It was a difficult order to fill. Several architects and designers tried and failed.

As it often happens, Starbucks's eventual savior was an unlikely one. Speaking in his lazy Carolina drawl, Wright Massey sounds nothing like a designer, much less the creative brain behind a fanciful and iconic retail environment. As Conlon put it, "Wright seems like a redneck from the country." But Massey's reputation as a commercial artist is so exceptional, I've heard at least three Starbucks executives take personal credit for hiring him away from Disney, where he'd been molding that company's mall-based Disney Stores. And Massey himself isn't unnecessarily humble about the significance of the design effort he spearheaded, which has since been imitated everywhere from airports to grocery stores to hospitals. "Starbucks wanted to reduce costs, but they didn't want any two stores to look alike," he told me. "It's called 'mass customization,' and it's very tough to do — it hadn't really been done before. They gave me a million and a half bucks and I did it in one year."

As Massey tells it, he had to do everything but enter into hand-to-hand combat with Starbucks executives to keep them from screwing up his work. (If he actually did need to fight, he would have been prepared. Massey kept a World War II–era army helmet and a buggy whip in his office; when people asked him why they were there, he would reply, "For days like this.") During Starbucks's midnineties expansion, the company had begun hiring former fast-food executives to help manage its growth, and these new hires held very conventional views of what the stores should look like. "The execs wanted stainless steel, not wood," Massey said with scorn. "They wanted five cash registers and more throughput. They wanted everything dark colored, so you couldn't see any dirt. People in that company wanted to make the cups *Styrofoam!* These fast-food execs just didn't get it — the ritual of it and the feeling. They just wanted stores that were easily maintained and clean."

So Massey refused to let any of them see his team's work while it was in progress. Allowing such an unorthodox approach was a huge risk for the company. "This wasn't like betting just a chicken or a pig, it was betting the farm on Wright's ideas," said Conlon. Many among the Starbucks brass thought Massey was insane — literally. Every week, the company sent in a therapist to speak with him, to make sure he didn't crack. "They thought I was crazy because I wasn't like them, but I thought *they* were crazy," Massey said. To those who didn't share his brutal honesty and focused work ethic, he could be downright caustic. "He would say just the darnedest things," recalled Brooke McCurdy, who spent much of her time undoing the damage caused by those darnedest things. "I don't think he sees the value in the grease between people that makes things run smoothly — the pleasantries. But I think that's what made him able to get so many things done."

To properly inaugurate his tenure at Starbucks, Massey decided to organize a communal mocking of his new employer. One day, he sent a group of design and development employees down the street to Home Depot with instructions to buy a variety of things used to build a Starbucks store — switches, faucets, floor tiles, and so on. When they returned with the receipt, Massey eagerly pointed out that the company was paying much more for these materials than his staff just had. "I told them, 'No wonder you're losing your ass,'" he recalled. Soon, he isolated his employees completely, cloistering them away from the corrupt influence of what he saw as a spendthrift company culture.

Massey claimed a loft space on an unfinished floor at the vast new "Starbucks Support Center" south of downtown Seattle, and for the next few months he held his design group prisoner there. Few visitors were allowed, and most employees didn't even know the place existed. Inside, an eclectic group of graphic designers, interior decorators, architects, and (for no apparent reason other than their familiarity with "feelings") poets did artsy things in hopes of arriving at a unique, imaginative look that Starbucks could call its own. They constructed tables out of scrap and old doors; they drew the siren in various attitudes, including "Bad Hair Day Siren"; they painted whimsical images and stream-of-consciousness phrases on walls. This last method yielded one of the company's most distinctive design elements: the nonsensical yet inspirational wall mural, a medley of swirls, colors, and expressions like "Journey with . . . / relax celebration / mug of steaming reflection / heart meeting under happy stars."*

This band of artistes wasn't starting from nothing, however. Over the years, Starbucks had introduced many useful refinements to its layout. For example, some café owners had assumed the espresso machine was a noisy eyesore and removed it from view, but Schultz placed it front and center so the customer could see the barista work her magic — again, pure coffee theater. The notion of letting customers add their own cream and sugar was also new, as was the practice of ordering and picking up drinks in different areas to reduce congestion. Some elements of the store environment were off-limits to the design

---

*I made that one up. My favorite actual Starbucks quasi-poem comes from a napkin, with three phrases of what appears to be a failed haiku surrounding a stylized leaf: "I will embrace it / Roasting / Bring me a perfect warm."

team, like the sacred white cup.* If Starbucks was to be a soothing haven from the outside world, televisions were likewise out. (Schultz
claims a cable executive once handed him a blank check in exchange
for the privilege of playing his channel inside Starbucks for a few hours
each day, but he handed it right back.) And nothing was allowed to interfere with the all-important coffee scent in the stores. "What is lost
on most people is the importance of aromas," said Ted Lingle, head of
the Specialty Coffee Association of America. "I have friends who say
that when they walk into a bean store, they know instantly how successful it is based on how it smells."

Everyone wanted something different from the end design — with
Schultz jockeying for a classic Italian look and the fast-food veterans
hoping for a bright plastic hell they could hose down at the end of the
day — but Massey ultimately delivered a look that closely obeyed the
"Big Dig" findings. The soft and fuzzy specter of the "Starbucks Experience" hung over every aesthetic judgment. Colors were subdued, either earth tones or gentle pastels. Whimsical flourishes like waves and
swirls of steam abounded. Counters curved around merchandise displays to reach a circular handoff platform, spotlit from above by a
handblown glass light fixture. Plastics and glaring metallics missed the
cut, in favor of natural materials like warm woods and stone. There
was even a rationale for the shape of the tables: they were small and
round, ostensibly to preserve the self-esteem of customers drinking
alone, since a circular table has no "empty" seats.

The new experience-focused design engaged each of the customer's senses, from the obvious (sight, taste) to the not-so-obvious, like
touch, which the designers managed to connect with through display
bins that showed the coffee bean in various roasting stages. Customers
could thrust their limbs into the product and feel the same kinesthetic
ecstasy Schultz wrote about. In fact, Starbucks poured much of its

---

*Although a former fast-food executive once proposed offering a thirty-two-
ounce size. After vicious debate, wiser heads prevailed, prohibiting this monstrosity from seeing daylight. Starbucks introduced the twenty-ounce "venti" instead.

store budget into a "touch zone" from knee- to eye-level, and then skimped everywhere else. (The ceilings, for instance, were often just spray painted a dark shade.) Noses and ears received consideration as well: a heady coffee aroma saturated the air, as did the carefully chosen music, which changed in mood throughout the day to reflect the needs of customers in each "day part." This music was so well selected, actually, that the company became something of a musical tastemaker, purchasing the Hear Music record label in 1999 and later receiving its own XM Satellite Radio station and dedicated section in the iTunes store. (There were also plenty of sounds Starbucks wanted customers *not* to hear in its stores, which is why it placed noise-dampening shrouds over the Frappuccino blenders.)

But the key virtue of Massey's layout, in the eyes of the bottom-line-watching executives, was its cost-effective versatility. In keeping with the hazy mysticism of the new Starbucks image, the design came in four different color schemes, corresponding both to the four elements of antiquity and to the stages of the coffee-preparation process. "Grow" featured earthy greens, "Roast" consisted of fiery reds and coffee browns, "Brew" brought out watery blues and (again) coffee browns, and "Aroma" included airy pastel yellows and greens. The four color templates, mixed with various furniture combinations, allowed for a total of twelve potential designs — enough, apparently, to inspire executives to claim that each Starbucks store was like a unique snowflake. "You're not going to see any Starbucks that's like another Starbucks," claimed one district manager, as though a customer accustomed to the "Brew" palette might wander into a "Roast" store and become so disoriented that he would have to ask a barista if this new and wonderful place was in fact a Starbucks. It was still cookie cutter, of course — there were just a few more shapes.

The rigidity of Massey's system was in many ways its greatest asset; by forcing Starbucks to pick from a few preselected colors and furnishings, it allowed no way for store costs to exceed a set limit. Massey compiled a playbook containing an image of each individual component used in the stores. The company stockpiled these parts in warehouses in California and New Jersey, and shipped a set out en masse when a store was about to begin construction. For contractors, it was like receiving a huge model airplane kit: they just had to glue everything together. The whole process happened far more quickly than ever before, with total store development time now cut from twenty-four weeks to eighteen weeks. Costs fell from the $350,000 average down to $290,000, which, when multiplied by just the sixteen hundred new stores Starbucks planned to build by 2000, would result in a whopping $96 million saved.

None of this could happen, though, without first getting the endorsement of Starbucks's supreme committee of one. Before Schultz visited the designers' secret lair to inspect their work, the group built full-scale models of each store, complete with furniture and espresso equipment. "When Howard came down there, I was yabbering like a cat on a hot tin roof, trying to explain everything," Massey recalled. "So Howard said, 'Wright, if you have to explain it, it doesn't work. Just let me experience it.'" After wandering silently through the environment for a few moments, Schultz turned and said, "Tear this stuff down right now and get it into every store in America." Recalled Massey, "He never said another word about it — that's how sure he was."

The company followed Schultz's edict with aplomb. To its base of 425 stores at the beginning of 1995, the company added 250 stores that year, then 340 the following year, then 400, then 470, then 600. Starbucks didn't just hit two thousand by 2000; by the end of that year, it had almost *double* that, a total of thirty-five hundred coffeehouses.* "It was suddenly very obvious that everyone else was an

---

*The company didn't retire the "Grow, Roast, Brew, Aroma" designs until 2005, when it began building new stores with three new templates: "Classico," a woody, European look; "di Moda," a slick, angular, more cosmopolitan design; and "Origins," a cheerfully colored template that is supposed to look like a Middle Eastern marketplace.

amateur," said Don Schoenholt, the specialty-coffee guru. "Everybody else was working with Formica and old wood panels, but Starbucks was going in with professional architects. And whatever it is that they haven't figured out yet, they're really good at hiding it." That was exactly the point. With its consumer-tailored image firmly in place, the company soon set out to erase any blemish on the "Starbucks Experience."

Phase 4: Refining the Formula

By the late nineties, Starbucks had put so much distance between itself and its competitors that it almost seemed they were in an entirely different business. Chains like Tully's and Gloria Jean's were busy staving off bankruptcy, and modest successes like Peet's and Caribou Coffee were executing cautious growth plans; Starbucks, on the other hand, had snared a huge clientele, claimed turf in every major American city, and developed a powerful brand. All that was left for it to do was to milk every cent it could out of those loyal patrons. "In a rare moment of honesty, I heard one employee say, 'We're supposed to try to sell everything to you,'" Jim Romenesko, the Starbucks Gossip webmaster, told me. "Starbucks has this incredible ability to squeeze every dollar out of customers."

The company has excelled at the task by any measure. As of this writing, Starbucks has had fourteen consecutive years with at least 5 percent growth in same-store sales, an astonishing streak for a company that has saturated America with so many stores. Essentially, this means Starbucks has been plunking new cafés across the street from its existing cafés and *still increasing sales at the existing cafés.* (Just in the past four years, the average Starbucks has boosted its sales from $798,000 to more than $1 million.) The typical Starbucks customer spends $4.05 per visit for coffee, compared to the fast-food industry's average of $4.34 a person *for an entire meal.* Schulz has often said, "There's no secret sauce here. Anyone can do it." But no. Not just anyone can carry out the microscopic refinements that have turned Starbucks stores into streamlined money machines.

Starbucks already heeded the basic laws of merchandising — like making sure every customer walks past the pastry case before ordering, and placing the highest-margin merchandise just to the right of the register (since most people are right-handed) — so most of these fine-tunings weren't obvious. "Anything we did, we tried to make it invisible to the customer," said Paul Davis, a former president of Starbucks North America. Aside from the customer's need for a third-place experience, Davis explained, patrons really only care about three things: cleanliness, order accuracy, and, above all, speed of service. Lines have always been the company's top complaint, and Starbucks has gathered a mountain of statistics about the psychology of queueing. According to the "retail anthropologist" Paco Underhill, a Starbucks consultant, people are generally content in line for about ninety seconds. After that, their sense of how long they've been standing there begins to distort; those who have waited two minutes feel like they've waited three minutes, and so on. It helps to give customers things to look at and to have an employee greet them, but there's really only one solution: get them through the queue as quickly as possible.

Starbucks fought the menace of slow lines with a system of inventive and effective refinements. (They were so effective, in fact, that Britain's National Health Service adopted the company's "interlocking queues" system outright in its hospital clinics.) "Starbucks was renowned for how fast they'd turn a line around," said George Howell, of Coffee Connection. "They were the model." Here's a sign of how far the drink-preparation process has evolved over the years: in the early days, the employee who took a customer's order would place a cup next to the barista in a specific position to indicate the desired drink. An upside-down cup with the logo facing forward and slightly left, for instance, meant "skim decaf cappuccino."* Today's system is simpler (they use felt-tipped pens), and the whole drink-making process is far more efficient. Starbucks's service target is now three minutes from when the customer walks in to when the beverage is served. (Here, some regular Starbucks customers might protest that this three-minute rule has never applied to their store, crammed as it is each morning with commuters ready to claw each others' eyes out. The company was actually angling for a three-minute *average*.)

Back at Starbucks headquarters, store operations specialists work obsessively to cut down the time it takes a barista to make any given drink; they call the coffee business "a game of seconds." When they discovered that baristas sometimes had to dig into the ice bin twice to get the right amount for a venti Frappuccino, they designed a new "volumetric" scoop that cut fourteen seconds off of the prep time. Unbeknownst to most customers, Starbucks now uses automatic espresso machines that grind, tamp, and pull espresso shots at the push of a button, while steam wands equipped with temperature sensors stop foaming the milk at precisely the desired moment. This strips the luster from the "handcrafted beverage" idea, yet a latte-making process that once took a full minute now takes thirty-six seconds, which allows Starbucks to nearly double the amount of money it can make in that period of time. According to the *Wall Street Journal*'s secret shoppers, the company makes the fastest latte in the business.

Sometimes, the company's strategies for shaking extra cents out of customers' pockets can seem a bit shifty. Take the "venti" cup. When Starbucks adopted the twenty-ounce size and bumped the eight-ounce "short" from the menu, it effectively killed off what was once America's standard coffee serving size — and it helped itself to an extra twenty-five cents per "tall" drink for just two cents' worth of added product. (Don't even get coffee snobs started on the atrocity of the twenty-ounce cappuccino, a drink intended as a five-ounce jolt, not a lake of milk.) Then

---

*How this didn't fail every time is a total mystery.

there are the promotions done in the name of "fun," such as customer "conga lines" where everyone tries a sample of a drink, that Starbucks puts on knowing every fifth sample leads to a sale.

But mostly, you have to at least chuckle at the incredible amount of thought that goes into even the smallest decision at Starbucks today, like the new summer Frappuccino flavors it announces each spring. As you read this, minions in the company's research and development kitchens are trying to figure out what the hot colors in the fashion world will be a year from now. The flavor they eventually pick will correspond to the color they expect to be trendiest; after all, people want to look good while carrying the product. (For example, Starbucks unveiled vanilla and coconut "Crème Frappuccinos" in 2002 to capitalize on the expected popularity of the color white.) Starbucks also uses the twenty-five hundred employees at its headquarters as guinea pigs for its latest recipes. New hires fill out questionnaires about flavor preferences on joining the company, and they periodically receive a summons to come sit in a small tasting room and register their thoughts on different drink and food formulas. It's a lot of work just to achieve subtle variations on the theme of "java chip" or "mocha."

Sometimes, this development process goes fantastically wrong. In the midnineties, before the advent of the Frappuccino, Schultz wanted to bottle and sell a cold, carbonated coffee beverage called Mazagran, which was based on a concoction the French Foreign Legion drank in Algeria in the nineteenth century to keep cool. As if the name weren't unappetizing enough, Mazagran was to come in flavors: berry, vanilla, spiced, and "fiery." The drink went through a brief test run before Starbucks concluded that the world wasn't ready for spicy, bubbly coffee. ("Mazagran made Mountain Dew look like table water — it was quite a jolt," Bedbury told me. "It was either the drink of your life or a no-go.") Another aborted idea was Starbucks brand *caffeinated* fruit juices; Schultz says someone even suggested producing coffee-flavored tanning lotion. And the misfires weren't confined to the realm of coffee and caffeine. In an effort to further infiltrate its customers' lives,

Starbucks produced a lifestyle magazine called *Joe* that lasted just three issues. It built "media bars" with CD-burning stations, which were little more than a waste of cash in the age of the iPod. The company also launched two full-service restaurants: "Circadia," a bohemian place equipped with a bar, and "Café Starbucks," a bistro. Both bombed. Even Starbucks employees considered them an embarrassment. "Café Starbucks?" Harry Roberts snickered. "Oh, that place was a *joke*."

Yet it didn't really matter if Starbucks lost money on these projects, though some lost a phenomenal amount of it. The incredibly lucrative coffee drinks neutralized all of the company's blunders. "You could make so many mistakes at Starbucks because there's so much profit in the espresso," said Engle Saez, a former Starbucks marketing executive. "It covered up everything." The raw coffee Starbucks buys is cheap, but the lattes consumers find so irresistible are not; for a drink that costs, say, $3.40, at least forty cents of that is pure profit. Revenues pile up so quickly at Starbucks that even a financial catastrophe barely makes waves. In 2000, the company wrote off nearly $60 million in losses because of a slew of disastrous Internet investments (Schultz was trying to make the company into a "lifestyle portal"), but the hit still didn't cancel out its gigantic profits for the quarter. Having secured the affections of tens of millions of weekly customers, it could do no wrong.

Starbucks just took the heaps of money it earned from its stores and built new ones. Then it took that money and built more. The more money it made, the more stores it built—and now they seem to be everywhere. But if things go according to Schultz's plans, Starbucks's growth has only just begun.

—4—

Leviathan

Here's a little parable about the ubiquity of Starbucks today. Even when I was just beginning to research this book, I already knew exactly how I wanted to open this chapter on the vastness of the company's domain. In dramatic fashion, making the reader tremble with anticipation, I would reveal one of the great secrets of our time: the location of the single town in the continental United States that is geographically farthest from a Starbucks. As I envisioned it, the Starbucks-free village would become famous as a pristine spot in a country saturated with chain stores and strip malls. Visitors would flood in; perhaps a university would spring up, or at least a bizarre commune. And if the appreciative locals should wish to erect a statue of me in the town center — clad in a toga, with a falcon perched on my shoulder — how could I stop them?

Bristling with this civic spirit, I contacted Michael Pilon of Map Muse.com, a Web site built around an interactive U.S. map that shows the retail locations of dozens of companies, including Starbucks. When I outlined the mystery of the nation's most decaffeinated town for him, Pilon immediately grasped the gravity of the project and agreed to use his mapping software to find the answer. Soon, he had a winner: a farming community in northern Montana called Turner (population 298), which was a full 201 miles from the nearest Starbucks store. I did a quick check of the local businesses — Sunford Grocery, Grabofsky Livestock and Grain, a salon called Image 'N' That. Perfect. The proprietors of Miles Gun Hut might scare off potential commune members, I speculated, but overall, things seemed ideal. Feeling pleased with my investigative work, I filed the information away and continued researching.

I should have known better. My strategy had one glaring flaw: between the day I got Pilon's results and the day I started writing these words, five months passed. In those five months, Starbucks built another six hundred stores. So, when I decided to double-check Turner's Starbucksless status before calling the people at the local saloon to break the news, I got a shock — not one, but *two* new Starbucks stores had opened close enough to the town to spoil its possible fame as a chain-free oasis. No problem, I thought; I'll just go with the runner-up, the town of Eureka (population 974) in the mountains of central Nevada, 198 miles from the nearest Starbucks at the time of Pilon's analysis. But this one too suddenly had Starbucks outlets in the vicinity. The third-place finisher — Cozad, Nebraska — likewise had a problematic Starbucks close at hand. After spending an amount of time I'd rather not disclose searching for other candidates, I settled on the community of Saco, Montana, as the new champion. But let's be honest: this answer's shelf life is probably short. As I write this, Starbucks is likely putting the finishing touches on a store in nearby Malta or Lewistown.

And that's actually the point of this whole exercise, anyway: there's no escaping Starbucks. If your quaint little neighborhood still remains untouched, it's really only a matter of time before you find yourself standing in front of what was just recently a bank, mouth agape, watching the siren beam that smug, knowing smile down at you. Wherever you go, Starbucks goes — this is the company's mantra. Its goal is absolute unavoidability. "We want to dominate," the former Starbucks marketing chief George Reynolds told the *Boston Globe* in 1994, in a moment of candor that may have contributed to his exit from the company soon thereafter. "We want to reach critical mass. The economics are better for us."

Needless to say, Starbucks doesn't like to frame its omnipresence in terms of dominance or "critical mass." What the company truly offers its customers, executives say, is *convenience*. Take just one example of this convenience in action: on a recent spring afternoon in Manhattan, three men in standard office-worker attire strode out of the Morgan Stanley building, near Times Square, then paused on the sidewalk, looking pensive. "Should we go to *that* one or *that* one?" asked the lead man, gesturing toward both ends of the block with his thumb. Do we even need to ask what he was referring to? The trio headed west and walked into a Starbucks on the corner — and sure enough, another Starbucks stood at the other end of the very same block. As a matter of fact, the men had their pick of *twelve* different Starbucks stores within a three-block radius. How's that for convenience? Manhattan is so loaded with convenience, actually — with 170 nuggets of it and counting — that mayor Michael Bloomberg once suggested the borough could build fewer public toilets because "there's enough Starbucks that'll let you use the bathrooms."

One of the truly odd things about Starbucks is that its cafés have always seemed utterly pervasive, even back when they really weren't. In 1996, when Starbucks had just seven hundred stores, it cooperated with NPR on an April Fool's Day radio story. "National Public Radio has been able to confirm that Starbucks will soon announce their plans to build a pipeline costing more than a billion dollars," proclaimed *All Things Considered* host Noah Adams, "a pipeline thousands of miles long from Seattle to the East Coast . . . that will carry freshly roasted coffee beans." NPR went out of its way to hint that the story was a joke, even including a reference to a protest group called Mothers Opposed to the Coffee Aqueduct, or "MOCA." Nevertheless, the story seemed a little too plausible; in fact, I've talked to some people who *still believe it's going to happen*. Never mind that the idea was patently ridiculous, and that a single Starbucks goes through maybe a few hundred pounds of coffee a day, hardly enough to warrant a multibillion-dollar pipeline. This was *Starbucks* we were talking about, the company that could put two stores ten yards away from each other and still pack them both. Starbucks already had such an aura of success, people assumed it could do whatever crazy thing it wanted.

It's tough to say which boggles the mind more: the sheer scope of the Starbucks empire or the staggering speed with which it arose. From a base of just one hundred stores fifteen years ago, Starbucks has grown into a thirteen-thousand-strong coffeehouse armada. It operates cafés in all fifty states and in thirty-seven countries; you can find it in airports, libraries, casinos, hospitals, and even churches. No chain has ever become so ubiquitous so quickly. Sure, Starbucks is no McDonald's, which serves fifty million customers a day at its thirty thousand restaurants, but give it time. The company now opens more than two thousand coffeehouses per year, an average of six new stores a day. And what's more, McDonald's arrived at its current total by selling franchises, which means its franchisees actually built all of those outlets, not the company. But Starbucks doesn't franchise; the company designs and constructs each store itself, making its breakneck expansion that much more remarkable.

Achieving this sudden omnipresence was no simple task — after all, dozens of other coffee companies were racing to expand as well — yet Starbucks so thoroughly routed its competition that it now commands 73 percent of the specialty-coffeehouse market. And the company is devastatingly efficient; every ten weeks, Starbucks opens as many new stores as its closest competitor, Caribou Coffee, has *total*. So how did Starbucks pull this off? As we've seen, it had an alluring design and great marketing, but plush couches and speeches about the romance of espresso didn't make the company ubiquitous — it still had to find the right locations for its thousands of stores. Thus, Starbucks owes its dominance of the urban landscape to its incredibly sophisticated real estate machine. Through a combination of cunning store-placement strategy and ruthlessness with competitors, the company attempted to make it so customers couldn't help but go to Starbucks. As former Starbucks marketing executive Engle Saez explained, "Starbucks doesn't have a lockdown patent on the environment; it doesn't have a lockdown patent on the experience; and it doesn't have a lockdown patent on the bean or the roast. All of those things can be duplicated. So what it comes down to is dominance of real estate. That's one area where no one can out-muscle Starbucks."

Of course, no one really tries to top Starbucks anymore. The company is so good at placing its stores that they almost never fail; of the first thousand coffeehouses it opened, only two closed. "They were just in such a different league, by virtue of their scale and by virtue of their iconic status," said Tom Danowski, a former executive at Seattle's Best. "It was almost comical to compete with them. They were just in such a different game." The only real question left is whether Starbucks will surpass McDonald's and become the biggest chain on the planet. Howard Schultz has declared that his aim is to reach forty thousand stores, a goal some even consider conservative. Think about it: for McDonald's, placing two stores on opposite corners of the same street would be pure folly, but for Starbucks it's routine. Which do you think has more growth potential?

In truth, no one knows when the Starbucks explosion will stop. In 1995, *Forbes* magazine predicted that the coffeehouse boom would die a quick death, with one analyst grousing, "It's horse pucky, and it's not going to be around much longer." That same year, a *Washington Post* reporter wrote, "Some local executives [have] wondered whether the District [of Columbia] — with fourteen Starbucks bars and outlets owned by numerous other chains — has hit its limit." There are now over two hundred Starbucks stores in the DC area. Most pundits have learned by now to stop declaring the market saturated if they don't want to look foolish. Starbucks has to slow down sometime; we know that much. Yet exponential growth defines the company. By design, this machine doesn't have an off switch.

The System

The headquarters of the marketing consultancy Airvision sits atop a modern Seattle high-rise, and from its airy deck, one can take in glorious, panoramic views of the glimmering waters of Puget Sound. This makes sense: the firm's founder, Arthur Rubinfeld, knows a bit about finding first-rate locations. For ten years, Rubinfeld headed Starbucks's real estate development division, leaving the company with forty times as many stores as it had when he started. A compact, neatly dressed man in his fifties, Rubinfeld — like his old boss Howard Schultz — is fiercely competitive, and he has an uncanny ability to get under a person's skin. (When I declined his offer of pretzel rods, for example, he shot me a look that conveyed both shock and disappointment that I would turn down such a golden opportunity.) His was not a job for the polite or the complacent. "I used to always say, 'Never stop and never settle,' which gives you a piece of my personality," Rubinfeld told me. "At Starbucks, you want the most highly visible location that offers the most convenience to your customer. So let's go get it."

Rubinfeld's former colleagues at Starbucks have often criticized him for taking more than his fair share of credit for the company's success. In his book, *Built for Growth*, Rubinfeld tends to portray himself as Starbucks's one-man executive dynamo, and when talking to me, he occasionally launched unbidden into descriptions of his favorite accomplishments.* But braggadocio aside, Rubinfeld brought a rigid, methodical approach to the company's expansion that was vital to its future dominance. Years ago, McDonald's built up its vast kingdom by following the motto, "Put your sugar along the trail of ants, and never

---

*You may have also noticed by now that former Starbucks executives seem compelled by some invisible force to write books about their deeds at the company. In addition to the already-published tomes by Schultz, Rubinfeld, Scott Bedbury, and John Moore — a former marketing department employee we'll encounter later — books are forthcoming from Harry Roberts and from the team of Jerome Conlon and Wright Massey.

make the trail turn." Under Rubinfeld, Starbucks took that philosophy to its apex, crunching statistics by the dozens to deduce the best sites for its stores. The system he developed turned the company into a nearly infallible judge of retail locations — a machine, as Rubinfeld likes to put it. "There's nobody near Starbucks's machine," he said. "The machine is unstoppable."

Back in the company's early years, however, the Starbucks real estate department was *very* stoppable — many landlords wanted nothing to do with it. "In those days, people wouldn't even talk to us," said Art Wahl, who worked on some of Starbucks's first real estate deals, in the 1980s. "They'd laugh at us and ask, 'How are you going to make money selling *coffee?*' The landlords would flat tell us we couldn't afford the rent." Starbucks made up for these disadvantages with tenacity. Yves Mizrahi, Rubinfeld's predecessor as the company's development boss, explained that Starbucks had to pick specific targets and work for them relentlessly: "When we were developing Starbucks, we were fighting with the bagel guys, the video guys, and especially with the other coffee guys. Everyone wanted that one corner in Anywhere, USA, and we always got it." The doggedness of Schultz and his employees often won the day.

As the Starbucks brand gained cachet, landlords began clamoring for the company's coffeehouses, allowing it more freedom to place its stores according to strict guidelines, some of them quite shrewd. For example, if you drive *toward* the downtown core of any major American city, you'll notice that most every Starbucks you pass is on your right. Why? The company's real estate team long ago figured out that the hassle of making a left turn across traffic to reach a Starbucks, then another left to get going in the original direction again, could be enough to dissuade a hurried morning commuter from stopping in. By building each store to the inbound driver's right, the company made that daily latte even more (wait for it . . .) *convenient*. Here's another one: Why would Starbucks want to locate its cafés next to video stores and dry cleaners? Because they double a potential customer's contact with a given Starbucks. The company knows that cafés draw patrons in proportion to the number of people who happen to walk by, and unlike other businesses, video stores and dry cleaners require two visits: one to drop something off and one to pick it up. So for every time a prospective customer needed to rent a movie, he would have *two* chances to buy a Frappuccino.

But obviously, the system was much more sophisticated than a few rules of thumb. Before Starbucks considered building in a particular spot, it weighed the area's average education level (better-educated people were more inclined to patronize Starbucks), average household size, average income, the number of cars that pass within an eighth of a mile, the daytime versus nighttime population, and scores of other statistics. In keeping with the McDonald's maxim, Starbucks made itself into an unavoidable obstacle in people's daily paths, instead of trying to draw them out of their normal routines. The goal was to end up with the highest-visibility location possible — to "shout the name out" to passersby, as Rubinfeld explains it. They called the ideal site for a store "the corner of Main and Main," and indeed, Starbucks is fanatical about corner locations. "We put in place a very efficient real estate machine that has targeted intersections in every major market across the country," Rubinfeld told me, continuing with the "machine" motif. "People are working those intersections constantly, just waiting for a lease to come to term."

The operative word there is *every*, because the overarching objective of the company's real estate apparatus was to be *every*where in *every* city as quickly as possible. Starbucks didn't dip its foot gingerly into the water to test a city's reaction; it flooded new markets with stores, suffocating any major competitors under the deluge. Starbucks strikes quickly and decisively, a fact stand-up comedians apparently feel they must comment on at least once a month. (For example, former late-night talk show host Craig Kilborn: "There's a new Starbucks game out. I bought the game and played it. Then I woke up this morning and there were six more games.") The company could whip out a store in six weeks and, because of exhaustive preplanning, reach its maximum sales volume almost immediately. Starbucks was extraordinarily adaptable, able to cram its modular design components into the smallest retail spaces. Who could possibly keep up?

The company often orchestrated store openings specifically to terrify anyone who would dare challenge it. "Starbucks didn't just open in a town — they'd scare the daylights out of you," said Don Schoenholt, the specialty-coffee guru. "It was like, *boom!* 'We're here, baby!'" Case in point: in January 1996, Starbucks ensured that its entrance into the Toronto market wouldn't go unnoticed by opening its first five stores *on the same day*, then *another* five on the same day the following month. When I asked Rubinfeld about this show of brute force, he made no attempt to deny that the move had little to do with satisfying customers and everything to do with frightening competitors. "Of course that's why we did it," he said. "You understand the personalities behind this, right? Toronto's a city of millions of people. So what are you going to say? 'Let's go open stores there. Oookay, how about here first?' No. That's mediocrity. What you want to do if you've got a major competitor in the marketplace there is find out how you can break through the noise. How can you make a statement?"

Besides, Starbucks didn't need to worry about overbuilding, because its growth strategy across North America was as systematically thought out as a military campaign. This, too, followed a plan: the "hub" and "spoke" expansion model. First, the real estate department put together a database ranking every U.S. metropolitan area according to the qualities Starbucks found especially desirable — high income, high population, and high education. San Francisco headed the list; apparently, Saco, Montana, was at the bottom. With typical Starbucksian cuteness, they categorized these metro areas into tiers: "grande" markets, which could bear twenty-five-plus stores; "tall" markets, which could handle ten to twenty-five; and "short" ones, of less than ten. Then Starbucks just went down the list. The company began its campaign in each market by building a costly flagship store in the middle of the city's most thriving district. This central urban area was the "hub." Starbucks peppered each "hub" with stores at a predetermined rate — at least ten per year in a "grande" market — until it reached the point where analysis showed it could make more money from building a new store in a suburb. Now came the "spokes" with which the company surrounded the established "hub," essentially walling off its turf.

Before Starbucks entered any new neighborhood or town, it would supplement its statistical rundown with a few tricks of the trade. Real estate employees checking out a potential site would peek in the windows of nearby dry cleaners, to make sure the clothes looked like they belonged to affluent professionals. They examined where the oil stains were in parking lots, to see where people actually shopped. They even checked the ethnic foods aisles in the supermarkets, trying to find out if the locals were up for culinary experimentation.* If everything checked out, Starbucks loosed another volley of stores — and the barrage only gains in intensity with time. In 2006, for instance, Starbucks declared that it would build 250 new outlets in Chicago by 2011, which would give the city an astonishing 580 stores; the company refers to this supersaturation tactic as "infill." By showering a major market with outlets all at once before moving on to the next region, Starbucks both capitalized on economies of scale and guaranteed its dominance over the area, forcing competitors to try to establish beachheads in lower-tier cities. So it went, all across America: blanket the "hub"; construct dozens of "spokes"; move on to the next battlefield.

The one exception to the "hub" and "spoke" strategy was New York City, a territory that was dear to both Schultz and Rubinfeld. (The two first met while living in the same Manhattan apartment building back when Schultz was still a housewares salesman.) In 1994, Starbucks announced it was making its much-anticipated foray into "New York," sending competitors into a rush to open expensive stores in the heart of the city and carve out their piece of the market. But Starbucks was

---

*In a related story, legend has it that McDonald's agents — always targeting the kids — used to measure the length of the milk aisle in local markets to gauge the number of children in the area.

toying with them. Instead of planting stores in the "hub," the company first built "spokes" in Westchester and Fairfield counties, where many rich and influential New Yorkers lived. As the competitors in Manhattan struggled to keep their hastily assembled stores afloat, Starbucks sat back and let the anticipation for its arrival escalate. Finally, it opened truly monolithic Manhattan stores — like the cavernous four-thousand-square-foot Astor Place Starbucks — and overstaffed them to cater to demanding New Yorkers. The competition jumped ship, and now Starbucks is all you see. "That was a brilliant strategy," Rubinfeld said with a grin. "It was a total mindfuck. You can put that in your book."

After scattering its coffeehouses throughout a city long enough, Starbucks would soon run out of locations for new stores that wouldn't draw customers away from existing ones. Cannibalization, as it's called, was inevitable: if Starbucks wanted to continue "infilling" a market, it essentially had to steal customers from itself, thereby risking lower sales. For Starbucks, this wasn't much of a dilemma. The company would rather subtract from its own sales than let a competitor come in — and besides, Schultz had never been queasy about putting his stores across the street from each other.* But strangely enough, whenever the company cut into the clientele of one of its own stores, any loss in sales was temporary; new customers would take the place of the old ones within months, and both stores would soon be going full tilt. Each new store just created new demand. When I asked Dave Olsen, the Starbucks coffee expert, why there seemed to be no breaking point for this, he pointed out that most people drink coffee every day, making virtually everyone in an area a potential regular. "We're looking at the number of *customers*, not the number of stores," he said.

The only significant issue was making sure people noticed that the new stores existed. Sometimes this was easy. For example, when Starbucks

---

*This, incidentally, is a major reason why Starbucks doesn't franchise: Schultz always intended to blanket cities with outlets, but franchisees would surely protest every time the company wanted to jam in another store and endanger the franchisee's sales.

entered Harrisburg, Pennsylvania, in 2004, the grand opening attracted four local television crews and a hundred spectators. But failing free exposure like that, Starbucks had a clever stratagem for publicizing its new outlets on the cheap: get others to do it for you. John Moore, a former Starbucks marketing department employee, explained that Starbucks "had this down to a science." Each store opened with its own miniature marketing campaign, which was usually tied to a local charity. Allying with a charity was more than just public relations; it also earned the company access to huge networks of people. Starbucks typically designated a day when a portion of the new café's sales would go to the charity, giving the nonprofit an incentive to do much of the marketing legwork itself. "What it's all about is word of mouth," Moore said. "If a store donates a percentage of sales to a charity for a day, that charity will want as much money as possible, so they'll go out and tell as many people as possible to go out and buy a latte." Scott Bedbury, the former marketing chief, told me that another favorite method for attracting notice was to build a store in a children's hospital. "Call it marketing; call it PR," he said.

Put these pieces together, from the right-hand turns to the hubs and spokes, and you can see why Rubinfeld insists on calling Starbucks a machine: the company expands on a huge scale with unprecedented efficiency. This store-building prowess sometimes produces amusing results. In 2003, Starbucks constructed a store in the community of Casa de Oro, just outside San Diego, which the company publicized with banners and a daily countdown as "San Diego County's 100th Starbucks." But this ended up being for naught; it was actually number 101. As the *San Diego Union-Tribune* reported the day after the store's debut, "A Starbucks in the Midway area that also opened yesterday beat it by nine minutes when it opened at 5:07 a.m." Oops. Another issue came up when customers dared to name a store their "favorite Starbucks," only to find that the company had built another one even nearer to their home or workplace. This put the customer in an awkward position, the *Washington Post* writer Joel Achenbach observed: "Should you switch? Or show loyalty to the original? Or is the whole point that they're fundamentally the same?" Starbucks actually has a solution to this quandary — go to the one that triggers fewer flashbacks. A company executive once explained that if a store's color scheme "reminds you of something from your childhood that you intensely dislike, you can go three stores down to a different Starbucks and say, 'I like this better. I just feel better here.'"

That people can say things like this without being considered deranged is just one of the strange symptoms of Starbucks's ubiquity. Some effects are more serious, however. According to U.S. Department of Transportation data, the number of short stops made by morning car commuters (say, for a latte) went up nearly 400 percent between 1995 and 2001, leading to greater fuel waste, higher pollution, and worsened gridlock as more drivers pulled on and off the road. Somewhat predictably, the travel analyst Nancy McGuckin dubbed this traffic-snarling phenomenon the "Starbucks Effect." The company has even been known to inspire flagrant criminal activity in its customers. In 2002, a reporter for the local newspaper in Chagrin Falls, Ohio, spent three full weeks staking out the town's Starbucks in order to report that an average of thirty-six people jaywalked across busy North Main Street every morning to get to the café.

If some Americans feel unsettled at seeing Starbucks wherever they look, company executives are steadfastly unapologetic — remember, the stores are supposedly there to make our lives easier. When I asked Rubinfeld if this justification for the company's omnipresence was perhaps overly simplistic, he replied, "Coffee has always been about convenience. It has to be easy to get in and get out. So why is this new to you? Why is that surprising?" It seems likely that people would grow to resent the audacity and invasiveness of it all, I said, especially since it's the company's *goal* to become inescapable. "Well, initially there was a big, audacious issue to it," Rubinfeld said. "But it's a convenience-driven product, so people said, 'They're serving me better, and I care all about me.' Whether you know it or not, Starbucks is offering you convenience."

One Goliath, Many Frustrated Davids

Success is a relative concept when you're competing against Starbucks, but of all the chains that attempt to joust with the company, Caribou Coffee has so far been the most successful of the lot. It holds the unique distinction of being the only coffee chain with more stores than Starbucks in a major market — Minneapolis, Caribou's home turf, where it maintains a slight edge of a few dozen outposts. Caribou is also the only coffee company that boasts a leader who founded and sold a lucrative cookie company, set a number of long-distance bicycling records, and ran strong but unsuccessful political campaigns to unseat both an incumbent senator (Georgia Republican Paul Coverdell, in 1998) and a sitting Speaker of the House (Newt Gingrich, in 1996). "It's funny," Caribou CEO Michael Coles said, "when I raced bicycles, my nickname was 'Caffeine Coles.' It didn't have anything to do with coffee, though — it was because I was so high energy. So I like to think I was destined to be in the coffee business."

Coles found himself drawn to his current field largely because of one of the coffeehouse industry's strangest quirks: there is no real runner-up to Starbucks. Given the craze for espresso that took off in the nineties, one would expect that *someone* else had made money off of the new national thirst, but Starbucks had completely dwarfed every challenger. When Coles started looking for a new calling after he sold his first business, the Great American Cookie Company, for a small fortune ("God bless the mall," he said), he was astounded at the yawning gulf between Starbucks and everyone else. "I looked at how big Starbucks was at the time, but I couldn't find out who was the second-biggest coffee company. After some digging I found out that the second-biggest was Caribou, and I just couldn't believe it — it was second-biggest with about 150 stores. I kept Googling it because I couldn't even believe it. I thought, here was an opportunity."

By some measures, Caribou has cashed in on this opportunity; the company now operates about 450 stores — up from 180 when Coles took over in 2003 — and it completed its initial public offering on the Nasdaq exchange in 2005. With its trivia challenges at the cash register, its unpretentious and kid-friendly atmosphere, and its mountain lodge design — complete with crackling fireplace — Caribou has thrived as a sort of anti-Starbucks.

But despite its modest success, Caribou also epitomizes the struggles every coffeehouse chain has faced in trying to hold on to a slice of the market. For one, it has long had problems at the top — the company has endured several management shake-ups, and its stock nose-dived soon after the IPO. Caribou has had a healthy dose of bad luck, as well. In 2000, the company's founders, John and Kim Puckett, sold their ownership stake to the investment fund Crescent Capital, an arm of the First Islamic Investment Bank of Bahrain. For obvious reasons, this connection became problematic after September 11, 2001. By the next summer, the inevitable rumor that Caribou funded terrorism started making the rounds on the Internet. Sales plummeted; it got so bad that Caribou had to shutter its Chicago operations completely. Of course, First Islamic (which swiftly changed its name to the comfortingly vague Arcapita) wasn't supporting terrorism at all, but it did require its businesses to obey some of the tenets of Shar'ia, or Islamic Law, which punishes theft with amputation, condemns homosexuals to death, and may or may not encourage routine wife beating. (Caribou only had to abide by the financial rules of Shar'ia — like its prohibition against collecting interest — but being linked to the other, more controversial parts doesn't make for great public relations.) In many ways, Caribou's plight exemplifies why there is no number two to Starbucks, not even an Apple to its Microsoft. Through mismanagement, carelessness, or plain ill fortune, every single challenger has faltered.* And with those that didn't, Starbucks got ruthless.

---

*To clarify: in this chapter, "the competition" and related phrases refer to other coffee chains. Independently owned coffeehouses are a different matter, which we'll discuss in chapter 5.

As an example of carelessness, consider Starbucks's institutional competition: huge coffee brands like Nescafé and Folgers. For decades, the specialty-coffee industry braced itself for the seemingly imminent thud of one of these eight-hundred-pound gorillas landing on the coffeehouse scene, crushing all comers underneath the gigantic bankroll of Procter and Gamble or Philip Morris (which own Folgers and Maxwell House, respectively). But the major brands never even tried; they just ran new variations on the old commercials. For instance, in a 2001 spot for Folgers powdered "Caffe Latte mixes" that ran frequently on MTV, three hip twentysomethings sit on a couch sipping coffee, looking bored. In chimes a voice from above: "This isn't one of those coffees you sit and sip as the world passes you by." Thus inspired, the youths tear the cushions off the couch and ride them down a snow-covered hill. Apparently the kids are into proper sofa maintenance these days, because no one bought it.

The entire point of the gourmet coffee movement escaped the fast-food giants as well. If anyone could have matched Starbucks in a contest of store-building skill, it was McDonald's, but the way McDonald's took its shot at the coffeehouse market makes one think that the company *wanted* to fail. Consumers associated coffeehouses with sophistication and community, yet McDonald's dubbed its concept "McCafé," pretending it had no idea that, to most Americans, nothing said "cheap, plastic, and tacky" like slapping the prefix *Mc-* in front of a word. Though McCafés have seen success in Europe and Australia, they are basically just dressed-up McDonald's outlets. "They went as far as fake lace curtains and some kind of veneer wood on the front counter, as if that would vault them into Starbucks's league of design," scoffed Rubinfeld. Meanwhile, Starbucks was decimating McDonald's coffee sales, taking them down by a third over the last decade.

Those who did appreciate the coffeehouse's allure didn't do much better, though, thanks to a chronic amateurishness that seemed to afflict other coffee chains. Companies like Gloria Jean's, Diedrich, and Coffee People always struggled just to keep their doors open, whether from mismanagement, disastrous IPOs, or poor real estate selection. (On more than one occasion, Diedrich built a store, only to find out *after* it opened that the business center in which it stood was closed on weekends.) When I asked Harry Roberts, the former Starbucks marketer, why so many chains struggled just to make money off four-dollar lattes, he simply responded, "It's harder than it looks."

Tom O'Keefe, at least, has made the thrashing somewhat entertaining. Though his company, Tully's, has yet to make a cent of profit from its 110 U.S. stores, O'Keefe has managed to spark an amusing rivalry with Schultz — even if it has the competitiveness of a contest between the Green Bay Packers and your neighborhood Pee Wee football team. One August day, I went to the Tully's flagship store in downtown Seattle to meet O'Keefe, and after waiting a few minutes I asked a barista if he was somewhere in the store and I just hadn't recognized him. "Oh no," he replied. "You can't miss him. He definitely changes the energy of the place." When O'Keefe arrived, I understood what he meant. Seconds after walking in, O'Keefe was already careening around the store like an excited puppy — slapping backs, cracking wise, adjusting the volume of the music, and passing out coffee samples. He seems like the type who sleeps about an hour a night, and once he sat down, limbs always somehow in motion, I saw why: he started popping whole coffee beans into his mouth and chewing. "Fabulous, oh god, it's fabulous," he raved.

As with almost everyone I spoke to in the coffee industry, merely mentioning Starbucks to O'Keefe was sufficient to trigger a miniature dissertation on the company. "We're twelve feet higher than the big mermaid," he told me, referring to Tully's new central office and roasting plant, which reaches slightly higher in elevation than Starbucks's nearby headquarters. "We've got a big, thirteen-foot-high T." The altitude advantage is pretty much the only one Tully's holds in the rivalry, however, save for a few public relations coups. Once, Starbucks offered a guarantee of "Lattes for Life" as a prize at a charity auction, and, to Schultz's chagrin, O'Keefe put in the winning bid. Now, Schultz's assistant sends O'Keefe a $100 Starbucks gift card every month, which he's only too happy to use. "I bought it for $5,000, and I probably got $100,000 worth of publicity out of it," he crowed. He has also been known to show up at Starbucks company picnics and volunteer for the dunk tank, all in an effort to needle Schultz. "I say it's a love-hate relationship," O'Keefe said. "I love him and he hates me."

Schultz would never put it this way, but his colleagues aren't as diplomatic about O'Keefe. "Fuck him," Howard Behar blurted out when I mentioned O'Keefe's name, quickly adding, "Excuse my language." Many contend that O'Keefe's outrageous gestures are only designed to divert attention from the red ink on Tully's balance sheet. Like many others who have floundered, O'Keefe had no coffee experience before founding Tully's. "These people don't have a clear stance," said Kevin Knox, the former Starbucks roaster. "Look at Tully's — that guy is just some real estate guy. Another one is Caribou. What do these people stand for? These are just business guys who wanted to make some money."

The Iron Fist of the Mermaid

Companies like Tully's didn't need help from Starbucks to shoot themselves in the foot, but with those that showed signs of promise, Starbucks could be absolutely merciless. If Schultz chafed at losing volleyball games at the company picnic, he grew apoplectic whenever another coffee company outmaneuvered Starbucks. To avoid giving his competitors so much as an inch of ground, he would even pay the rent on a retail space just to keep it empty.

Schultz hired people who shared his distaste for losing, especially in the real estate department, which battled with other companies most directly. The preeminent example of this was Tracy Cornell, a dealmaker who easily matched Schultz in competitive drive. In her decade-plus career at Starbucks, Cornell found and locked up a staggering nine hundred retail sites in North America.

"I'm a deal junkie — that's what I get off on," Cornell told me. "I think, honestly, that I can sell anything." Cornell was so aggressive, in fact, that Schultz at first considered her a potential liability and pondered firing her. But she was just too effective to lose. "Tracy is absolutely Attila the Hun when it comes to making deals," said Art Wahl, the Seattle real estate broker. "She'd run through a wall to talk to someone about putting in a Starbucks." On one occasion, when Cornell was in San Francisco hunting for sites, the landlord of an attractive retail space refused to talk to her because of his dislike for Starbucks. Cornell soon discovered that the landlord was a physician, so she made an appointment with his office, pretending to be a patient. When he walked in to see her, she went into her pitch. "I got the deal done, I can tell you that much," she recalled, obviously savoring the memory. "At the end of the day, I got the site."

Keeping cutthroat agents like Cornell on the payroll certainly helped Starbucks tyrannize the competition, but nothing signaled Schultz's willingness to win at all costs like the company's entrance into San Francisco — home of Peet's, the company's spiritual father, which was still owned and operated by Schultz's old mentor Jerry Baldwin. When Baldwin sold Starbucks to Schultz in 1987, the agreement included a noncompete clause that kept Starbucks out of the Bay Area until 1992. As soon as the noncompete expired, Baldwin received an ominous letter from Schultz, offering to buy out Peet's. "The implied threat was, 'We'll crush you,'" Baldwin later told the *Los Angeles Times* of the letter. Baldwin was furious. He'd given Schultz his start in the coffee business, and now the guy was threatening him? Shortly after Baldwin declined Schultz's offer, he learned just how serious his former pupil really was: Starbucks opened up a store on Chestnut Street in San Francisco, just a few doors down from a Peet's. "That's Howard — he's a streetfighter," said Dawn Pinaud, the early Starbucks employee. "He and Jerry were *friends*, but he wanted to take him out by taking away sales. I mean, the store was right across the street. When I first saw it, I said, 'Oh my god, is he insane?'"

It didn't end there. Since Starbucks considered San Francisco its most potentially lucrative market, Schultz continued the onslaught, to the point where one California real estate agent told *Seattle Weekly*, "They [Starbucks] seem to have a thing about moving in next door to Jerry." (Incidentally, Peet's has thrived despite the clash. Within the coffeehouse industry, its profitability is second only to Starbucks, in part because Baldwin expanded very slowly and carefully.) Those who know Schultz insist his actions weren't malicious, but just business. "I don't know what Jerry was thinking," Roberts said. "For us not to open in San Francisco at all would be ridiculous. Did he expect that we would give him that market forever? In Jerry's mind, Starbucks was still his. We're talking about emotion here, not logic." Schultz himself defends aggressive moves like these as an unavoidable reality of the marketplace. "The real estate business in America is a very, very tough game," he told *Business Week* in 2002. "It's not for the faint of heart."

The Peet's case notwithstanding, Starbucks was usually successful in its attempts to buy a strong competitor out of the way — an approach that often won the company feelings of undying hatred from devotees of the coffeehouses it purchased and liquidated. The first (and most notorious) instance of this occurred in 1994. Starbucks wanted to break into the Boston market, yet it faced two strong and entrenched competitors: Dunkin Donuts, which was already everywhere in Boston; and George Howell's Coffee Connection, one of the nation's most prominent coffee institutions. Fearing Starbucks's advance, Howell had been rapidly opening stores to defend his territory, yet he was growing miserable; he wanted to ponder coffee's aesthetics, not build a chain. So Starbucks made Coffee Connection — to use Rubinfeld's words — "an offer they couldn't refuse": $23 million in stock. (If you're wondering, this would be worth nearly $600 million today.) Schultz hastened to promise Coffee Connection's loyal customers that there would be "very few changes" in its operations, telling the *Boston Globe*, "The name will stay the same. And the coffee will stay the same, roasted in Boston and guided by George Howell. We don't want to create anxiety and tension." Within two years, however, Schultz flipped all of the Coffee Connection stores into Starbucks outlets, closed its Boston roasting plant, and laid off much of its staff.

Over the next decade, Starbucks repeated this strategy a number of times. It bought and converted the fifty-six-store Pasqua Coffee Company chain, the seventeen-store Torrefazione Italia chain, most of the two-hundred-store Diedrich chain, and — when it wanted to make its entry into the British market with a bang — the sixty-five-store Seattle Coffee Company. About this last move, which made Starbucks a common sight in the UK virtually overnight, Seattle Coffee Company cofounder Scott Svenson quipped, "Better to work with Starbucks than to work against them."* When Starbucks finally admitted it was hopeless at making tea, it bought the Portland-based Tazo Tea Company. And Seattle's Best customers thought they'd walked right into George Orwell's *1984* when they stopped in for a drink one day in April 2003 and noticed a small placard on the counter announcing, "Today we are pleased to announce that Starbucks has purchased Seattle's Best Coffee." (O'Keefe claims Starbucks has also offered to buy Tully's, which several Starbucks sources denied. "He was just trying to get under Howard's skin by putting his stores in right next to ours, but why would Starbucks want to buy him then?" Cornell explained. "It would just be buying redundant space.")

Reactions to Starbucks's cutthroat tactics vary. Some sigh at the futility of trying to battle such a relentless and aggressive heavyweight. Others credit Schultz and Starbucks for doing so much to make coffee a high-profile product; Nick Cho, of the Washington, DC, independent café Murky Coffee, likes to say that Starbucks enabled him to sell four-dollar lattes in the first place. (Herb Hyman, the founder of Coffee Bean and Tea Leaf, goes even further: he cackles with delight when he thinks of all the money he's made off his Starbucks stock.) And many commend Starbucks for its hard-nosed approach. This *is*

---

*We'll delve into Starbucks's campaigns abroad, as well as the cultural imperialism debate, in chapter 9.

America, after all, where a modicum of ruthlessness in pursuit of success is considered a healthy part of the entrepreneurial spirit.

But a growing number of people, both in America and abroad, are beginning to take exception to Starbucks's domination of the coffee market and its omnipresence in the urban landscape. Consumer choice keeps dissolving into Starbucks ubiquity, and company spokespeople just smile and cheerily announce that consumers' lives are becoming more convenient. It didn't matter if you liked Torrefazione or Coffee Connection or Pasqua — you would go to Starbucks regardless. By undercutting all challengers and making its stores unavoidable, the company made sure of that. And as I learned from Howard Schultz when we met in his Seattle office one afternoon, this is only the beginning of what he has in mind for Starbucks.

The Belly of the Beast

If you are at all inclined to view Starbucks as a sinister corporate villain bent on global domination, you'll only become more convinced of this after your first glimpse of Starbucks Center, its monolithic headquarters in an industrial area south of downtown Seattle. From atop a 150-foot-high clock tower, a giant replica of the top of the siren's head — just the eyes and the crown — peeks out at passersby. She looks eerily sphinxlike up there, her huge, blank eyes gazing off across the city. The image repeats on each of the four sides of the tower, which gives one the impression that the siren has a panoramic view of her domain. And that she's *always watching.* Even Chris Gimbl, a longtime Starbucks spokesman, admits the effect is a little unsettling. "Yeah, it can seem kind of ominous," he told me as we walked through the building's labyrinthine hallways. "Some Starbucks people have tried to explain that she's watching over the port — you know, to protect it — but that's too over the top for me."

As befits a sprawling international megacorporation, Starbucks Center is an enormous structure of nearly two million square feet, enough to accommodate twenty-five hundred employees and a few big-box retailers. When Sears first constructed it in 1912 as a distribution center for the West Coast, it was America's largest building west of the Mississippi. Now, it's just the biggest office building in the Northwest. Some floors in the squat, brick structure have more than three football fields' worth of space; Sears employees used to transport parcels around the complex on roller skates. The building is, quite literally, a gigantic Starbucks, and for reasons that go beyond the familiar decor and the shiny espresso machines that dot the hallways. Because Starbucks Center is so mazelike inside (Gimbl even got disoriented a few times while showing me around, and we also ran into a veteran employee who greeted us, "Oh hi! Where am I?"), the floor plan is laid out so that each level is exactly the same. That is, the Yukon conference room on floor four is in precisely the same spot as the Yukon room on floor five, which is a clone of the Yukon room on floor six, and so on — which just goes to show that homogeneity and monotony are design directives Starbucks never fails to embrace.

Naturally, reminders of the company's growth are seldom far from view at Starbucks Center. In one open atrium area, the flags of various Starbucks-colonized nations hang around a garage door–sized black scoreboard that displays the company's store counts in each of the countries where it operates. When I pointed out that the board was a few hundred stores behind, Gimbl replied, "Well, keeping it up-to-date would be a full-time job."* On a more symbolic level growthwise, the company maintains several potted coffee trees, which sit in a spacious skylit community area set up exactly like a huge Starb — actually, I'm sure you can guess what it's set up exactly like. Bright-eyed employees in casual attire, each of them holding a steaming mug, chatted at the tables. "The trees have really thrived in here," Gimbl volunteered, prompting a cocked eyebrow from me. Coffee plants are typically leafy

---

*A quick side note: A Texas man who calls himself "Winter" actually *has* made a full-time pursuit out of visiting and cataloging every Starbucks store on the planet. He's made it to about sixty-five hundred locations so far.

and lush, but these were yellowed and scraggly, with only a few scattered berries. "I do use 'thrive' a little bit subjectively," he clarified. "I mean, this is not coffee you'd want to process and drink."

As Gimbl and I walked through the muffled silence of fields of cubicles — the headquarters follows an "open plan," which translates as "pretty much nobody gets an office" — a few messengers intercepted us with urgent news: "They're looking for you. Howard is ready now."

Schultz is not a man one keeps waiting. Though he is no longer technically the company's CEO, Schultz is still the undisputed chieftain of the Starbucks tribe. Instead of managing the company's day-to-day operations, he spends his time trying to "touch as many people as possible" — visiting stores, playing the company's public face, and calling its branches around the world: Europe in the morning and Asia at night. What's more, when I visited, he had a professional basketball team to run. With about fifty other smaller investors, Schultz bought the Seattle SuperSonics in 2001; his 42 percent stake set him back $84 million. (Which isn't necessarily a lot of money for Schultz. He also owns a $14 million vacation home in the Hamptons, and according to *Forbes* magazine, his net worth exceeds $1.1 billion.)

The Sonics investment has been something of a disaster for Schultz's public image in Seattle. Before dabbling in sports franchise ownership, Schultz fit in nicely with the city's pantheon of young male business titans, like Amazon.com's Jeff Bezos and Microsoft's Bill Gates. Local newspapers referred to him affectionately as "Mr. Coffee," and many Seattleites found it hard to understand why anyone wouldn't adore Starbucks (which happened to have made a lot of them rich). Sure, there was one dustup in 1994, when Schultz rerouted the driveway at his new multimillion-dollar Lake Washington mansion through a small, disused area of adjacent Viretta Park, later nicknamed "Vendetta Park." The court battle with a group of incensed locals over the hundred-foot crushed limestone path took years to resolve. (Schultz had to remove part of the driveway.) "Howard was being stupid," Roberts explained. "He was full of himself. He came to community meetings about it with two-thousand-dollar suits and five lawyers."

But Schultz didn't become truly controversial until the purchase of the Sonics. At first, he tried to Starbucksify the team, even giving players his home phone number "just in case they need to talk." The franchise lost millions each year, though, and Schultz soon grew unhappy with its lease agreement for Key Arena, the team's home court. He began acting petulant in public, griping about certain players to the media and throwing now-legendary tantrums during games from his courtside seats. He pouted about the need for a better arena, exhorting the fans, the city, and the state government to pay for a new facility (a suggestion many denounced as "welfare for billionaires"). As I was walking into the executive enclave on the eighth floor of Starbucks Center, Schultz was in the middle of a media firestorm over his threat to move the Sonics out of Seattle — perhaps the most effective means known to mankind of turning an entire city against you. (Indeed, a few months after we spoke, Schultz sold the team to a group of investors from Oklahoma City.) He might as well have proclaimed that he'd peed in everyone's lattes over the years. "If people want to make me the villain, that's their prerogative," he grumbled to the *Seattle Times*.

So the Schultz I met was subdued, to say the least. After shaking my hand, he slouched so far back in his stuffed armchair that I had to wonder how he was still able to breathe. His eyes flitted listlessly around his office, a cluttered and less majestic place than one might expect, with a bile-green carpet that bordered on the unsightly. Aside from the spectacular view of downtown Seattle and a set of artsy black-and-white photographs on one wall, there was little to indicate that this was the workplace of anyone more important than a moderately successful lawyer — which is just how Schultz likes it. When I pointed out the bottle of Mazagran (the failed carbonated coffee drink) displayed on his desk and the rack of *Joe* magazines (the failed lifestyle quarterly) in the corner, he explained that they were there to ward off complacency by reminding him of past missteps. "We don't want to take anything for granted," he said. "I really believe that our success is not an entitlement, that we have to earn it every day." But make no mistake: it's not like Schultz suffers from a lack of self-esteem. Even on off days, Schultz is the consummate top dog. Dressed smartly in a tailored blue shirt and dark slacks, he exuded an air of unshakable confidence, like a man who has come to see it as part of the natural order of things that people jump at his command. Those who know Schultz say he can turn the charisma on and off at will, a by-product of his years as a salesman. Today, the charm switch was definitely off.

I asked Schultz if he agreed with those — including his former right- and left-hand men, Behar and Orin Smith — who have claimed that Starbucks changed the world. "It's a pretty arrogant thing to say, 'We changed the world,'" he replied. "I don't know if I'd say it like that. I think we have managed to, with a simple cup of coffee and a very unique experience, enhance the lives of millions of people by creating a sense of community, by bringing people together and recognizing the importance of *place* in people's lives. In the last few years, I think it's become fairly evident that we're having this effect around the world." This is the kind of statement that made Schultz a marketing icon; he can steer any question toward the concepts he wants to associate with the brand, turning his answer into a brief celebration of the benevolence of Starbucks. The lofty words tend to arrive in avalanches. Explaining what his company has done for the once-debased coffee bean, for example, Schultz told me, "We've been able to raise it to a unique level in this country in terms of its manifestations of the social experience, bringing people together, community, *humanity*, all of these things."

Mention coffee around Schultz, and the next thing you know you're talking about the human condition. When I asked how these leaps made sense — how a latte can become a key to transcendence and how, as he often claims, a company with 125,000 employees could possibly be "passionate" — Schultz adopted a serene, sagelike grin. "It's very easy to be passionate about something that tastes so good," he said. "And I think the culture of the company self-selects people who are passionate, and probably people leave who do not feel it. It's not just something that you can prescribe and hand to somebody. It's just . . . it happens. It's imprinted on the DNA of the company."

If Schultz sometimes sounds like a victim of wishful thinking, this is because he genuinely believes his company can do what most people deem impossible; and considering how far Starbucks has risen when next to no one thought it viable twenty years ago, it's hard to blame him. This is a company that forever changed the way people consume the most popular beverage on the planet. After his near-religious experience in a Milan espresso bar, Schultz took two cheap and simple ingredients, coffee and milk, and used them to spark a national craze, develop a powerful brand, twist Wall Street around his little finger, and expand his caffeinated empire faster than any other chain in history. Why *wouldn't* he think Starbucks is capable of anything? But Schultz doesn't just believe things that seem impossible; he believes things that *are* impossible. In a remark about Starbucks's ability to incorporate "romance and theater" into its design, he told me, "I think the art and mystique of Starbucks has been our ability to do that in a company that could be described as a chain. It's *not*, because every store, although the same, is different." It sounds like something a stoned college student might say — *every store, although the same, is different* — but to Schultz, the true believer, it makes perfect sense.

This conviction that Starbucks can achieve the unachievable helps explain Schultz's dismissal of any concerns about resistance to his company's ubiquity. Once people "get underneath the hood and see the conscience of the company, the benevolence of Starbucks," he said, they welcome it into their communities without reservation. "I think the issue of ubiquity was more of a concern people had three or four years ago than they appear to have today," he continued, "because of the kind of company we are, the reputation we have." Schultz might see no downside in exponential expansion, but many others view the matter differently. "It's going to become like McDonald's," said Jim Romenesko, the Starbucks Gossip webmaster. "When I was a kid, going to McDonald's was special, but then they just ran it up until it got out of control. Starbucks is just going to lose appeal as it grows. I already see it happening." Robert Thompson, the Syracuse University pop-culture professor, pointed out that Starbucks has long thrived on its gourmet image, yet utterly pervasive companies never maintain their air of distinction. "Anyone can get Starbucks now," he told me. "There's no exclusivity to it anymore. They've moved into volume, volume, volume." Regardless, Schultz claims his company shall overcome all doubt. He concedes that "when things get big, they don't usually stay good," but insists that Starbucks is different. "No company our size has ever really done this before," he said. "We have created an anomaly in the marketplace, and in doing so, we are for the most part being given the respect that very few have garnered in the past."

Starbucks, Schultz believes, is an enterprise fueled by destiny — he's been sure of this since that fateful day in Milan. In his book, Schultz compares himself to the wizard Merlin, who went through life going backward in time, forever alienated from others by his knowledge of what the future held. "Sometimes I think I know how he must have felt," he wrote. "My vision for the future, my aspirations of what kind of company Starbucks should be, are so easily misunderstood." In a sense, Schultz is probably right to believe in fate. If he had never voyaged out to Seattle and just continued selling housewares, another company would have brought gourmet coffee to the masses, but surely no one could have replicated the dramatic, overwhelming success of Starbucks. So when I asked Schultz if he would have been happy if things had turned out differently — if Starbucks had only blossomed into a chain of maybe a hundred stores — he was momentarily taken aback, as if the question didn't make sense to him. And maybe it didn't. "I would not have been happy if I knew the opportunity was greater than one hundred stores and we stopped," he began. "But I don't think anyone then or now believed the runway we would have would be this great. And sitting here today, it's going to be greater from this point on to the future than it has been in the last fifteen years. That's going to be the *stunner*."

But what if the world is already stunned enough?

~PART TWO~

Getting Steamed

—5—

Storm Brewing

On the afternoon of July 12, 1789, a young French journalist and rabble-rouser named Camille Desmoulins vaulted himself onto a tabletop at Paris's Café de Foy, drew a pair of pistols from within his coat, and — losing for a moment his lifelong stammer — let out an impassioned cry: "To arms, citizens!" In eighteenth-century France, this sort of thing actually happened all the time; café patrons generally just tried to get the overexcited speaker off the furniture by telling him something like, "Hey, you start storming the Bastille and we'll totally meet you there later." But at that moment, with bread prices intolerably high and the monarchy utterly despised, Desmoulins's speech drove those at the Café de Foy into a frothing rage, and the crowd charged off to pick a fight that would eventually snowball into the French Revolution.

That this bloody national uprising began in a coffeehouse is hardly a surprise. Coffee is a remarkably incendiary beverage, with a long history of sparking debate, dissent, and even outright violence; some thinkers of ages past went so far as to blame "that dark and evil bean from Africa" for the human sacrifices made by the "black-skinned savages of that continent." Cafés have nurtured the ideological seed-lings of revolutions from Europe to Russia to America, a fact that led many fearful governments to stock them with spies, if they permitted them to operate at all. Coffee-inspired unruliness so terrified the grand viziers of the seventeenth-century Ottoman Empire, for instance, that they briefly made consumption of the brew a crime punishable by death. (Those caught drinking it received a brutal thrashing on the first offense, and on the second offense they were just sealed inside a leather bag and pitched into the Bosphorus River.) One might think that jitter-inducing caffeine, not coffee, is the real culprit behind all the friction and strife. But consider this: tea contains the very same drug, yet it has precisely the *opposite* reputation — that of a great paci-fier, a symbol of polite society. It may seem far-fetched to think that cof-fee has some unique power over us, but at the same time, a cup of English Breakfast never made anyone want to fight the powers that be.

For reasons that may forever remain mysterious, discord sticks to cof-fee like a shadow, and today this turmoil has taken a new form. Ironi-cally, the outrage that coffeehouse-goers used to channel into toppling the government now has a new target: the coffeehouse itself. Actually, just *one* coffeehouse — Starbucks. In a way, this is surprising; one of the company's signal achievements was its ability to take the countercultural bite out of coffeehouses and transform them into beverage-dispensing day spas. But in the process, Starbucks created an entire subculture of people who abhor its way of doing business. After all, Starbucks is the first coffeehouse to ever actually *become* one of those reviled powers that be that café patrons have always resisted. The coffeehouse as a hotbed of radical ideas is largely dead, and though it trades on this romantic im-age, Starbucks is the one that did it in. Indeed, thinking of the coffee-house as a haven for intellectual discourse is difficult when the one in question operates thousands of clones, wants to sell you the latest Cold-play album, and serves five-dollar milkshakes for adults. It's tough to imagine Camille Desmoulins hopping up onto a purple velour couch and hoisting a venti iced mocha for liberty.

Chances are, he'd be hoisting a metal *USA Today* box through the front windows of a Starbucks instead, as a group of bandana-masked protesters did, to much fanfare, during the 1999 World Trade Organization riots in Seattle. This climactic moment — images of which reached millions of Americans through television and newspapers — constituted the official beginning of a backlash against Starbucks. The company had finally reached a point where it was no longer an up-and-coming Northwest coffee company, but another massive corporation. And to those of a certain Left-leaning bent, Starbucks was more than that: it stood for everything rotten and deceitful about corporate America. On top of all of the attention, accolades, and cash the company has earned over the years, it now attracts an equal measure of controversy. Just as in the nineties, legions of customers still flaunt their green-and-white cups as status symbols; the difference is, today you'll also find some customers ducking furtively into Starbucks stores with unmarked mugs, petrified that they might be spotted patronizing a company that many in their peer group consider downright evil.

But wait a minute. Starbucks is supposed to be in the business of fostering social harmony — filling souls, not just bellies, and all that. Why the hand-wringing about a *coffee company?* Because for some people — neighborhood activists, human rights workers, and ordinary, Big Business–wary Americans among them — Starbucks touches a special nerve. Megacompanies like McDonald's and Wal-Mart are easy targets, their transgressions so obvious that it's pointless to debate them; anyone who walks through the golden arches knows they're taking the express route to heart disease, yet they pack the place regardless. But in the eyes of its critics, Starbucks is a far subtler threat, its methods more insidious. For one, the company has buffed its public image to such a high sheen that unless you've spent time investigating its effects on the world, you would think Starbucks was a branch of the United Nations. Think about its core product: coffee seems benign, yet it's fiercely addictive. And look at its expansion technique: the chain sneaks into the crevices of a city, swiftly and silently reaching ubiquity. Plus, to grow so fast and make so much money just seems sinister, like the company really *is* aiming for global domination. Little wonder, then, that Dr. Evil, the power-hungry villain in the *Austin Powers* movies, kept a secret lair at the top of Starbucks headquarters.

Everyone has an opinion about Starbucks, and those whose feelings on the company range toward burning hatred have expressed their derision in a variety of creative ways — boycotts, pickets, petitions, vandalism, and more. Take Jeremy Dorosin, a California scuba instructor who felt so wronged by Starbucks's customer service that he paid $40,000 for several large *Wall Street Journal* ads denouncing the company.* Or consider a few examples of the inventive sabotage techniques favored by the anticorporate wing of the Starbucks-hating crowd. In 2003, vandals jammed the locks of twenty-three Houston Starbucks stores with toothpicks and glue in the dead of night, rendering the cafés inoperable. That same year, a group of San Francisco pranksters disabled the locks at seventeen stores, then plastered up FOR LEASE signs and a faked memo on Starbucks letterhead declaring that in the interest of good taste, "This location will cease operations as of today." ("We hope that you will continue to visit us here until that time," the letter added cheekily.) In 1999, hoodlums in Portland, Maine, shattered one store's windows on four consecutive weekends. "Customers say it's been really inconvenient," late-night host Conan O'Brien remarked about the incident, "because, several times now, they've had to use the Starbucks across the street."

The list goes on and on: a sit-in in Madison, Wisconsin; spray-painted "corporate whore" screeds in Chicago; a string of aggressive urination incidents at a store in Durango, Colorado; ball bearings fired through the windows of three San Diego stores. Starbucks has become

---

*To be fair, Dorosin's anger was slightly out of proportion with Starbucks's transgression against him: selling him two defective $300 espresso machines, then refusing to replace them with $2,400 models. When the company offered a compromise, Dorosin upped the ante, demanding Starbucks apologize for mistreating him by sponsoring a multimillion-dollar center for runaway kids.

such a perennial target that on particularly volatile occasions, police protect it in advance. When New York City hosted the Republican National Convention in the summer of 2004, for example, several Starbucks stores stayed open behind walls of riot cops, and the company instructed its employees not to wear their uniforms in public for fear of drawing hostility. For some, protesting Starbucks is a knee-jerk reaction. After a Seattle police officer shot and killed a black man who was trying to flee a traffic stop in his car in 2001, the Reverend Robert Jeffrey of New Hope Baptist Church had an odd response: he called for a boycott of Starbucks. Obviously, the company had nothing to do with the incident, but Jeffrey had picked up on a neat trick — if you want attention for your cause, protest Starbucks and you'll get it.*

So what, precisely, has Starbucks done to incur this ill will? The lineup of charges against the company is quite diverse, but they fall into five main categories. According to its critics, Starbucks is

★ Killing the character of neighborhoods and employing predatory tactics to take out locally owned coffeehouses.

★ Causing the suffering of millions of Third World coffee farmers by paying unfair prices for beans.

★ Peddling a product that is harmful to our health (and to our delicate palates).

★ Exploiting its employees and crushing their attempts to unionize.

★ Homogenizing the planet and destroying cultural diversity by saturating the world with its stores.

There are plenty more where those came from — like the accusations that Starbucks secretly pushes a liberal agenda, and even that it once

---

*Jeffrey tried to justify the boycott by claiming that all of corporate America deserves blame for keeping black people down, but he also admitted that protesting Starbucks was a far more effective publicity grabber than the usual candlelight vigils and rallies.

attempted to exploit emotions about 9/11 to sell more of its Tazo Citrus drinks — but those are the most significant of the lot. These five allegations trace the effect a corporation has on every part of the world it touches: local neighborhoods, suppliers, customers, employees, and the very fabric of world culture itself. Figuring out the truth behind the charges levied against Starbucks, then, should give us a picture of what its influence on the world really is. And that is the objective of the second half of this book: to investigate the ethical debates about the company's interactions with different segments of society — from coffee growers to mom-and-pop coffeehouse owners — and to discover the hidden ways that Starbucks affects our lives.

When I spoke with Howard Schultz, he insisted that the allegations against his company were "all noise," just the bitter grumblings of those who reflexively hate any business where you can't buy things made from hemp. Yet if this were no more than "noise," Starbucks wouldn't have to pay upwards of $500,000 a year to provide Schultz with bodyguards and personal security services. (In 2003 alone, the company shelled out $677,334 to protect him.) Nevertheless, Schultz has consistently expressed bewilderment at the suggestion that there are people who don't adore Starbucks unconditionally; in response, he simply reiterates his belief in the company's essential magnanimity. "You have to have the *courage* to believe in the *purpose* of the company," he told me, wringing the maximum meaning out of the noble nouns. "And the courage we have is that we recognize that our success is going to create people that are going to misunderstand us or target us for something. Over time, we're going to have detractors because we've gotten big and successful."

Of course, this is at least partially true; any company as huge and lucrative as Starbucks will inevitably draw critics. But Schultz also believes his company has become a magnet for controversy *because* it's so benevolent — in other words, because protesters know Starbucks is a progressive company and therefore assume it will be inclined to heed their criticism. (Ronnie Cummins, the head of the Organic Consumers Association, has basically granted Schultz this point. Cummins has organized several protests of the company over its use of milk containing bovine growth hormone, and he acknowledges that his group only picks on Starbucks because a conglomerate like Kraft would never pay it a moment's attention.) Schultz also likes to point out that Starbucks gets an unfair share of anticorporate agitation because of its high visibility. "Starbucks is both this ubiquitous brand and a place where you can go and break a window," he told *Business Week* in 2002. "You can't break a can of Coke." But this is only the logical result of a strategy Schultz himself emphatically embraced: if your stores are convenient to visit for a Frappuccino, they're also convenient to vandalize. Ultimately, Starbucks brought this controversy on itself with its rapid expansion and its constant self-promotion. "For a big corporation, they're phenomenal and progressive in many ways," explained Kevin Knox, the former Starbucks roaster. "But they promote themselves as being even better than they actually are. So they open themselves up to be analyzed according to the highest standards."

The unique thing about the Starbucks backlash is that all of the ethical questions about the company are very much up in the air. In fact, despite the picketing and window smashing, many believe Starbucks is a model corporate citizen. It doesn't take much investigation to deduce that a Big Mac won't do your arteries any favors, but can you say with such certainty whether coffee is good or bad for us? Or if a new Starbucks in your area will help or hurt the local economy? As we'll see, many of the things people commonly assume about Starbucks, the coffee production chain, and the life-giving bean we so worship are dead wrong.

And one of the biggest misconceptions of all may also be the most widespread. Many proclaim it as if it's beyond doubt: Starbucks has systematically hunted down America's mom-and-pop coffee shops and driven them out of business, draining character and cash out of neighborhoods in the process. But while the company's effect on communities is up for debate, Starbucks's ubiquity has had astonishing and entirely unexpected consequences for its independently owned competition.

Green Alert

Whenever Starbucks announces plans to enter another thriving community, there's always a subset of alarmed locals who react as though the town were under siege from the Mongol horde. Yet even by these standards, the residents of the Hosford-Abernethy neighborhood raised a considerable amount of hell when the company declared its intent to build a store there in the spring of 2004. As the liberal nerve center of the already hyperliberal city of Portland, Oregon, the community has long been a tough sell for chains; shortly before the Starbucks revelation, the riled-up citizenry had scored a triumph over McDonald's, which had to scuttle its plans to open nearby because of strong resistance. Now, the locals were fighting Starbucks's occupation of a marquee space on a multipronged intersection known as Seven Corners. This did not fit with the pro-mom-and-pop neighborhood plan, and people let Starbucks know it in a flurry of protests and pickets. To say that relations between the company and its prospective customers were troubled would be putting it lightly. At one demonstration, a nine-year-old girl with a moss-green hat pulled over her ears took the microphone and announced that Starbucks was a "cancer."

The conflict reached its climax one night that May — on the eve of the store's scheduled debut — when a hooded and masked man, who was later given the folk-hero nom de guerre "The Nightworker," made a last-ditch attempt to stop the Starbucks from opening: he tossed a Molotov cocktail at the store's front windows. But unbeknownst to the amateur bombardier, by then the chain had learned to use reinforced glass, so the homemade firebomb just bounced off the building and burned out on the sidewalk without causing much damage.

One could easily dismiss this act of anticorporate terrorism as an over-the-top anomaly, but there's a noteworthy point to consider here: some people are so afraid of what a Starbucks will do to their neighborhood that they'd sooner see the store burned to the ground than risk letting it open. Moreover, these worries seem to apply to Starbucks more than to any other similar chain. If that retail space had gone to, say, Bath and Body Works, the opposition to it would never have risen above a few grumbles about what-is-the-world-coming-to and never-thought-I'd-see-the-day. Certainly, no one would have tried to *firebomb* it.

When residents resist Starbucks's advances, they do so out of worry over a unique set of local effects: changing neighborhood character, soaring property values, increasing tourism and traffic — in short, things we usually group under the touchy concept of "gentrification." To some, the company is inextricably linked with this controversial phenomenon; a 2001 Brookings Institution report on the topic even listed the arrival of Starbucks stores as a sign of gentrification in progress, along with new art galleries, music clubs, and businesses that offer valet parking. Locals also chafe at the idea that Starbucks will bulldoze its way into their neighborhood no matter what anyone says, and they fear that any cash spent at the chain will stream back to its corporate headquarters, sucking the community dry. "I don't want to be an elitist and say there's not room for everyone," Charles Kingsley, who worked on the neighborhood growth plan for Hosford-Abernethy, told me. "I know we can't be exclusively local. But I also know that with local businesses, money circulates a lot longer in the local economy, which makes a big difference." Under this logic, Starbucks could endanger not just the identity of a neighborhood, but its very survival as well.

Anxieties about gentrification and corporate strong-arming have launched many communities into full-blown civil-defense mode. Thousands have signed petitions to keep Starbucks out of cities from Santa Fe, New Mexico, to Athens, Georgia. (Taking this a step further, the town of Excelsior, Minnesota, turned its antipathy toward the company into a tourism slogan: "Secede from Starbucks nation.") Sometimes, the sheer volume of a community's collective loathing is enough to turn Starbucks away. In 2002, for example, the chain called off plans to construct a store in London's posh Primrose Hill neighborhood after local authorities received thirteen hundred letters of objection, including one from the actor Jude Law, who lived in the area. The emotional trauma of having a Starbucks open nearby can even reopen age-old psychological wounds. "They should not come at all," one resident of San Francisco's Japantown community told the *San Francisco Examiner* about the chain's plan to build a coffeehouse there. "We've been through too much, the Japanese people." A small army of four thousand petitioners cajoled Starbucks into abandoning that proposal as well.

Schultz denies the charge that his company disregards the feelings of local residents, offering a counterexample: "There was a community in Westchester County, New York, called Katonah that didn't want Starbucks, so we said 'fine.' We don't want to go where we're not wanted." Some doubt his sincerity, however, because outcomes like this are so incredibly rare. Constant hostility from neighborhood activists has given the company such thick skin that things have to go horribly, firebombingly bad before it considers backing down. Starbucks reacts to local opposition with practiced cool, always playing up the advantages of having an outlet nearby. After all, it declares, we're trying to build community. Did we mention we just got back from a four-day retreat about "human connection" and never even thought of mentioning money?* Oprah *loves* us. How could we be bad? "It's a fine balance to know where you're wanted, where you'll be accepted, and where you should wait," Arthur Rubinfeld, the former real estate chief,

---

*Current Starbucks CEO Jim Donald actually boasted of having done this in a 2005 issue of *Fortune* magazine: "We just had a four-day leadership conference. The theme was human connection. We didn't once talk about sales and profits. We talked about how we continue to grow and how we connect."

told me. "Obviously people fear what they don't know, right? They didn't know what was going to happen. This was not the Wal-Mart-ization of the American landscape. This was the communal *integration* of the American landscape, *driven* by the coffeehouse." (In a characteristic touch, he added, "That's a pretty good one. You even smiled at that one. You can use that in your book.")

When the Starbucks-as-Shangri-la approach falls flat, the company sometimes delves into psyops. Scott Bedbury, the marketing veteran, says one effective strategy is to ask innocently at community meetings whether any independently owned local businesses offer benefits like stock options and health insurance for part-timers — both of which Starbucks, to its credit, has long provided. Since very few mom and pops do the same, then comes the crushing blow: the suggestion that Starbucks is *too enlightened* for this backward-thinking neighborhood. "It surprises me," Bedbury writes in his book by way of example, "that a community as progressive as this one would rather have businesses that don't offer these benefits to the people who work here."

But often, Starbucks just grits its teeth and plunges forth despite the hostility, knowing the opposition will likely need to change local laws to negate the company's right to open a store. "We would say, 'We respect your opinion, but we'll go with the zoning — can we come in here or not?'" Rubinfeld said. Sometimes the answer would be no, and the company would still do it. For instance, the Ocean Beach, California, planning board asked the company not to move in, but since the request wasn't legally binding, Starbucks did anyway. The company has figured out that it's only a matter of time before the tides change and the furor blows over. In fact, the day after the Portland firebombing attempt, reporters spotted several black-clad protesters sitting under the plywood-covered bank of shattered windows at the Seven Corners store, their signs flat on the ground. The picketers' hands were otherwise occupied — with Starbucks drinks, compliments of the store's staff.

A Tale of Two Cities

So let's say your petition has failed, the protests you organized weren't strident enough, and the carefully constructed leaflets you sent out — perhaps featuring a cartoon of a mermaid spanking a cute puppy — didn't sway public opinion. Now a brand-new Starbucks sticks its green tongue out at you from within a cluster of charming restaurants and antiques stores. What can you expect, other than the sinking feeling of defeat? Will this tentacle of the great coffee monstrosity drain the life out of your neighborhood, or will it actually enhance the community?

It depends. Taking the usual approach to this question, we'd want to examine the existing research into how chain stores and locally owned independents each affect a local economy. Without fail, these studies have found that more cash recirculates locally when customers patronize an independent, because mom-and-pop business owners hire local accountants, buy merchandise from local vendors, blow through their profits at local strip clubs, and so forth; chains just funnel the proceeds to some distant corporate bank account. One such investigation, conducted in Chicago's Andersonville neighborhood by the firm Civic Economics, found this discrepancy to be quite significant. After probing the books at ten chain stores and ten independents, the researchers discovered that for every $100 spent at a mom and pop, an average of $73 of that recirculated in the local economy, while the figure for chains was just $43. Which makes sense; strictly speaking, the whole purpose of a chain store is to tap into a community's cash pool and reroute the funds to company investors.

According to Stacy Mitchell, author of *The Hometown Advantage: How to Defend Your Main Street Against Chain Stores and Why It Matters*, we also need to bear in mind that chain stores can undermine a community by making it more bland. "People want to visit a neighborhood because of its uniqueness and charm," she explained. "There's a danger if you're an urban neighborhood or downtown, and you're not offering anything that can't be found at a mall, where there's weather control and plenty of parking. You risk losing that advantage."

But the typical approach doesn't quite work with Starbucks, because it's not like other chain stores. Sure, its profits flow straight to Seattle, but some believe this bloodletting is justified by the benefits that the Starbucks stamp of approval confers on an area. Let's look back for a moment at the main gentrifying effects that accompany a new Starbucks, which the Brookings Institution report lists as follows: changing neighborhood flavor, increased tax revenue, displacement of poor residents, escalating property values, and fresh commercial activity. Flourishing places like Hosford-Abernethy in Portland might shudder at the thought of these forces altering a neighborhood they already love as is, but literally thousands of depressed towns and communities salivate over them. Fundamentally, their government leaders and planning boards are *seeking out* gentrification, with all of the new development and skyrocketing income it entails. For every community that starts into the usual rending of garments at the prospect of a new Starbucks, ten more are begging the company to build a café and give their town an aura of affluence. So when we're attempting to measure the local impact of a new Starbucks store, we must first figure out whether the company really *does* have the power to change an entire community's fortunes, for better or worse.

Some, especially those in more prosperous locales, openly scoff at the idea that Starbucks wields so much influence. Knowing that a Starbucks has little to offer them besides cookie-cutter predictability, these thriving communities often look down their noses at the chain. For example, a Waltham, Massachusetts, city councilor told the *Boston Globe* that when it comes to Starbucks, "Not to sound like I'm bragging, but Waltham is above such trivial concerns." For good measure, he added that any town looking to Starbucks for validation "must have some sort of inferiority complex." During the company's hard-fought (and ultimately victorious) 2006 battle to enter Palm Beach, Florida, America's third-richest community, a typical letter from an irate local read, "I find it inconceivable that . . . an influx of T-shirted coffee drinkers, slopping down the Avenue, dropping their paper cups who-knows-where would be a panacea — or even a help — for any Palm Beach store or resident."

But if you doubt that Starbucks really affects a city's image either way, consider how damning it can be *not* to have them. When Schultz visited Detroit in 2006 to give a speech, local reporters pressed him to explain what it meant that the city had only five Starbucks stores — even the Detroit Metropolitan Airport had more. ("It means Detroit is still ghetto, that's what it means," one local explained to the *Detroit News*, which ran a story arguing that the dearth of Starbucks was a symbol of the city's economic struggles.) Baltimore mayor Martin O'Malley triggered a widespread sense of indignation among his constituents after he allegedly begged Starbucks to build a coffeehouse in his city. (O'Malley later claimed he "just ran into them," and it was all a misunderstanding; still, Baltimore got its first stand-alone Starbucks soon thereafter.) We could even formulate a makeshift Mermaid Index: the number of Starbucks a city has per hundred thousand residents happens to be a fairly accurate gauge of its quality of life. San Francisco proper, with seventy-five outlets for its 744,000 inhabitants (score: 10.1), rates highly; Cleveland, which has just nine of them for its 478,000 people (score: 1.9), not so much. And Detroit (score: 0.4) might want to have its mayor put in an emergency call to Seattle.

Consequently, long-struggling communities often react to the arrival of Starbucks the same way some citizens of developing nations react to getting indoor plumbing. When one finally opened in Lexington, Kentucky, in 2002, a local business owner was actually quoted as saying, "Hallelujah!" There's something almost delusional in the way people talk about their new Starbucks. When the company debuted in Muskegon, Michigan, for example, the president of the local chamber of commerce crowed, "Having them locate in Muskegon is a symbol that we are a community of the future." To Robert Vallee, a councilman in Franklin, Massachusetts, a Starbucks store is nothing less than a magic key to new prosperity: "We want better education, performing arts, things like that. This town is ready for a Starbucks."

To win one, city planners have dangled incredibly generous incentives in front of the company's real estate department. In one case, the Los Angeles suburb of Alhambra gave Starbucks $136,000 in public redevelopment funds and pledged that the company would get a deal on rent — essentially paying half of the store construction costs and ensuring easy money for a company that reported a profit of well over half a billion dollars in 2006. Such offers flow into the company's regional offices every day, and Starbucks often waits for the deal to sweeten over time. The people of Clearwater, Florida, bargained with Starbucks for two years before scoring one: "Now the rest of the world may sit up and take notice," a city planner proclaimed afterward. Sharon, Massachusetts, negotiated for *five* years to get one.

In effect, these communities are banking on the idea that a Starbucks store will help produce the gentrifying effects they covet — new investment and tourism, higher quality of life, and the rest. So is there a payoff? According to Carol Hilsenkopf, of the Cornelius, Oregon, chamber of commerce, her town's new Starbucks had an immediate impact. "We're absolutely thrilled," she told me. "People look at that and say, 'This is a place to be.' Since Starbucks came, we've had four or five new businesses locate nearby." A sparkling Starbucks store can also make a historically bleak place seem that much more livable — to the point where real estate agents in Hyde Park, on Chicago's South Side, include the distance to a new Starbucks in their home listings. Arthur Rubinfeld boasted to me of having received stacks of letters from thankful homeowners who credit a nearby Starbucks with boosting long-stagnant property values. Even Ray Oldenburg, the father of the "third place" idea who later refused to endorse the chain, offered surprising praise for Starbucks's ability to help revitalize a depressed town. "To their credit, they brought Naperville [Illinois] back to life singlehandedly, and now it's one of the five most livable cities in the country," he said.

One might ask if the company is really causing all of this, or if Starbucks is just smart enough to piggyback onto a community at the right time. In other words, is Starbucks the horse pulling the gentrification cart, or, as the Brookings Institution researchers imply, is it merely a symptom of gentrification already in progress? No one contests that a Starbucks can give a neighborhood a more boutiquey, affluent appearance, but for the most part, the company's stores seem to be an *effect* of gentrification, not a cause. Though Starbucks has sometimes cooperated with the basketball star Magic Johnson to open coffeehouses in historically blighted urban areas, it generally targets communities that are either well-off or going in that direction. As one real estate agent who has closed more than one hundred Starbucks deals told me, "Starbucks rarely comes in and says, 'We're going to save the day.' They're looking for neighborhoods that are on the up." The company uses a very sophisticated real estate formula to find the best locations for its stores, and it's difficult to imagine that Schultz would put profits or his closely guarded brand at risk by building cafés in communities that weren't firmly headed toward prosperity.

In truth, how we characterize a Starbucks's impact on an area may come down to a matter of taste — whether you see the company's arrival as revitalization, gentrification, or plain homogenization. As the company's supporters love to point out, Starbucks has a near-spotless record when it comes to churning out stores that are immediately popular, so how can anyone claim it isn't wanted? "I find it very ironic that Starbucks often wants to go into a neighborhood and there's a backlash, then it opens and it's doing its maximum volume pretty much out of the gate," said Harry Roberts, the former Starbucks marketing executive. "A market like San Francisco is wildly successful for us, but people down there have put up billboards against Starbucks. Why? The place is packed! What are they afraid of?" Obviously, being popular doesn't necessarily mean a business is good for the community — Wal-Mart has no trouble attracting customers, despite its drawbacks — but many towns are happy just to have a bustling, chic storefront in their midst.

Never mind that Starbucks isn't adding anything unique, or that it makes an area resemble a strip mall that much more, or that encouraging locals to spend $4.50 every day on coffee may not be the most prudent route to economic stability. For a struggling area, a Starbucks is something to be excited about. And with good reason: the company might not *cause* a local economic revival, but it's almost always a *sign* of it.

The Hosford-Abernethys and Berkeleys of the world aren't interested in this kind of "revitalization," however, because they don't need it. Above all, their citizens want to feel that the neighborhoods in which they live are filled with an inimitable charm that makes them unlike any other place, which describes everything Starbucks is not. If you're not adding something distinctive to the community, they say, you're weakening it; so even though a new Starbucks would draw customers in droves, it still poses a threat. This argument makes some at Starbucks positively indignant. "I was just in a Starbucks near my daughter's apartment in New York — she can't afford high rents so she lives on the Upper Upper East East side," Dave Olsen, the longtime Starbucks coffee expert, told me. "That store attracts people from all over: bicycle messengers, moms with strollers, old farts, students with computers — everybody. So how does anyone look at that picture and say she shouldn't have that? That's arrogant. It's bullshit."

But no one is saying these people shouldn't have a community gathering place. They're saying they'd rather it be a unique, locally owned coffeehouse run by good ol' mom and pop — the very people whose blood seems to drip from Starbucks's fangs each time the company occupies a new neighborhood.

Mortal Combat

America adores its small businesses. They're the quintessential underdogs, representative of all the principles — independence, following one's dreams, striving to succeed — that make this country . . . well, *rich.* Starbucks, the unstoppable corporate steamroller, threatens this ideal more or less by definition. With the exception of airports and a handful of small, chronically undercaffeinated towns, Starbucks competes with independent coffeehouses most every time it enters a new market. Often, Starbucks will move in *right next door* to a scrappy mom and pop, prompting a community-wide gasp. The only thing it could do to make its intentions clearer would be to put up a sign saying, WE ARE HERE TO DESTROY YOU.

This experience drives some coffeehouse owners batty with panic. After a Starbucks opened in 1999 near an eclectic Seattle café called Coffee Messiah (motto: "Caffeine saves"), its owner, Howard Bialik, gathered a group of regulars and cast "coffee spells" at the new store, culminating with the would-be shamans dumping coffee grounds on the Starbucks's doorstep. If anyone entered the premises with a Starbucks cup, his employees told him to get out. Finally, Bialik was arrested by Seattle police for allegedly plastering the Starbucks's windows — plus a trash can, a telephone pole, and a bus sign — with Coffee Messiah stickers. (Bialik later claimed that he only handed out the stickers to others, and the city of Seattle decided not to press charges.)

Bialik's terror, at least, is understandable. If a Starbucks opens up right next to an independent, one of them has to crumble, right? And considering the chain's track record and massive war chest, it probably wouldn't be Starbucks. Indeed, the idea that the company is systematically eliminating locally owned cafés through predatory tactics seems so obvious that few think to question it. Take the Delocator project, a Web site designed by three Los Angeles artists in 2005 as a means of combating this trend. The site's sole function is to list independently owned coffeehouses in any ZIP code the user types in. Its fight-the-corporate-coffee message proved popular enough that Delocator.net attracted over a million hits just in its first month. In a brief manifesto, the project's creators explain why they undertook this crusade: "Currently, independently owned cafés are under attack; and their numbers have been sharply decreasing for many years." But this statement isn't merely a bit off the mark — it's completely false. The *opposite* is true: the number of independent coffeehouses in America is exploding, and it's mostly thanks to Starbucks. Paradoxically, the surest way to boost sales at your mom-and-pop café may be to have a Starbucks move in next door.

This isn't to say that Starbucks is helping on purpose. The company has certainly *tried* to pick off its locally owned competition in a variety of ways, a few of them yielding modest success. In his book, Rubinfeld maintains that Starbucks always "respected good local operators that provided high-quality coffee and unique environments," but he never claims the company didn't try to pull out the rug from under them by bidding on their leases. In one much-discussed case, Starbucks offered to triple the rent that a Mill Valley, California, coffeehouse owner was paying for his space and to throw in a $30,000 signing bonus to top it off. Norman Weintraub, who ran the café, didn't find out about Starbucks's proposal until his landlord told him he'd have to match the terms or clear out. (Weintraub paid, but not happily.) When the company's massive bid came to light in the media, Starbucks representatives said what they always say: that the landlord was behind it all, greedily trying to squeeze extra cash out of everyone, and that Starbucks would never knowingly undercut a mom and pop. (Occasionally, the company has proved the truth of this argument in court. A Canadian judge ordered one landlord to pay over $80,000 in court costs and legal fees after he secretly pitted Starbucks against a beloved Toronto café called Dooney's in 1995; the landlord's scheming had led to a gigantic contractual mess. As soon as Starbucks signed a lease to take over the Dooney's space, public outcry forced the company to sublet it back to the café and take out full-page ads in the *Toronto Star* explaining that it had not intended to force out Dooney's.)

Scheming landlords aside, Rubinfeld insists that there's nothing unethical about offering to pay rates many independents could never afford — that's just the way the market works. "What happened [in Mill Valley] was sort of like, 'Get over it,'" he told me. "If Starbucks didn't take that corner, then Petco would, or Chico's, or someone else. You could call it controversial. You could call it whatever you want." In the hypercompetitive atmosphere of Starbucks headquarters, no one was going to weep for those who couldn't keep the pace. "Putting mom-and-pop coffee shops out of business was discussed a lot within Starbucks, but I don't think management lost any sleep over it," said Jerome Conlon, the "Big Dig" researcher. "They just put together strategies to combat it in public forums and moved on." The fact that Starbucks drew fire for commonplace practices — like negotiating noncompete clauses in its leases — only increased management's belief that it was unfairly maligned. "You know, it wasn't that long ago that we were the underdog, and people were rooting for us and raving," Schultz said. "Then we started succeeding, and people said, 'Wait a minute . . .' So I think it's human nature."

But while Starbucks technically isn't doing anything worse than competing aggressively when it poaches leases, there's something alarming about the eagerness with which it has approached the task. "It was sort of piranha-like," Tracy Cornell, the real estate agent who once posed as a medical patient to get a space, told me. "It was just talking to landlords, seeing who was behind on their rent. All I needed was an opening like that, where the landlord wanted out. I was looking for tenants who were weak." Another former Starbucks employee claimed that she was present at a real estate negotiation between Rubinfeld and a strip-mall landlord, wherein Rubinfeld kept pointing out occupied units and asking if the tenants kept up with their water bills.

If there is a piece of real estate Starbucks wants, it charges ahead, regardless of who occupies it — even if it's someone who considered Schultz a friend. Roger Scheumann, who worked with Schultz at Starbucks as a teenager, says he was in the midst of leasing a location in Bethesda, Maryland, for his tiny coffee chain when Schultz stormed in and made an offer to buy the building. (The landlord declined.) "It was typical Howard — very hard-charging," Scheumann shrugged. "We

got all cranked up about it, but he was just being himself, competing."
Incidents like this have made some coffee-world gossips believe Schultz
will go to any length to beat potential rivals. "Howard doesn't play
fair — you know that, right?" said Fortune Elkins, a prolific coffee
blogger. "Howard will buy the building next to you and put up a sign
that will block yours. He will buy the lease next to yours. He will
even — it has been alleged — go to the zoning commission and pay to
make traffic go one way toward Starbucks. Howard doesn't screw
around."

The idea that Starbucks even controls the direction of traffic in our
cities is a *little* much, but Elkins is correct in one regard: Starbucks will
park a store next to any competitor it can't oust by other means, in
hopes of siphoning away business. "Back in the nineties, Howard
Schultz let it be known that 'If we can't buy you out, we'll squeeze you
out,'" said Martin Diedrich, whose Diedrich Coffee chain was profitable until a disastrous IPO and overzealous expansion plans dragged it
into debt. The first time he ever saw Schultz in person, Diedrich was at
work building his third coffeehouse, in Newport Beach, California, on
a Sunday afternoon. Despite the dust that coated the windows, Diedrich made out the shape of a limo pulling into the dirt parking lot
outside. A figure hopped out and walked up to the window, clearing
away the grime and cupping his hands so he could peek inside. It was
Schultz. "I was standing right in front of him, and as soon as he saw I
was there, he immediately jumped back into the limo so he wouldn't
be recognized," Diedrich recalled. Soon thereafter, he says, Starbucks
made its debut in Orange County, and each of its first three outlets
was "literally within a block" of his three coffeehouses. "I have to believe it was intentional," Diedrich said. "It couldn't have been mere
coincidence."

A complete list of the company's aggressive actions could fill volumes. "I don't have any stores where Starbucks isn't within two blocks
of me," said Oren Bloostein, owner of the nine-store New York chain

Oren's Daily Roast. "They've opened in the same building as me. They've tried to get my lease terminated. They've approached my landlord, to see if he would somehow find a way to kick us out." Penny Stafford, who runs a small coffeehouse in Bellevue, Washington, says employees from a Starbucks down the street have passed out samples right on her doorstep; she is now suing the company in federal court, claiming Starbucks is an unregulated monopoly. When the chain entered Saratoga Springs, New York, it offered the owner of a café called Madeline's Espresso Bar the lowball sum of $105,000 to sell her business. (It had grossed $750,000 the year before.) After she turned the company down, Starbucks planted a store across the street. A company representative later called the buyout bid a "goodwill gesture," telling *US News and World Report,* "If she was clearly afraid of us, here was an opportunity to get out."

But generally, independents have little reason to be afraid. For most locally owned coffeehouses, a new Starbucks nearby is actually cause for celebration.

The Revenge of Mom and Pop

When Starbucks first besieged Los Angeles in 1991, Herb Hyman was as alarmed as any local coffeehouse owner would be. Though his successful Coffee Bean and Tea Leaf microchain had enjoyed a decades-long relationship with the Hollywood elite, Hyman worried that this juggernaut from Seattle would crush the business he had worked thirty years to build. Starbucks even promised as much. "They just flat out said, 'If you don't sell out to us, we're going to surround your stores,'" Hyman recalled. "And lo and behold, that's what happened, and it was the best thing that ever happened to us."

Soon after declining Starbucks's buyout offer, Hyman received the expected news that the company was moving in next to one of his stores. Instead of panicking, as many have done (Martin Diedrich started hyperventilating when he heard Starbucks was opening near him, for example), Hyman called his friend Jim Stewart of Seattle's Best Coffee, who had plenty of experience competing with Schultz. He asked Stewart what really happened when Starbucks built a store nearby. "You're going to love it," Stewart replied. "They'll do all of your marketing for you, and your sales will soar." His prediction proved correct. Each new Starbucks created its own buzz, drawing out people who had never strayed from Folgers to try a latte: After they were hooked, these converts started exploring other coffeehouses, and it just so happened that there was another one right across the street. The increased attention to coffee immediately boosted Hyman's sales. "I told my people to get real estate wherever Starbucks went — it didn't matter how much it cost," he told me. "We bought a Chinese restaurant right next to one of their stores and converted it, and by God, it was doing a million dollars a year right away. It was just incredible." With the extra profits, Hyman built up his company and sold it off for a tidy sum, and he credits Starbucks for much of his success. He's not alone.

"Anyone who complains about having a Starbucks put in next to you is crazy," said Ward Barbee, founder of the specialty-coffee trade magazine *Fresh Cup*. "You want to welcome the manager, give them flowers. It should be the best news that any local coffeehouse ever had." Barbee, a legendary coffee-industry personality who died in 2006, was no great fan of the chain's product — in fact, he often boasted that he invented the phrase, "Charbucks, home of the Scorchiccino" — but he long maintained that Starbucks unwittingly does more to help mom-and-pop cafés than it does to harm them. "They didn't close the independents," he told me. "There are more now than there have ever been."

While almost all of the chains that have tried to replicate Starbucks's success have plummeted toward insolvency, business has been good for locally owned coffeehouses that keep their ambitions in check. Here's a statistic that might be surprising, given the dominance of the Starbucks empire: according to Specialty Coffee Association of

America figures, 57 percent of the coffeehouses in America are mom and pops. Even between 2000 and 2005, long after the ascendance of Starbucks, the number of independent coffeehouses in the United States increased more than 40 percent — from 9,800 to just under 14,000. Starbucks's share of the market keeps inching upward (over the same period, it tripled its U.S. store count, from 2,700 to 7,500), but the proliferation of its stores hasn't fazed the mom and pops at all — quite the opposite. The failure rate for new coffeehouses is incredibly low — only 10 percent, according to the market research firm Mintel — which means a sizable majority of the independents stay in business regardless of where Starbucks drops its stores. "This isn't like the restaurant business, where the vast majority fail," explained Dawn Pinaud, the early Starbucks employee. "Very rarely does Starbucks ever put people out of business."

It's so rare, actually, that of the scores of specialty-coffee industry sources I spoke with for this book, not one could recall a nearby Starbucks hurting sales at one of their coffeehouses for longer than a few months. (Or at least they wouldn't admit it.) Kelly Traw, the head of marketing at Espresso Specialists, Inc. — the nation's top espresso machine vendor — put it like this: "Despite all of the furor about Starbucks coming into town, they've probably never put any of our customers out of business — the ones who are doing it right." But how can this be? If Starbucks is saturating cities with stores and doing its best to draw sales away from locally owned cafés, shouldn't mom and pops be on the wane?

One reason this isn't the case is because Starbucks doesn't enjoy the same competitive advantages as other megaretailers. Look at why Wal-Mart has decimated its locally owned competition: it has lower prices than any of its rivals, its hours are generally longer, and its range of products is larger. None of this is true of Starbucks. The company's prices are typically higher than even the most quality-obsessed independents, and as a rule, it never gives any kind of discount on its drinks. Starbucks stores often close in the early evening, yet locally owned coffeehouses can lure in students and night owls well into the wee hours. And while all coffee bars offer the same basic beverage lineup, mom and pops have the ability to serve a variety of freshly made sandwiches, salads, and so on; the fare at Starbucks, on the other hand, sometimes stretches the definition of what one can reasonably call "food."

Independents can easily contend with Starbucks if they just pay a little attention, and, crucially, if they resist the temptation to mimic their corporate rival's every move. "Anybody can compete with Starbucks," Scott Bedbury told me. "It costs frickin' nothing — the price of an espresso machine and eight hundred square feet. You can't compete with Wal-Mart, though." Many coffeehouse owners have tried to joust with Starbucks by making their businesses more like it: imitating its decor and toning down any eccentricities. But this is the strategy that caused nearly every chain to fail. You can't beat Starbucks at being Starbucks. As the coffee consultant Bruce Milletto explained, nimble independents have a huge advantage over a slow corporate behemoth. "The indie can always compete with the chain, and even do a better job," Milletto said. "You can turn on a dime and switch strategy tonight. You have the ability to produce a better product, and you can design and market your coffee bar to your community."

Company executives know Starbucks can do little to dislodge those independents who are perceptive enough to offer something different. "The purveyors who understood how to differentiate themselves from the chain stayed and did really well," said Rubinfeld, with little enthusiasm. "The ones who never had a good product to begin with went away." Some of the shrewdest independents have even stolen one of the chain's signature moves, to great effect. "These guys at Starbucks are seriously good at locating coffee bars," wrote one of them, David Schomer of Seattle's Espresso Vivace, in a primer on how to compete with Starbucks. "Just open your coffee bar next to one." As Schomer knows, in a side-by-side comparison, customers will often choose quality and uniqueness over efficiency and uniformity.

Naomi Klein, creator of the antichain "No Logo" movement, has lambasted Starbucks over its habit of clustering stores and opening next to mom and pops, but in the coffeehouse business, a cluster of cafés can do better as a group than each café would alone. Just as a thicket of restaurants or gas stations will amplify business for everyone by forming a nexus people instinctively gravitate toward when they think *food* or *gas*, a Starbucks and an independent can work in tandem to draw more coffee drinkers. It's like a reverse Wal-Mart effect. Independents also benefit from Starbucks's mainstream appeal. Said Milletto, "They give people a safe place to have their first specialty-coffee experience, and once they have that, they find it easier to venture out." Stories from around the country bear this out. For example, the *Omaha World-Herald* reported that after Starbucks blitzed Omaha with six stores in 2002, business at locally owned cafés was up as much as 25 percent, with many new mom and pops opening up. And Martin Diedrich, who had watched Starbucks open "within a stone's throw" of each of his coffee bars, likewise reported increased sales. "I didn't suffer whatsoever," he said, his near heart attack notwithstanding. "Ultimately I prospered, in no small part because of it."

The coffee community isn't unanimous on the verdict that Starbucks boosts independents, however. Corby Kummer, the *Joy of Coffee* author, says that mom and pops are getting harder and harder to find when he travels around the country, a claim not supported by industry statistics. Many can't get beyond the fact that the company clearly *intends* to leach sales from locally owned coffeehouses. Several coffee shops have indeed gone under thanks to Starbucks, but most agree that these occasional casualties were generally subpar and deserved to be pruned away. "Starbucks has managed to establish a minimum standard of service and quality," said Timothy Castle, a specialty-coffee consultant and writer. "They make it very difficult for people to survive in this business who are not doing a good job. You have to be better than them to survive, which is hard to do."

Some even go so far as to credit the company for making the whole business viable in the first place. Without the work Starbucks did to popularize espresso and to educate customers in the vagaries of coffee connoisseurship, who can say if the coffeehouse industry would have ever grown this prosperous? "Everyone I know in the business who's doing well — none of us would be where we are if it wasn't for Starbucks," said Joe Monaghan, the Seattle coffee industry veteran. "My roof and my kids' shoes and my daughter's college education — that's all thanks to Starbucks and Howard."

This is fundamentally the company's position on the matter. "It's kind of ridiculous to say Starbucks put people out of business," Howard Behar, the former right hand to Schultz, told me. "If anything, we created an industry. We legitimized something that was kind of bohemian." Schultz put this argument much more stridently to a *Seattle Weekly* reporter in 1994, when the issue of Starbucks targeting independents was first gaining momentum. "It's ironic to me," he said. "I came back [from Italy] with the drink caffe latte in 1982. That word was not in existence in this town before we opened up our first coffee bar in April of 1984 in downtown Seattle. We created this business. We created a tremendous opportunity not only for ourselves, but for others. We're not asking anything for it. It's great. . . . Why there's animosity toward us is a question you have to ask others." When I asked Schultz if he still held to these words, he reaffirmed them without hesitation. "We created an industry that did not exist," he said. "We created a beverage experience, both in terms of the makeup and the ingredients of a drink that only existed in Italy. We created a language that didn't exist. We changed the culture and enhanced people's lives through a simple cup of coffee, and we've done it around the world. Absolutely."

Whether or not you buy Schultz's claim, the truth is this: all parties involved — Starbucks included — are fortunate to have found themselves selling such an incredibly lucrative product, for which the world's appetite only continues to increase. Few trades exist in which consumers allow retailers to charge a huge price for something that costs next to nothing to produce, and gourmet coffee is certainly one of them. It's hard to go wrong with it. "You can't do better than a cup of coffee for profit," said Dan Cox, a former SCAA president. "It's insanity. A cup of coffee costs sixteen cents. Once you add in labor and overhead, you're still charging a four hundred percent markup — not bad! Where else can you do that?"

The enormity of the coffee market makes it impossible for even a behemoth like Starbucks to monopolize the industry. Americans alone drink three hundred million cups of coffee every day, which makes the seven million customers Starbucks serves daily around the world seem almost tiny by comparison. And the size of the pie keeps growing. Mintel, the market research firm, expects national specialty-coffee sales to more than double between 2006 and 2011, hitting a lofty $18.8 billion. The air is so thick with cash that things seem to work out for everybody.

Everybody, that is, but the people who grow the coffee.

—6—

A Fair Trade?

In theory, the International Coffee Organization should be one of the most influential agencies on the planet. As the leading advocate for the world's twenty-five million coffee farmers, its global sway ought to be right up there with OPEC, another regulator of a vital liquid fuel. After all, oil and coffee are the two most-traded commodities in existence, and if either were to suddenly vanish, the gears of the world would grind to an immediate halt. Without coffee, half of Western civilization would be crippled by blinding headaches; morning commuters would wander around in a daze, mumbling to themselves and clutching empty travel mugs; the long-haul trucking industry would simply cease to exist. In short, coffee growers prevent the world from descending into animal-pelt-wearing, fire-god-worshipping anarchy.

So given the devastating power at the ICO's fingertips, it might come as a surprise to learn that the organization's offices are a shoestring affair, crammed into a row of unremarkable gray buildings down a quiet alley in London's West End. Here, just thirty-five people work to improve the welfare of those twenty-five-million-plus coffee growers. In addition to a comprehensive coffee library (complete with page-turners like *Coffee: Commercial and Technico-legal Aspects* and *Coffee and Upper Gastronomical and Sensory Functions*), the headquarters houses a small United Nations–style assembly hall, where emissaries from bean-producing nations hash out the terms of the global coffee trade with representatives of multinationals like Nestlé. The negotiations are rather one sided: the conglomerates hold the power, and the growers have none. It's an imbalance that goes back centuries — but things have never been as uneven as they are right now.

When I visited the ICO one damp autumn morning, sawdust floated in the entryway and the halls echoed with the racket of drills and hammers. The place was a jungle of plastic sheeting. This was just the standard disorder from building renovations, yet it would have been difficult not to see the chaos as somewhat symbolic of the constant turmoil that plagues the world coffee market. Essentially, today's bean growers play the lottery with every harvest. In any given year, prices can be as erratic as an EKG during a heart attack, jolting dramatically up and down with no warning. The farmers' fortunes depend, literally, on the weather. And as if to underscore the unpredictability theme, Néstor Osorio — the man who has to deal with the effects of this volatility — breezed in for our meeting a half hour late.

The past few years have been difficult ones for Osorio. His arrival as executive director of the ICO, in March 2002, coincided almost exactly with the lowest inflation-adjusted coffee prices in history: 41.5 cents per pound, far below the growers' cost of production. (For the sake of comparison, prices had ranged as high as $3.18 per pound four years earlier.) A dignified, neatly dressed man with an aristocratic air, Osorio doesn't attempt to paint a happy face on the situation. He knows the hardships of the grower's life firsthand, from the months he spent on his grandfather's coffee farm as a child back in his native Colombia. If the current predicament for coffee producers doesn't make him panic, it's because his quarter century of experience with the economics of coffee has taught him that stability is the exception, not the rule.

"The history of coffee is a history of crisis," Osorio told me, interrupting himself briefly to request that his assistant bring in two cups of the beverage. ("Here, it's compulsory," he said with a smile. "You have to drink coffee. Not tea.") In major coffee-producing countries, he explained, the price of a pound of coffee means far more than we could imagine; it's the difference between a farmer sending his children to school or out to work in the fields, between subsistence and deprivation. "The social structure of coffee is in essence a structure of small farms in South America, Central America, and Africa," he said. "In these countries, the entire economy depends on very few crops, like coffee, bananas, and sugar. In places like Uganda and Ethiopia and El Salvador, coffee continues to make up over fifty percent of their total export revenues. This is why the political situation is so volatile in these countries." A sharp drop in the price of coffee can sink nations like El Salvador into extreme poverty or even violence.

The coffee historian Antony Wild claims this most recent coffee crisis has led to "the largest enforced global layoff of workers in history," with the World Bank estimating that six hundred thousand coffee workers are now out of work in Central America alone. In response to the terrible market conditions, farmers have undertaken desperate measures. In 2002, growers in Acapulco, Mexico, amassed an 8.4-million-pound hill of coffee beans — enough to brew more than two hundred million cups of the stuff — and crushed it into fertilizer. The following spring, London's *Financial Times* reported that the skies over vast areas of Guatemala were black with smoke from farmers torching their own coffee plantations. From Colombia to Ethiopia, farmers razed their coffee trees and replaced them with coca plants, opium poppies, and qat — a euphoria-inducing stimulant popular in eastern Africa. When the cost of raising and harvesting a pound of beans far exceeds the market price, the coffee trees just aren't worth keeping in the ground. If it can't put food on the table, the crop becomes kindling instead of a beverage.

The great irony of it all is that this disastrous slump for growers has occurred in an era when coffee has enjoyed its highest profile in history. As desperate Central American farmers were destroying their own crops, Starbucks was bringing ever-greater numbers of people into its flock of hazelnut latte addicts and reaping huge profits in the process. The divergence in fortunes between growers and roasters over the past twenty years has been nothing less than staggering. In the late 1980s, as global coffee sales hovered at around $30 billion, farmers earned a steady $10 billion or so of the pie. The market has more than doubled since then — soaring to well over $70 billion on the strength of the designer-coffee boom — yet according to Osorio, growers have received an average of just $6.2 billion a year since the turn of the millennium. Farmers are actually making less now than they were in the eighties, when the market was significantly smaller.

With this yawning chasm between the fortunes of the two groups staring us in the face, the conclusion we tend to draw is that Starbucks, the most prominent coffee baron of all, must be the villain here. Indeed, many agree with this sentiment. Social justice advocates have frequently accused the company of selling "sweatshop coffee," and the loudest among them are those pushing consumers to only drink coffee that has been certified Fair Trade. The idea behind this movement is simple: for any beans that bear the Fair Trade seal, consumers know the growers who produced them abided by a set of ethical and environmental standards, receiving a good price in return — at least $1.26 per pound. Despite the sluggishness of mainstream coffee companies in embracing the concept, Fair Trade coffee sales in the United States have skyrocketed; since the Oakland-based company TransFair USA began certifying Fair Trade coffee in 1999, sales shot up from two million pounds the first year to forty-four million pounds in 2005.

Fair Trade coffee owes its meteoric success to one fact: we feel especially guilty about the social and environmental costs of the coffee we drink. As many coffee lovers realize, four-dollar lattes and chocolaty Ethiopian beans are undeniable luxury items — and what could be more inhumane than having farmers in the developing world suffer to

produce our little indulgences? This sense of guilt about the consequences of our daily cup has fueled the rise of a bewildering array of
conscience-soothing labels, few of which consumers actually understand. What, exactly, is the difference between "shade-grown" and
"bird-friendly" coffee? Do I have to decide if I feel more of an affinity
for shade or for birds? If coffee is "eco-friendly," is it good for both parties? Or do birds not like the shade? The guilt-plagued consumer
grows confused, wondering if there's any way to enjoy a cup of coffee
without making the world a worse place.

It doesn't need to be that complicated; the solution to the coffee
crisis sits right before us. For all of its good intentions, the Fair Trade
movement can't lead the world's coffee growers out of their current
predicament. Strange as it sounds, only gourmet coffeehouses like
Starbucks can improve the lot of impoverished farmers in a lasting
way — not because of Starbucks's mixed and often halfhearted efforts
to help coffee producers, but because of the specialty-coffee industry's
unique ability to reshape and uplift the coffee world. If you want to advance the welfare of farmers and their families, you'll have to indulge
your taste for high-quality beans as often as possible. But before we can
see why this is the case, we need to understand how coffee growers got
into this mess in the first place.

Coming to America

When most of us stop to ponder where coffee comes from, the image
that pops into our heads first is probably that of Juan Valdez, the musta-
chioed Colombian spokesfarmer, standing alongside his mule sidekick,
Conchita. Actually, Valdez isn't so much a spokesman (his dialogue is
generally limited to "*Buenos días*") as he is a mysterious supernatural
force. Created in 1959 by a Madison Avenue advertising firm as a repre-
sentation of the prototypical contented coffee grower, Valdez's purpose
in life is to materialize out of thin air in various locations (bedrooms,

trains, grocery stores), hand puzzled consumers a can of pure Colombian coffee, then disappear as a voiceover reminds everyone that Juan's is "the richest coffee in the world." The coffee *must* have been good, because no one ever seemed even slightly apprehensive about drinking something given to them by a grinning, poncho-wearing guy who had been hiding out in their cupboard with a farm animal.

The Juan Valdez ad campaign was a masterstroke on the part of its sponsor, the National Confederation of Coffee Growers of Colombia. By etching the "richest coffee in the world" tagline into consumers' brains through constant repetition, the ads earned Colombian farmers premium prices on the coffee market. In a way, this was just making the best of a tough situation. Osorio told me that coffee has been the country's "nucleus" for generations, with Colombia historically second only to coffee goliath Brazil in total production. The nucleus metaphor is apt. The crop isn't just the country's social core; it's bound to the land with the same kind of inescapable force that unites protons and neutrons. For better or worse, Colombia is stuck with coffee.

This is true of dozens of Latin American nations, but not one of them chose this fate. Remarkably, the Americas couldn't claim a *single* coffee plant three hundred years ago; remember, *Coffea arabica* originally hailed from the highlands of Ethiopia. Today, on the other hand, coffee trees cover almost half of the permanent cropland in northern Latin America. And amazingly enough, all of this is the work of a single obstinate Frenchman, whose single-minded mission to bring coffee across the Atlantic changed the destiny of an entire continent.

This Frenchman's name was Gabriel Mathieu de Clieu, and when his quest began, in the autumn of 1720, he was an ambitious young naval officer on leave in Paris from his post on the Caribbean island of Martinique. De Clieu was acutely aware of the fact that the early eighteenth century was a terrible time to be a coffee drinker; beans were both scarce and costly. At the time, the Dutch trading empire controlled the continent's two major coffee sources — plantations on the Indonesian island of Java and trade routes with the Yemeni port of

Mocha — and as with any monopoly, they made the most of it.* Continental coffee aficionados had little recourse in the matter. They couldn't grow the beans themselves, as coffee trees withered in European soil without meticulous supervision. Dutch hegemony appeared inescapable.

De Clieu thought he could change things and become a national hero in the bargain. His plan was simple: (1) he would chaperone a few coffee seedlings back to Martinique, where he assumed they would take to the rich tropical earth; (2) a forest of riches would sprout up for France; (3) honors, titles, and rewards would descend on him. Easy. Conveniently, France had just acquired its first coffee plant, which resided in Paris's royal Jardin des Plantes. A few years before, King Louis XIV had gone through lengthy negotiations with the city of Amsterdam to obtain just one five-foot-tall coffee tree. Since then, the garden's botanists had doted over its cultivation.

De Clieu presumed the king would surely part with a sapling or two for the glory of France, but his formal requests for coffee sprouts won him nothing but rejection and scorn; he was too lowly a minion to merit even a leaf from the king's prize. De Clieu prowled the sprawling grounds of the royal gardens for days, hoping to swipe a coffee sprig when no one was looking. The opportunity never came. He grew desperate.

But he didn't lack for ideas. According to his letters — written a half-century later — de Clieu recruited a beautiful noblewoman to convey the full significance of the cause to the royal physician, a man with after-hours access to the gardens. He got his plant shortly thereafter, in a physician-assisted moonlight raid on the Jardin des Plantes. Loot in hand, de Clieu fled to the coast, and in October 1720 he set sail for Martinique aboard the merchantman *Le Dromedaire*. To protect

---

*What's more, these two places — Mocha and Java — were significant coffee sources for so long that their names became synonymous with the drink. (Centuries later, Howard Schultz would give the former word its current meaning by naming his new hot cocoa and espresso concoction a "mocha.")

his fragile charge from salt water and the ship's rats, de Clieu constructed a makeshift greenhouse out of spare glass, wood, and wire. All he had to do now was keep it alive through the long voyage.

Unseen dangers lurked in the shadows, however, imperiling his mission to caffeinate the New World.* As de Clieu told it in his letters, the first menace surfaced a couple of weeks into the journey, when the ship's passengers awoke in the dead of night to find themselves under attack from a Tunisian corsair. *Le Dromedaire's* twenty-six cannons soon convinced the pirates to call off their assault. Just days later, another threat emerged: de Clieu caught a fellow passenger inside his cabin, looming menacingly over the greenhouse — a man who, suspiciously, spoke French with a Dutch accent. Before de Clieu could stop him, the Dutch spy managed to rip a branch off the tiny seedling. Yet the tree survived. After this, de Clieu scarcely let the plant out of his sight.

Still, his vigilance couldn't hold back Mother Nature. A few hundred miles from de Clieu's destination, a tempest nearly snapped *Le Dromedaire* in half. Then the fickle Caribbean winds stopped blowing entirely. The ship was becalmed for over a month in an area sailors called the "horse latitudes," because dead winds and low rations sometimes forced them to eat the larger, four-legged passengers on board. As stores of drinking water dwindled, each passenger was limited to a half cup of water per day; the noble de Clieu chose to share his ration with the coffee plant. "I would have died of thirst to keep alive the plant . . . upon which my happiest hopes were founded and which was the source of my delight," he later wrote.

By the time the ship finally sighted the black sands of Martinique, the seedling had shriveled to the size of a pinkie. De Clieu took no chances with its cultivation. When he reached his estate in Precheur, he planted the feeble sprout in easy view of his house, surrounding it

---

*And here, I hasten to note that there is considerable debate about how much of the following took place only in de Clieu's imagination — but at the very least, the guy had impressive dramatic flair.

with thorn hedges and ordering his slaves to guard it at all hours. As he'd hoped, the coffee plant flourished in the tropical climate, under the shade of the native mahogany and rosewood trees. Within five years, it had spawned two thousand new coffee trees on the island, and de Clieu sent seeds along to Guadeloupe, Santo Domingo, and other nearby French colonies. (De Clieu did end up getting his reward, eventually becoming governor of Guadeloupe and a chevalier in the French Legion of Honor.) By 1777, this one sapling had sired over eighteen million coffee plants on Martinique alone; at the end of the century its offspring were producing coffee cherries from Mexico to Brazil and throughout the West Indies.

According to coffee lore, the seedling de Clieu brought to Martinique is the father of most of the coffee trees in Latin America today. The trees thrived in the hot, humid climate of Central and South America, and European colonists kept planting and planting. Coffee trees went in as fast as workers could clear the land — so many of them, in fact, that coffee beans, through a sudden abundance of supply, became affordable for ordinary Westerners. The colonists considered it the perfect cash crop for the New World, and they convinced the natives that coffee cultivation would act as a social motor and propel them to European-style prosperity. Three centuries later, the populace is still waiting for the payoff. They have little choice. Coffee is both the hand that feeds Latin America and the noose around its neck.

A Day's Work

The working conditions on the Americas' first coffee plantations were horrific, and Brazil swiftly emerged as the market leader, not just in production but in brutality toward its labor force. Like de Clieu's stealth mission, the story of the bean's journey to Brazil is another entertaining (but much shorter) coffee legend. In the late 1720s, the French and the Dutch jealously guarded their Latin American coffee plantations, hoping to prevent other powers — especially the Portuguese — from getting a piece of the market over in the Brazilian territory. But in 1727, they let down their guard. The two needed a third party to help resolve a border dispute between French Guiana and Dutch Guiana (now Suriname), so they invited Brazil's Lt. Col. Francisco de Melo Palheta to act as a mediator. Palheta, it turned out, had an even greater gift for subterfuge than de Clieu; while he was supposedly fostering peace between the French and the Dutch, he was also (*ahem*) achieving harmony with the French governor's wife. And after the two nations reached an agreement, she bestowed on Palheta a farewell gift: a bouquet of flowers, with coffee seedlings hidden inside.

Unfortunately, this is just about the only lighthearted anecdote one can tell about Brazil's early coffee cultivation. Over the next 150-odd years, Brazil imported more than three million slaves to work the country's coffee *fazendas*, nearly five times the estimated number of slaves the United States brought in over its entire history. These slaves endured grueling seventeen-hour workdays, with their masters granting breaks only to sing prayers and sleep in locked dormitories. Because of this daily ordeal, the slaves' average life expectancy from the moment they set foot in Brazil was just seven years. The coffee-slave bond defined the country; as a member of Brazil's parliament pronounced in 1880, "Brazil is coffee, and coffee is the negro." By the time Brazil abolished slavery in 1888, the country's coffee hegemony was indisputable. At the dawn of the twentieth century, Brazil produced five times as much coffee as the rest of the world's countries *combined*.

Coffee growers are better off today, but the nature of their work remains much the same: the world's best beans are still sown and harvested by hand on remote equatorial farms, just as they were centuries ago. It's tough work, performed in some of the world's most difficult terrain — sheer mountainsides, teeming rain forests — but it couldn't be any other way. Arabica, the strain of coffee that accounts for two thirds of the world's beans (and *all* of the good ones), is a remarkably finicky plant. If the temperature varies too much from sixty-eight degrees Fahrenheit, it aborts; if the ground it rests in gets less than four or five inches of rain per month, it wilts; if you try to plant it at an altitude lower than four thousand feet above sea level — you get the idea. For the diva-ish arabica plant, only lush, mountainous, tropical regions will do. In other words, coffee likes to grow in areas that are a complete hassle to reach — Indiana Jones territory. "In places like Colombia and Africa, you have to travel along these very bad roads with thousand-foot dropoffs on the side to get to coffee country," said Dave Olsen, the Starbucks coffee expert. "The thing I'm probably most thankful for is that I didn't end up rolling down some steep mountainside."

During the harvest season in Latin America, which begins at different times of year depending on altitude, workers of all ages flock to the plantations to pick coffee cherries. Migrant workers walk for days to take part. Children work alongside their parents and grandparents to help defray the cost of school supplies, a fact that has sparked outrage from some industry critics, who have accused Starbucks and its rivals of supporting "child labor." The kids certainly work, but not everyone considers it a *bad* thing; for rural children in Latin America, working with your family to harvest coffee is as much a part of growing up as naptime or Little League is in America. "No one ever thought of it as 'child labor' or anything," explained Martin Diedrich, who grew up on a coffee farm in Guatemala. "My brother and I had to work on the farm every day. If there was no work on my farm, Dad would make us go to the neighbor's farm, and we'd work at local wages. It was just what you did to get by."

The child-labor charge is a good example of our tendency to assume we know the score about coffee farms in the developing world and are thus entitled to proclaim what's best for growers. Even those who work extensively with the farmers themselves are sometimes prone to embarrassing gaffes. For instance, Rebecca Wagner of Green Mountain Coffee Roasters, a Vermont-based company that sells large quantities of Fair Trade coffee, recalled showing a farmer the artwork on one of Green Mountain's Fair Trade coffee packages; it depicted a worker happily placing coffee cherries in a wicker basket. "He looked at it and said, 'That basket is *huge!*'" Wagner told me, laughing. "He said they could never carry that much at once — which I guess just shows that we don't know anything."

Journalists and other white-collar types who get a chance to work in the fields as a coffee picker typically express surprise at how exhausting it is to pluck little berries all day. Since coffee has always been such a cheap and ubiquitous commodity, maybe we just assume the trees down in Latin America are filled with gleaming, full coffee cans. But producing a raw coffee bean actually entails a great deal of labor. Let's say you're a typical American coffee drinker, clocking in at about twenty pounds of roasted beans consumed per year.* Keeping this buzz alive requires the full yield of twenty coffee trees (a mature tree only ends up producing one pound of roasted beans per year), each of which demands hours of cultivating, fertilizing, pruning, and so forth. The vast majority of the tree's output actually goes to waste. When we speak of coffee "beans," after all, what we're referring to are the seeds of coffee cherries — round, vivid red fruits the size of large blueberries, which grow in clusters around the tree's branches.

While we're clearing things up, this "tree" really looks more like a stout shrub, covered top to bottom in slim, dark green leaves. Though they can grow more than thirty feet tall in the wild, coffee plants are kept at around seven feet on farms for ease of harvesting. Ideally, taller trees will shield the coffee shrubs from the full strength of the sun's rays, for reasons of quality and environmental health. This is why the "shade-grown" designation has become a hot one. Coffee producers, always looking to boost yields, long ago discovered that sun-drenched coffee plants produce significantly more berries, albeit at a cost to overall quality. But the environmental consequences of this practice are

---

*The American per capita average is ten pounds, based on the three billion pounds the United States imports each year, according to the ICO — but that figure includes those who don't drink coffee as well.

considerable. Sun-grown coffee leaches nutrients out of the soil much faster than shade-grown plants, spoiling the land and triggering erosion. Plus, the more forest canopy farmers remove, the worse things get for the migrating birds who need a place to lodge for the winter. (So to answer the question from the beginning of this chapter, "shade-grown" and "bird-friendly" coffee are fundamentally the same thing.)

Making the seeds from these coffee trees palatable takes finesse; any missteps result in rancid coffee. First, the berries must be harvested at their peak ripeness. At dawn each morning during the harvest season, pickers set out through the mountain mists into the fields, wicker *canastas* strapped to their waists. They search for deep crimson-colored cherries, rapidly plucking them off and dropping them in the basket; they're paid at the end of the day according to how many baskets they've filled. (On the massive coffee plantations in Brazil, however, mechanized coffee harvesters that look like soccer goals on wheels harvest the unripe cherries along with the ripe and just weed out the offenders later on.) Each coffee berry contains a double-sided seed — which splits into two beans — underneath a layer of sweet pulp. Farmhands wash the cherries to sift out twigs and leaves, send the fruit through pulping machines to extract the hard seeds, and spread the beans onto vast concrete patios to dry under the sun. Twice an hour, workers rake the beans to make sure they dry evenly. After a week or two of this treatment, they pour the raw, pale green beans into sixty-kilogram burlap sacks, ready for sale to the coffee roasters.

In the 2005–2006 crop year, the globe's coffee plantations generated 14.3 billion pounds of coffee beans in this way. Tropical developing nations supplied almost all of it, while temperate, industrialized nations consumed 80 percent of it. To put it bluntly, poor countries grow coffee for rich ones. Over the past three centuries, this relationship has remained unchanged; the "social motor" that the coffee industry supposedly represented never revved up. Although the plantations are no longer overseen by European colonists, there might as well still be a patronage system. A small army of middlemen — importers, shippers, exporters, and local coffee "coyotes" (or bosses) — each take their cut from the farmer's sale price, leaving growers broke and powerless to change things. Because they generally have no access to credit, farmers can't even raise the cash to escape the cycle. And if they go hungry, their cash crop won't help. You can't eat coffee.

Dozens of generations of coffee production have taught farmers from Honduras to Rwanda how to cope with this difficult way of life. But not even the most resilient among them can survive the lowest coffee prices in history, which reached their current depths courtesy of a very unlikely culprit: Vietnam.

Free-Market Freefall

When the head of the organization dedicated to improving the lot of coffee farmers throws his hands up in frustration while discussing how best to carry out his job, you might call that a bad sign. But Néstor Osorio has every right to be aggravated. Consumers around the world are racing to pay preposterous amounts of money for a cup of coffee, yet growers are struggling as never before. When he tries to suggest simple, painless ways to help these millions of people *not starve*, the governments of the First World nations that are buying the incredibly cheap raw coffee refuse to obstruct free trade.

The whole problem seems almost nonsensical: if I pay ten dollars for a pound of coffee, how could the farmer who produced it possibly get that measly 41.5-cent average?* In part, that's just the wacky way the free market works, but there's a political angle to the crisis as well. The source of the growers' current predicament lies in the sometimes brutal intersection of power politics and the open market.

Things weren't always so volatile for farmers; in fact, the ICO once

---

*Some might ask a slightly different question: if coffee is so cheap, why is a latte still four dollars? We'll get to that in a few pages.

administered a deal between producing and consuming nations to guarantee a stable price for growers. But it needed a dictator's help to pull this off. Back in the 1950s, conditions for coffee producers stood roughly where they do today: in a state of chaos, with the fates of millions depending on the whims of the weather. A single frost in Brazil, which happens reliably every few years, would spark a buying panic, doubling prices overnight. Bumper coffee crops would cause massive gluts, sending prices plummeting because of reduced demand while sacks of coffee rotted in warehouses. It was like pegging the value of coffee to a Super Ball on the loose, and the exhausted producers clamored to put an end to it. Surely, a quota agreement would make more sense for everyone, they said — one that would serve growers by letting them control the amount of beans entering the market (thereby avoiding surpluses), and buyers by ensuring a stable coffee supply. The idea didn't fly because of one major dissenter: the United States, buyer of a quarter of the world's beans, which didn't want to impede the free market.

Fidel Castro made the United States reconsider. In 1959, Castro rose to power in Cuba, establishing the first Communist state in the Western Hemisphere. Three years later, after he helped terrify America with the prospect of nuclear assault during the Cuban missile crisis, U.S. leaders realized they had to do something to stop other impoverished Latin American nations from turning to Communism. Senator Hubert Humphrey declared in 1962 that maintaining stable coffee prices was "a matter of life and death," adding that "Castroism will spread like a plague through Latin America unless something is done about the prices of raw materials produced there."

Suddenly filled with this brotherly spirit, the United States and other consuming nations agreed to the first International Coffee Agreement that same year; the ICO was created to oversee the accord. For three decades, farmers got a stable price for their crop, and the major coffee brands had little to worry about besides their expensive ad campaigns. "The big companies like Nestlé were supportive of the quota system because they knew in October of each year exactly how much coffee would be available and what the price would be," Osorio told me. "The administrators loved it. They could just go off and play tennis at three in the afternoon. It was a well-organized world."

In 1989, this world came crashing down along with the Berlin Wall. Suddenly, the cold war was over — the threat of Communism had passed. With no fledgling Castros to worry about, the United States abruptly pulled out of the ICA. By 1992, coffee prices had plunged 50 percent. Three years later, a Brazilian frost tripled prices. The free market was restored.

As if things weren't bad enough already, the ghost of the cold war had one last trick to play on coffee farmers. The highest profile battleground in America's war on Communism, of course, was Vietnam. By the midnineties, Osorio explained, developed nations were acknowledging that they owed a "moral debt" to Vietnam, which they decided to pay off (through the World Bank) with funding for agriculture. And how did the Vietnamese government elect to use this cash? To plant coffee, which, as the discerning reader knows by now, is about as likely to yield widespread happiness as plowing one's life savings into a slot machine. With coffee prices temporarily high because of a frost, Vietnamese officials naively encouraged their citizens to plant as many coffee trees as possible.

But these weren't high-quality arabica trees; they were robusta trees, the hardier, harsher tasting strain that yields more berries and costs far less to maintain. It's filler coffee, used in supermarket blends to keep costs low. (The conglomerates first have to steam the robusta beans to remove the flavor, which coffee tasters compare to "burnt rubber" and "compost," then layer on artificial flavors to compensate. This is why we see so many instant coffees with names like Hazelnut Royale Cappuccino and Caramel Mocha Frothé.) The Vietnamese beans were so bad that locals had to load their daily brew with milk, sugar, butter, and fish sauce just to make it palatable.

Vietnam overwhelmed the market with bad coffee, which the conglomerates were only too happy to buy cheap. Within a decade, it had upped its annual coffee production by a factor of eleven, from 84,000 tons to a whopping 950,000 tons, suddenly making it the world's number two coffee producer, behind Brazil. "They did in ten years what Colombia did in a hundred years!" exclaimed Osorio. "It's no wonder they weren't prepared to handle it. The coffee has . . . *defects.*" Without the safety net of the ICA, this influx of coffee sent prices into a nosedive across the board; the bad bean glut even devalued the good beans. This is when farmers started discovering that it was cheaper to burn their crops than it was to harvest and sell them. The British humanitarian agency Oxfam estimates that, because of the global oversupply, five billion pounds of coffee go to waste every year — almost a pound for each person on the planet.

With free trade as the industrialized world's current mantra, Osorio sees no hope that the quota system will make a comeback soon. He's tried to advocate for it, but with no success; the coffee growers are fundamentally on their own. "In the free market period, there have been five critical years, five okay years, then five critical years again," Osorio said, exasperation showing in his face. "The quota system was a system of protection for farmers. It guaranteed a minimum price. Now, the market is regulated by a frost in Brazil, a drought in Vietnam — it's a free-for-all."

The ICO, other concerned nonprofits, and government leaders in producing countries have proposed a number of schemes to fix things without quotas, to little avail. All of them revolve around reducing the amount of coffee on the market. Pemex, Mexico's state-run petrochemical company, suggested using surplus coffee to soak up oil spills. Others devised ways to use it as fuel (Brazil's trains reportedly once ran on coffee beans) and even as animal feed, which would boost the low energy levels of the world's cows dramatically. Oxfam wanted the multinationals to burn 660 million pounds of beans to reduce the glut, a suggestion met with icy silence. ("It's a business," Osorio pointed out. "Who was going to propose to the board that they burn money?") The nature of the coffee market is so skewed that Hurricane Katrina actually *helped* farmers when it trashed two hundred million pounds of coffee in New Orleans warehouses. In what other industry do producers cheer when the fruit of their labors is violently destroyed?*

Fixing the problem for good without quotas is an almost impossible task, because there's no other easy way to control the coffee supply. Coffee beans are produced in more than one hundred countries around the globe, with small farms in extremely remote areas doing most of the work. How could you possibly coordinate the number of coffee trees these people cultivate? "Everywhere I go, I try to explain to farmers and representatives why they shouldn't plant more coffee," said Osorio. "But it's a matter of convincing tens of thousands of individual small farmers to do the same thing." Adding to the degree of difficulty, bear in mind that growers must decide how many coffee trees they should plant three to five years in advance, since that's how long the trees take to mature — and this is in a market where the weather can radically change prices overnight. Where do they even begin? Anything could happen between now and then.

Faced with this uncertainty and upheaval, some farmers have given up on coffee, taking out their arabica trees and replacing them with drug crops. Between 2000 and 2001, cocaine production in Colombia more than doubled, since uprooted coffee plantations cleared up extra acreage for coca plants. In Ethiopia, a country where a man offering a woman a handful of coffee beans is the equivalent of getting down on bended knee and proposing, qat production doubled after coffee export revenues fell from $830 million all the way to $165 million between 1998 and 2003.

The market, ever volatile, has recovered somewhat since the depths of the early 2000s, but Osorio knows it's only a matter of time before another crisis hits. (The ICO got the United States to sign on for another International Coffee Agreement in 2005, but the document con-

---

*Okay, maybe in the piñata industry.

tains no real reforms.) When we met, Osorio was nervously awaiting new crop statistics from Brazil, which, if they turned out too high, could wreck everything once again, no matter how much a pound of gourmet coffee is selling for at the supermarket. Which brings us back to that guilty feeling. With the future looking so bleak for growers, conscience-plagued coffee drinkers have devised a system of their own for buying beans — a system focused on fairness.

Just Java

If you ever feel inclined to look at modern American affluence from a new and jarring perspective, here's a method that never fails: ask some Latin American coffee farmers out on a shopping trip. Sure, this can be difficult to arrange, as you'll rarely get the chance to extend an invitation at, say, yoga class. But seeing the contrast firsthand makes the effort worthwhile.

I speak from experience. Early one June morning, I found myself standing in the parking lot of a Wild Oats grocery store in Vancouver, Washington, next to two visiting coffee growers, Daniel Balux and Reynaldo Vaszquez. I had met them the evening before at a reception hosted by the Portland-based company Sustainable Harvest, a top Fair Trade coffee importer that advocates for direct relationships between roasters and growers. (Farmers typically have no idea where their coffee goes when it leaves their farms.) Daniel and Reynaldo had flown up to Portland for the week to meet with representatives from companies that buy their beans, like Green Mountain and Whole Foods. As the reception attendees ate smoked salmon hors d'oeuvres and sipped microbrews in a rooftop garden that evening, the twenty-two-year-old Daniel — who works twelve-hour days on his farm in Guatemala and had set foot on a plane for the first time just days before — thanked the envoys for embracing Fair Trade. "I feel there's not a lot we can do for you," he said through a translator, "but you do so much for us by promoting our coffee." The next morning, the two would be visiting Wild Oats (an upscale natural foods chain) with a Sustainable Harvest cameraman in tow, to see their coffee on the American retail shelf. I accepted an invitation to tag along.

Even in the parking lot, it quickly became apparent that this would be a surreal experience. While waiting for the cameraman to get his equipment ready, Daniel, Reynaldo, and I watched in varying states of awe as a tanned and taut woman wearing enormous sunglasses parked her sports car and strode into the store, bracelets loudly jingling, never for a second breaking concentration from the mobile phone call she was conducting at a mild yell. Daniel, who does not typically perform his farmwork while gossiping on a cell phone, seemed impressed; Reynaldo, a fifty-year-old Nicaraguan grower and polished Fair Trade spokesman, less so.

You might be expecting me to report that Daniel and Reynaldo recoiled with disgust at the posh, climate-controlled store, where shoppers fussed over exorbitantly priced organic bananas and hormone-free, omega-3-enhanced, Grade AA brown eggs. Actually, they found the whole thing riotously funny. They laughed at the display of pink flip-flops, pointing out the comical frills. They rolled their eyes at the plastic coffee cup lids, space-age thermoses, disposable stir sticks, thermal cup sleeves, and individualized sweetener packets we use. (Daniel told me that where he lives, people generally just strain their coffee through a cotton shirt and drink up.) As Reynaldo was perusing a Fair Trade brochure in the store's coffee aisle, he noticed with a chuckle that one of the contented farmers pictured therein was a friend of his. Daniel was particularly amused by the bulk Green Mountain coffee dispensers; he assumed that people had to let the coffee fall into their cupped hands, until someone pointed out the paper bags that fit snugly over the plastic chute.

These bulk beans, for which farmers received the Fair Trade price of $1.26 per pound (or $1.31 if organic), were selling for $11.99 a pound — a markup of over 900 percent for those who roast and sell the product. Many farmers find this discrepancy infuriating, even when they received a price deemed "fair" from companies that like to boast about their support of progressive causes. As one frustrated plantation owner put it in the journal *World Coffee and Tea*, "From the producer's point of view, it seems truly ironic that a product that takes a year to grow, and that requires thousands of worker hours of difficult, delicate, and often dangerous work, should be so remarkably inflated by someone who simply cooks and displays the coffee." It's a good thing for roasters, then, that most coffee farmers have no idea about the markups charged for roasted beans. "They only know how much they get paid for the coffee," Daniel said. "They would be shocked if they knew how much it sells for here."

But Daniel and Reynaldo weren't at all troubled by the price gap; Reynaldo even good-naturedly ribbed Daniel because bulk Guatemalan coffee was selling for a dollar less than the other varieties (which was just a labeling error). They considered themselves lucky to be selling their coffee in such a prosperous place; Fair Trade contracts are scarce, and those fortunate enough to secure one seldom complain. "I feel happy that our coffee is bought and enjoyed here," said Reynaldo as he sipped a cup of coffee that, at $1.29, cost more than an entire pound of Fair Trade–certified raw beans. "It gives us all a feeling of security to be able to bring information back to our families and our children and share an experience that was very wonderful."

This $1.29 cup of plain drip coffee brings us back to an obvious question: if raw coffee is hovering around its all-time low price right now, why isn't the slump making a dent in those big numbers on the coffeehouse menu board? Well, because what you're paying for at a Starbucks or a local café isn't the coffee. Take the oft-mentioned $4 cappuccino, for example. According to statistics from the SCAA, only 5 percent of that price ($0.20) is the cost of the coffee itself, and that's for *roasted* coffee, which the coffeehouse has already paid to cook, package, and ship. In reality, a nickel more than covers the farmer's take for that cappuccino; that's less than the cost of the cup, sleeve, and lid ($0.07). So even radical coffee-market swings would scarcely affect the drink's price. At a coffeehouse like Starbucks, you're paying for dairy products (10 percent, or $0.40), labor and overhead (71 percent, or $2.84), and, of course, profit (11 percent, or $0.44). With raw beans composing such a tiny portion of the price of coffee drinks, upping farmers' rates significantly would cost the consumer virtually nothing — literally a few pennies per drink to double the grower's take. But since that's not how the free market works, farmers are stuck struggling.

The Fair Trade movement represents an attempt to change this by voluntarily giving growers a higher price, and Daniel and Reynaldo are proof that this approach can change the lives of those lucky enough to get their coffee certified. Their children can go to school, they have access to credit for farm improvements and training, and they see their futures as reasonably secure. The middlemen who sliced off excessive portions of their coffee's price have mostly been weeded out of the Fair Trade system, leaving the farmers with a much better share of the spoils. The system seems ideal, a utopian vision come to life.

That's how many consumers have treated Fair Trade, at least. By paying a dollar or two more for their coffee beans, shoppers with hyperactive guilt complexes get to feel that they're actually serving some greater purpose with a French roast purchase; this feeling is so addictive that TransFair USA, which administers the Fair Trade seal in America, has had to almost double the quantity of coffee it certifies every year. Some like the Fair Trade model so much, in fact, that they want to make drinking any other kind of coffee *illegal*. In 2002, the citizens of Berkeley, California (surprise, surprise), voted on a measure to ban the sale of beans that were not Fair Trade, organic, or shade grown. The proposition was headed toward victory, until someone noticed that the penalty for violating the law would be six months in jail, which, even in Berkeley, seemed a tad extreme. The measure's opponents (including Starbucks and Peet's) immediately sent out leaflets showing police officers leading a coffeehouse owner away in handcuffs, killing its chances of passing. (Apparently, many people had no problem with this image, though; the measure still won 30 percent of the vote.) Despite this setback in Fair Trade's forward march, the crusade has won many significant victories, with giants like Wal-Mart, McDonald's, Nestlé, and Starbucks now offering Fair Trade beans. (Starbucks, by virtue of its size, sells more Fair Trade coffee than anyone — eighteen million pounds in 2006 — though its commitment to the cause is relatively small.) The movement, by all outward indicators, has charmed growers and consumers alike.

But it hasn't won over everyone. Specialty-coffee roasters detest Fair Trade coffee almost universally; one even went so far as to tell me, "It's *un*fair trade." Strangely, many of the program's most unwavering critics are the same people who prominently feature Fair Trade beans in their coffeehouses. You'll seldom hear them condemning Fair Trade in public, whether from a reluctance to denounce their own product or from anxiety about attacking what's become a left-wing sacred cow. (There's also a legal problem: roasters who use the Fair Trade logo are contractually forbidden to criticize either TransFair USA or anyone with whom it does business.) But as the coffee writer and past SCAA president Tim Castle explained, they have few kind words for Fair Trade in private. "When they're honest about it, almost all of the roasters hate Fair Trade," he said.

Their inventory of grievances is extensive. The first sticking point concerns the restrictions on which farms are eligible for Fair Trade certification. In order to participate in the system, applicants must obey a set of rules that often seems more like a socialist wish list than a structure designed to help growers. All aspiring farms must be small, family-run plots that are part of democratic, worker-owned cooperatives. Private ownership and capitalist practices are completely off limits — even hiring day laborers can take your farm out of the running. Many say this restriction unfairly disqualifies good private farms, and some also call it culturally insensitive. The coffee world is full of families who have cultivated the same land for generations, beholden to no one; the idea of having others make their decisions goes against years of tradition.

Then there are the structural problems. Fair Trade certifiers refuse to interfere with merchants' market practices, which gives greedy retailers a free pass to take advantage of well-meaning consumers by charging ridiculous margins. In June 2004, for instance, the *Wall Street Journal* revealed that the British grocery chain Tesco was tacking on an extra $3.46 per pound to its Fair Trade coffee, even though the growers were only receiving $0.44 above the open-market price. (Consumer ire forced Tesco to revise its prices.) Here's a vexing question: what happens to Fair Trade farmers when the market price *exceeds* $1.26 per pound? "The whole Fair Trade thing is a mess," Dan Cox, the coffee consultant, told me. "The market price going above the Fair Trade price is where things really fall apart. Farmers ask, 'Hey, why should I deliver my coffee when I can get more money by breaking our contract?'" Fair Trade took flight in response to a crisis, and thus problems arise when the crisis wanes; the moment another massive frost strikes and coffee soars to $4.00 a pound, don't expect growers to happily take their $1.26. Besides, under Fair Trade, the farmers aren't even the ones who get the money — the cooperative does. Yet a corrupt co-op can be every bit as thieving as middlemen.

But the biggest division between Fair Trade advocates and specialty-coffee roasters is a philosophical one: the latter are focused on roasting the best-tasting beans possible, while the former care only that farmers receive a good price. These ideologies can clash spectacularly. Within the industry, it's an open secret that Fair Trade beans have historically been much lower in quality than their unsanctified cousins, and one doesn't have to be a coffee snob to pick up on the difference. Said Castle, "Fair Trade, I believe, keeps low-quality farmers in business at the expense of high-quality farmers. It may be ugly, but it's true." If a farmer is guaranteed his $1.26 no matter what, why should he worry about quality? Despite these shortcomings in taste, however, specialty roasters feel obligated to buy it anyway, to stave off the impression that their coffee might be exploitative. (There's a bit of a catch-22 here as well: if you buy *some* Fair Trade beans, are you then *admitting* the rest of your coffee is evil?) For high-quality roasters, the most frustrating part of all is that they often pay far more than the Fair Trade rate to secure the best beans, yet without the Fair Trade insignia, conscientious consumers tend to assume the worst.

Perhaps the most important objection to Fair Trade as a lasting solution for coffee farmers, though, is the reality that the movement can only go so far. As any economist will tell you, consumers buy food products based on two main criteria: taste and price. If Fair Trade coffee tastes worse and costs more than its competitors, then even major ethical considerations won't induce mainstream America to buy into the crusade. TransFair USA says its research shows that eight in ten consumers are willing to pay a premium for ethically produced goods, but what people say and what they actually do are two different things; it's tough to imagine the average coffee drinker in Nebraska voluntarily forgoing his preferred blend in favor of Fair Trade. As Osorio explained, the movement's growth has been impressive, yet its overall effect is limited. "How important is Fair Trade's contribution to coffee?" he asked. "I'd say it's important in terms of awareness — it gets people talking about the needs of farmers. But in terms of impact on the market, it's nothing. Zero-point-four percent of the world market is Fair Trade."

In other words, Fair Trade is not a viable solution to the global coffee crisis. It obviously helps the lucky few who buy into the co-op system and get their farms certified, like Daniel and Reynaldo. But advocating Fair Trade as a panacea is like trying to put out a four-alarm inferno with a squirt gun; although it might help a little, it's not going to extinguish the blaze.

There is a better answer to the problem, though — one that requires no co-op systems or guilt-inspired purchases of sour beans. It's quite simple. Just indulge your inner spoiled brat and demand the best-tasting coffee you can get.

Bucking the Big Four

Before I launch into an argument in support of the happy global effects of conspicuous coffee consumption at Starbucks and other upscale coffeehouses, I want to be perfectly clear about one thing: Starbucks has never *voluntarily* done much to help struggling coffee growers. On the rare occasions when the company has taken steps to better the lives of farmers, it has generally only done so because a consumer group was planning a protest or a boycott. When the farmer welfare issue first threatened to tarnish the company's public image in 1995, for example — after the U.S./Guatemala Labor Education Project began exposing the horrible labor conditions for Latin American coffee workers — Starbucks responded by issuing a much-publicized code of conduct for its growers. This move won the company wide praise in the media, yet those who looked closely noted that the "code" was nothing more than a toothless statement about Starbucks's beliefs and values. It contained no actual pledge that Starbucks would change its buying practices, only platitudes about how the company thought people should be treated with dignity and so forth.

The staving-off-protests strategy continued over most of the next decade. It's not that Starbucks did nothing at all — the company donated millions to the humanitarian charity Care and sporadically built schools, clinics, and coffee mills in needy communities. But it was stalling from making any substantive changes in the way it did business with farmers. Throughout the late 1990s and early 2000s, Starbucks fended off criticism by explaining that a thorough study on the issue was in the works, but this study was consistently delayed by something or other. It diverted attention to its new paper cup, made from 10 percent recycled fibers (which took eight years to develop) and to its purchases of renewable power. And besides, the company maintained, tiny Starbucks couldn't do much to change things anyway. (Despite its perceived ubiquity, it only buys a little over 2 percent of the world's coffee.) They offered rationalizations: "We would like to give [farmers] the support they need to make changes, but it's their country and their business, not ours," Mary Williams, Starbucks's longtime head green-coffee buyer, told *Seattle Weekly* in 1999.

When I spoke with the now-retired Williams seven years later, she held to this argument, and she unleashed a bit of her pent-up frustration about the actions of protesters as well. (Williams eventually grew so irritated with their claims, which she considered deliberately misleading, that the company barred her from meetings with consumer groups altogether.) "I remember once there was somebody outside one of our stores handing out a pamphlet with a starving child on the front, and the headline was 'Starbucks refuses to pay their coffee farmers a living wage,'" she recalled. "But Starbucks doesn't own these farms, and it doesn't control coffee pickers. Starbucks is so far removed from that poor child that it never could have made a dent in his life. These are countries where the culture is their own worst enemy." Even coming from the mouth of a corporate coffee buyer, this is an exceedingly cynical statement — if the company could never make a dent in farmers' lives, why bother to lift a finger at all? — yet much of what she says is true. Companies like Starbucks can try to inspire large farms to treat their workers better, but they can't order them to do anything. In this spirit, Starbucks recently announced an actual concrete policy change — it will pay growers a premium of up to $0.10 per pound if they can prove they obeyed certain environmental and labor codes. The program will be audited by a third party to ensure that the company sticks to it.*

But there's another, more significant reason why the sentiment

---

*Some farmers have criticized this program, pointing out that it costs them much more than an extra $0.10 per pound to do all of the things Starbucks is asking for.

behind that pamphlet isn't accurate: Starbucks's astonishing success at popularizing high-quality beans has actually been keeping the coffee industry's head above water. Let's take a second and go back to the source of all this misery for coffee growers — the glut of awful robusta coffee. The problem, remember, is that huge coffee conglomerates like Procter and Gamble are vacuuming up these cheap, acrid beans to save money, then chemically treating them and adding them to their canned blends. This leaves arabica producers with a smaller market for their crop, driving prices downward. For these farmers, then, low-quality robusta is the enemy. Their fortunes rise and fall on the world's demand for good coffee beans, and no one has done more to generate an insatiable global thirst for high-quality coffee than Starbucks.

Starbucks has done such an excellent job of making coffee connoisseurs out of average Americans, in fact, that competition for the world's best beans grows fiercer every year. As a result, specialty-coffee companies are paying more and more to secure a good supply, which is exactly the sort of trend that helps farmers. It's all tied to quality; if the brew tastes good, then the company that roasted the beans probably paid a decent price for them. Even Starbucks, the perennial punching bag of Fair Trade advocates, paid an average of $1.42 per pound for its coffee in 2006, which is $0.16 *higher* than the Fair Trade price. (Historically, though, Starbucks has typically paid a few cents less than Fair Trade rates.) The company has also won praise from Oxfam for doing 30 percent of its business directly with growers, leading all major coffee buyers. This isn't necessarily benevolence in action, mind you; it's only the reality of the marketplace. Every bit as much as farmers need its cash, Starbucks relies on loyal growers to satisfy its ever-increasing need for high-quality beans. If gourmet coffee roasters don't pay a stable price, their bean sources disappear.

In contrast, the conglomerates that suck up bad beans share none of these worries. Because they will remove the taste from the coffee and reinject it with synthetic flavorings, quality is not a concern; they'll just buy whatever's cheap. And the so-called Big Four coffee conglomerates — Nestlé, Procter and Gamble, Philip Morris, and Massimo Zanetti (which bought Sara Lee's coffee brands, including Hills Bros. and MJB, in 2005) — buy an enormous amount of coffee. All told, they provide 60 percent of America's coffee supply, and they make massive profits at it. According to Oxfam, Nestlé earns a profit margin of 26 percent on its world-spanning instant-coffee business. For coffee that will be chemically reconfigured anyway, the multinationals will gladly pay as little as $0.25 a pound for raw beans.

If you're seeking a culprit for the plight of coffee growers, look no further than the Big Four — and, by extension, those who purchase their exploitative coffee products. After all, these conglomerates have long been ratcheting up the amount of robusta in their blends, yet consumers have kept torturing their own taste buds without protest. In 1989, major blends like Folgers and Yuban were 50 percent robusta; today, they're 65 percent robusta. As long as people accept this ongoing trend, farmers will suffer. Oddly enough, the roaster Paul Katzeff — a man so steeped in Left Wing radicalism that he once protested farming conditions in El Salvador by pouring buckets of fake blood on the steps of a hotel where an SCAA convention was taking place — explained the state of affairs quite lucidly. "At Starbucks, they don't want to harm anybody, and they don't want to help anybody," he told me. "They just want to make money. They're neutral. I wouldn't say to Howard Schultz that he's a murderer for not buying enough Fair Trade coffee. But I will say to other companies who buy as cheap as they can that their actions are killing people — starving them, keeping a living wage from them."

This is why concerned coffee drinkers should revel in their gourmet habit. It's a simple formula: more demand for good beans leads to better prices for growers. Helping lift farmers from poverty, then, isn't so much a matter of hectoring companies like Starbucks (even if the company isn't the human rights champion it claims to be) as it is of making sure people never drink the cheap and exploitative coffee offered by conglomerates like the Big Four. Pushing consumers to cultivate a high-quality coffee habit might seem like just another utopian scheme, no different from Fair Trade advocates prodding people to buy based on ethics. But unlike Fair Trade, gourmet coffee is already an entrenched part of mainstream American life. Plus, while consumers don't always consider the ethical status of their coffee, everyone wants a high-quality product.

Finally, we have a humanitarian reason to pay four dollars for a latte: the more snobbish we are about the coffee we drink, the better things work out for the farmers who produce the beans. And really, the true problem has always been that we've *never* paid enough for our coffee. A dime for a cup of Joe was a fantastic value in decades past, but who ever said it was fair? As Kenneth Davids, a top coffee taster and the editor of the *Coffee Review,* points out, the best wines in the world sell for thousands of dollars a bottle, yet the globe's best coffee is cheaper per cup than a can of Coke. So those who feel guilty about spending a small fortune on coffee might want to tell themselves this: maybe they're just paying what it's actually worth.

~7~

What's in Your Cup

It probably didn't make anyone choke on their oatmeal, but still, readers of the *New York Times* on the morning of January 7, 1927, must have at least paused in bewilderment for a moment when they spotted the peculiar item on page 21, buried amid articles on steamboat inspection and contraband whisky confiscation. "COFFEE CHALLENGE," blared the headline, "Minnesota Drinker Invites All Comers to Championship Contest."

The drinker in question was one Gus Comstock, a barbershop porter in the remote town of Fergus Falls, near the North Dakota border. Comstock, it seems, was blessed with a unique gift: the man could drink *a lot* of coffee. Months before, he had set the first-ever world coffee-drinking record, downing sixty-two cups of it over a ten-hour span. But two challengers soon bettered this mark; H. A. Streety of Armadillo, Texas, declared that he had knocked back seventy-one cups in under nine hours, while Perry Wilson of Canyon, Texas, managed a seventy-two-cup effort in the standard ten hours. (Apparently, Texas was something of a coffee-drinking-contest talent mill.) Stung to the quick, Comstock announced his plan to take back the crown for good, pledging not to quit until he had surpassed his goal of one hundred cups of coffee consumed.

A few days after the *Times* story, a mob of spectators packed into the Hotel Kaddatz to witness Comstock's bid for liquid-intake immortality. The contender got off to a blistering start, downing fifteen eight-ounce cups of black coffee in the first hour, his incredible coffee-drinking ability dazzling the crowd. As the contest wore on, Comstock showed his versatility: he sometimes threw in cream and sugar, sometimes cream *or* sugar, sometimes nothing. After several hours of robust imbibing, Comstock took a short break and submitted himself to a physician's examination; aside from a mild fever, the doctor said, he was in "pretty good shape." But as the *Times* reported a few days later, "the rest threw Gus off his stride," and his swigs grew "somewhat labored" toward the end. Finally, Comstock had to give in after seven hours and fifteen minutes of action, with an impressive final tally of eighty-five cups — a record no challenger has broken since.

This quest for coffee-drinking greatness raises a few important questions. First, just how bored do you have to be before watching a guy drink coffee for seven hours sounds like an entertaining prospect? But more relevant to our purposes, what was in the coffee he was drinking? Shouldn't eighty-five cups of caffeinated coffee — more than five gallons of the stuff — have killed him or at least left him a quivering mess? Well, yes. Fortunately for Comstock, the competition-grade coffee at the Hotel Kaddatz must have been little more than hot water with a hint of coffee flavor. If he had tried his stunt at a present-day Starbucks with the chain's brawny drip brew, he would have consumed 13.6 grams of pure caffeine, well over the fatal oral dose of five to ten grams. In truth, he would have grown too shaky and disoriented from caffeine intoxication (an actual medical condition) to get even halfway to the record.

Comstock likely wasn't all that concerned with what was in those cups — fixated as he was on securing a prominent position in the history of Western civilization — but today's coffee enthusiasts obsess over the smallest details of their daily brew, down to the specific farm from which their beans hail. Unlike Comstock's day, when a man could get national media attention for drinking five gallons of coffee,* coffee lovers now focus on quality, not quantity. For modern aficionados of the bean, less is more; the perfect one-ounce shot of espresso is the gourmet coffee world's holy grail. And since café goers today are so finicky, coffee companies come up with ever-more extravagant claims about the quality of their wares — everyone wants the consumer to see their product as the finest gourmet indulgence available. As the coffee veteran Gary Talboy put it, "I've never met anyone in this business who claimed to sell *almost* the best-quality coffee."

At the top of the boasting heap sits Starbucks, a company that spent decades cultivating its image of luxury and refinement. Its beans, the Starbucks Web site tells us, are "the world's best." Every shot of espresso the company pulls has both a "billowing body" and a "dark, intense heart," which makes the product sound more like a mythological sea creature than something you can drink. The chain's marketing department is still as crafty as ever, but now, with forty million customers to please each week, Starbucks is having a tougher time maintaining its reputation as a top-notch roaster. How, customers might ask, can something be both a gourmet delicacy and a mass-produced product you can find at almost any grocery store?

In a sense, asking if Starbucks sells truly top-quality coffee is like investigating whether McDonald's dishes up the best hamburgers money can buy. Both are huge chains, which seems to disqualify them from the start; their focus on efficiency and throughput means they spend as little time as possible on each individual product they serve. But McDonald's doesn't portray itself as the Godiva of beef, nor does it charge the highest prices in the marketplace. Starbucks, on the other hand, undoubtedly makes its customers pay gourmet prices. In fact, according to British government statistics, in England a cappuccino now

---

*Actually, I guess that part hasn't changed much.

costs more than a line of cocaine. If consumers are paying that kind of money, shouldn't the product give them a similar thrill?

Or are they getting too much of a thrill already? After all, coffee drinkers don't just worry about the quality of what they're buying; they also wonder if their favorite daily habit is bad for their health. And despite Starbucks's marketing savvy and its real estate machine, one tiny molecule has always been a crucial component of the company's success: caffeine. Why else would the chain's customers need to come in *every day*, if not to stave off withdrawal from an addictive drug they must have just to feel normal? And our cravings for coffee can be fiercer than we realize, even overriding our other little joys in life. For instance, in one eye-opening 2005 survey sponsored by Dunkin' Donuts, pollsters found that respondents were more inclined to give up sex than they were to give up their daily cup of coffee.*

Though we often don't perceive it as such, caffeine *is* a drug. With 90 percent of Americans taking some form of it habitually, caffeine has become so commonplace in society that food and beverage manufacturers often don't bother to inform consumers if it's present in a product. But it's there, far more frequently than we realize. Here's an example: we all know that soft drinks like Coca-Cola and Barq's Root Beer contain enough caffeine to give us a decent jolt, but who would have guessed that Sunkist — an *orange soda* — has more of it than either of those two? Caffeine isn't some naturally occurring part of the soda-manufacturing process, nor does it have any noticeable flavor; it's always an additive, mixed in by beverage companies specifically for its pharmacological effects. What's more, fully 70 percent of American soft drinks contain it — a fact that has helped make caffeine the most widely used psychoactive drug on the planet.

Which, depending on your opinions about the issue, would make Starbucks the world's biggest pusher. That's not an exaggeration. To

---

*Which is puzzling, since a different Dunkin' Donuts–backed survey found that habitual coffee drinkers had sex more often than those who abstained — from coffee, that is.

some, caffeine represents an insidious public health threat — no better than a socially sanctioned form of amphetamine — and Starbucks has done more to promote and propagate the drug than anyone; the caffeine content in the chain's drip brew blows away every major competitor. That venti latte will give you more than a buzz, critics say; it'll destroy your body and debilitate your mind. When we add the worries about the company's calorie-packed pastries and whole-milk-and-syrup drinks to this stew of caffeine- and quality-related concerns, a dilemma becomes clear: health-conscious consumers have ample cause to second-guess their Starbucks habit.

Coffee is a cornerstone of modern life, and the busier we all become, the more we rely on it to pull us through the day. But how much do we really know about this little bean and its effect on our bodies and palates? It might seem a simple concoction, but coffee is deceptively complex; we've grown so accustomed to its presence in our lives that we generally fail to appreciate this. "Coffee is a very tricky and complicated beverage — much more so than wine," Kenneth Davids, one of the world's top coffee tasters, told me. "At any given moment, there's much more going on chemically. And when you roast it, there are so many changes inside the bean, it's almost volcanic." Fortunately for us, science — aided by some true coffee fanatics — has unlocked many of the secrets of this mysterious bean.

Painting the Tongue

The Italian port city of Trieste is an odd jumble of a place, situated precariously between the sapphire blue waters of the Adriatic Sea, the low-level chaos of post-Soviet Eastern Europe, and the forested hills of Italy's Friuli region. Crammed as far into the northeastern corner of the country as it can go without leaking over into neighboring Slovenia, the city is a multicultural hodgepodge of strudel shops, Vespa-riding Italians, monuments to James Joyce (who lived here intermittently for over a decade), chattering day-trippers from Ljubljana, and stately Habsburg dynasty–style buildings — remnants of Trieste's past glory as the main port of the Austro-Hungarian Empire. (For a while during World War II, the city even fell under the iron rule of *New Zealand*.) So while wandering through Trieste's gray streets and windswept plazas, one often has cause to ask: who does this place belong to, anyway? Apparently some Italians wonder about this as well; according to surveys, many of them aren't even sure Trieste is in Italy.

There's one easy way to tell that the city's heart is firmly Italian, though: go into any café and order an espresso. To Triestinos, coffee is not something one trifles with. In unremarkable coffee bars all over the city — places where the unappetizing shrink-wrapped sandwiches and bowls of potato chips look like they've been sitting on the counter since the Habsburgs' heyday — baristas treat each Euro-0.80 serving of espresso like a work of art, painstakingly measuring and tamping down the fresh grounds, then dusting off the portafilter with a paintbrush before locking it in and pulling the shot. Even in the bustling, rickety train station café, customers each get their foam-topped espresso in a white porcelain demitasse, with matching saucer. The baristas here have a lot to live up to. Since 1933, Trieste has been the home of illy caffè, the most quality-focused major roaster in the world; its square red logo graces the front windows of most of the city's coffee bars. And imagine the pressure the baristas must feel: at any moment, Ernesto Illy, the patriarch of the Illy clan — and a man who happens to be the globe's foremost authority on the science of coffee quality — might walk in to see if you're doing his beans justice.

Not that Illy is much of a threatening figure, especially at age eighty-one. With his cue-ball head, huge aviator-style glasses, and wiry frame, he resembles an Italian Ross Perot — only with smaller ears and, if you can imagine it, more energy. If his family name commands respect in Trieste, it's a respect based on admiration; Illy is a man who doesn't seem to have much use for pretension. Unlike many trade secret–guarding captains of industry, he is only too happy to share every detail of his life's work with the world. Indeed, the Illy clan has produced a book all about it, with help from scores of scientists: *Espresso Coffee: The Science of Quality*. (It's a ripping read, as long as you understand phrases like "plurimodal particle size distribution" and "optical microscopy of emulsified lipids.") When it comes to the science of coffee, the Illys don't fiddle around; both Ernesto (illy caffè's chairman) and his son, Andrea (its CEO), are chemists by training. After decades of research into every conceivable aspect of coffee preparation — including, for example, fourteen years spent studying different ways to grind beans — Illy has reduced the ideal shot of espresso to as precise a formula as man can devise. He has turned coffee into a science.

Illy calls espresso the "quintessential expression of coffee," which is a sentiment most of his fellow countrymen share. The term *espresso* refers not to a different variety of coffee bean or a specific roasting style, but to a method of preparation. In Italian, *espresso* means just what it sounds like, "express," and the name perfectly reflects the intentions of the drink's purported creator, a manufacturing plant owner named Luigi Bezzera. Seeking to shorten his employees' coffee breaks, Bezzera invented a machine in 1901 that brewed single, superconcentrated servings of the beverage as quickly as possible, using steam pressure. But the Italians soon discovered that espresso was more than a time-saver; it was a potent one-ounce distillate of the best the bean had to offer. As David Schomer, owner of Seattle's Espresso Vivace, explained, "The entire purpose of this venture is to make coffee taste as good as fresh-ground coffee smells. And espresso is certainly the best method for doing so, because the short brewing time pulls the best flavors out and leaves the negatives behind." Done well, the process yields a syrupy, naturally sweet elixir, with flavors so intense that they linger in the mouth for as long as twenty minutes after drinking. Done poorly, it produces an astringent, off-tasting fluid that has to be buried under heaps of sugar and a cupful of milk. Most of the world's espresso is of the latter variety.

That statement isn't meant as a slight to mainstream baristas but simply as proof that high-quality coffee preparation is incredibly com-plicated. This is where Dr. Illy comes in. "Between the coffee plant and the cup, there are one hundred fourteen steps where something can go wrong," he told me in his modest office, a room dominated by science texts and stacks of research papers. "Every mistake is a catastro-phe." The goal of the system Illy has devised is to defend these 114 steps from impurity, methodically eliminating any flaw that could taint the coffee. In this quest, no detail is too small to merit extensive study. For instance, when illy caffè hired the Italian architect Matteo Thun to de-sign its official espresso cup in 1990, the assignment came with a seventy-page document from Dr. Illy specifying how thick the cup needed to be, what the necessary dimensions were, which kind of por-celain to use, and so on; Thun later said that the only thing left for him to do was attach the handle. In Illy's view, science and research had dictated sensory perfection, and nothing could be left to chance. "We need to have zero defects, no?" he said with a smile.

The top candidate for evildoing in the coffee-preparation process is actually the bean itself. Since heat is the only ingredient roasters add to raw coffee, the beans must be perfect to begin with — the roaster simply unlocks the potential within. And as Illy explained, arabica beans are complicated little things. "Remember, *Coffea arabica* has forty-four chromosomes. We humans? Forty-six!" He paused to give me a mean-ingful look. "All other coffees have just twenty-two." Being such intricate organisms, arabica beans are prone to blemishes. Some defects are obvi-ous to the human eye, as with unripe black green beans (which taste like rotten fish when roasted) and waxy-looking sour beans (which have a vinegar flavor). But other common flaws are effectively invisible. "Dirty" beans, "stinker" beans, and "Rio" beans all appear normal, despite tast-ing of (in order of appearance) wood, rot, and medicine. If the raw coffee has defects, those defects will show up in the final product.

To avoid bad beans, every specialty roaster employs a small strike force of coffee-tasting experts known as "cuppers." Professional cup-pers taste hundreds of coffee samples each day, grading the quality of each with machinelike precision — the best ones can even pinpoint the country and growing region where a coffee sample comes from through taste alone. These cuppers don't take dainty little sips. Within the industry, the dominant belief seems to be that one's cupping skill correlates directly with the volume of one's slurp. Imagine the sound of Velcro being torn apart, but fed through a fully cranked-up bullhorn, and you have a reasonable approximation of a professional slurp. Now picture yourself in a room where these explosions are bombarding your ears from all sides as cuppers raise spoonful after spoonful to their mouths, add in a few comments like "I'm getting crab apples and paprika here," and you've practically attended a cupping session. (There's a justification for the violent sips, of course: they atomize the liquid and spray it over the entire tongue, revealing the coffee's full character.) On any given day, the cuppers might taste a chocolaty Sulawesi, a sweet and spicy Guatemala Antigua, a blueberry-hinted Ethiopia Harrar, and even what's called Kopi Luwak coffee, which, at $300 per pound, is the world's priciest coffee. Why? Because Kopi Luwak beans are harvested from the droppings of a catlike animal called the Indonesian palm civet; the creature eats ripe coffee cherries and partially digests them before passing them on enhanced, its special gift to the world. (The stuff is big in Japan.)

The cuppers' taste buds guide them to the most promising beans, but even in the finest coffee batches, defective beans slip through the quality-control defenses at the rate of one or two per hundred. To Illy, this is unacceptable. "A serving of espresso is approximately fifty beans," he said. "One bad bean can taint the other forty-nine like a rotten egg. These things can be perceived at much lower concentrations, because bad things are much more pungent than good things." (This sensitivity, he says, is a product of the evolution of our senses of taste and smell, which arose in part to defend us from rotten and harmful foods.) To fully safeguard our taste buds, the only solution is to examine each bean individually and to remove the offenders, a task illy caffè carries out with the aid of cutting-edge technology.

When Illy starts talking about the scientific nuts and bolts of coffee, it's best to grasp your chair firmly with both hands, hunker down, and just try to keep up for as long as possible while he volleys graphs and technical terms at you. He might be waxing lyrical on how espresso is like a beautiful woman one moment, but he's always seconds away from explaining the composition of the polymers in her dress. So, boiled down a bit from Illy's daunting explanation, the bean-sorting process works as follows. Defective and perfect beans might look identical to us, but one disparity betrays the stinkers: when you bounce light off them, they absorb slightly more of it than the good ones do. At the illy caffè roasting plant, four refrigerator-size contraptions shoot beams of light at every incoming raw bean — each machine examines four hundred of them per second. Whenever the cameras spot an offending bean, a puff of air immediately blasts it into a reject pile.

This optical seek-and-destroy system is relatively simple, but matters become mind-bendingly complex once the roasting process begins. Scientists have identified as many as fifteen hundred distinct chemical compounds in the coffee bean, and the intermingling of these chemicals during roasting is what ultimately determines how the coffee tastes. The temperature of the roaster, the duration of the roast, the method of cooling — all of these factors influence each individual compound differently. And there's also the unique structure of the bean itself to consider. As raw coffee heats up inside the roaster, water molecules inside the beans turn into steam and attempt to escape, only to run into a thick cellular wall that seals everything in. Each bean is like a miniature pressure cooker, containing a maelstrom of chemical reactions within; the stress is such that the coffee bean expands in volume by half, before finally popping. Think of the whole roasting process as being something like juggling fifteen hundred different objects at once while standing inside an erupting volcano.

But if this is a little too much to comprehend, we can simplify things a bit. As most everyone knows from the old grade-school experiment where you pinch your nose closed and try to taste an apple, flavor is mostly a matter of aroma perception. This is especially true of coffee. "Espresso is for the nose, not for the taste," Illy told me. Roasted coffee contains over eight hundred "aromatic volatile compounds," but only about twenty-five dominant ones. The distinct flavor and scent of roasted coffee, then, is an olfactory cocktail made from this set of twenty-five ingredients, many of which are easily recognizable to the untrained nose. In a laboratory analysis of roasted coffee, a gas chromatograph will pick out aromas ranging from vanilla, roses, Darjeeling tea, and honey, all the way to oddball scents like roasted meat, cabbage, sweat, butter, and the hard-to-describe "cat scent." (Let's just say it's a good idea to minimize it.)

As you would expect, Illy comes armed with an assortment of charts showing how different roasting techniques affect these important aromas and, thus, the flavor of the coffee. For any given aromatic compound — say, 4-vinylguaiacol, which smells like clove — he can pull out a bar graph that shows its intensity in the bean at five different roasting levels: raw, very light, medium (for Illy's "normale" style), dark (for Illy's "scurro" style), and super-dark (which is essentially the Starbucks roast). Desirable aromas always peak at the medium or dark setting, dropping off sharply on either side. "It is always diminishing when you overroast the coffee," Illy explained as he showed me the charts for various good aromas. Next, he displayed a graph in which the Starbucks-style roast yielded far more of a certain odor than the others. "This is the aroma of . . . if you had a fire that has been extinguished by a fire brigade," he said, trying not to smirk. "It's called 'wet fire' scent."

While most coffee companies offer dozens of blends and single-origin coffees in a variety of roasts, illy caffè sells just one blend in two roasts, and the product is constantly monitored and tweaked to produce the right aromas consistently. For Dr. Illy, there can only be one perfect espresso, and his tight control over every variable in the coffee-preparation process allows him to achieve it regularly. On a guided tour of illy caffè's Trieste facility — with a security guard trailing ten

yards behind at all times, ready to pounce if I brandished anything re-
motely resembling a camera — I saw the rest of Illy's directives put into
action. Pneumatic tubes transported the beans from the roasting plant
to the packaging center, where machines dumped the coffee into air-
tight tins and flushed them with nitrogen to preserve freshness, before
finally pressurizing and sealing the containers. At one of illy caffè's two
on-site concept espresso bars, a barista pulled me a shot according to
strict percolation instructions; the water must be heated to exactly 194
degrees Fahrenheit, then pushed through the coffee grounds for precisely thirty seconds at a pressure of 130 psi, thereby generating a layer
of khaki-colored foam on top called *crema.*

Given the array of chemistry equations, lab tests, and strict proto-
cols that underpinned the steaming cup I was raising to my lips, I half
expected the espresso to taste like brewed algebra. But this was like no
shot of espresso I'd ever had back in the States, where *espresso* usually
just means "pungent, extra-strength coffee." The brew was viscous
like a liqueur, with a honeylike natural sweetness, the result of cara-
melization of sugars inside the bean during roasting. Illy likes to say
that the ideal espresso shot "paints the tongue," which I suddenly understood after the first sip. Billions of tiny oil particles one micron
wide were coating my taste buds and slowly releasing the aromas contained within. My tour guide, a blond American expatriate, advised
me that I would detect hints of caramel, dark chocolate, and freshly
toasted bread, which is the sort of wine-connoisseurish thing my taste
buds typically refuse to do. To my astonishment, I could actually pick
them out.

Many coffee experts disagree passionately with the idea that such a
thing as the objectively proved perfect espresso exists. Taste, they say, is
subjective, particular to every unique tongue. Good coffee, then, is
just as much the result of art as it is of science. Said Schomer, "You're
talking about a sensory system of great complexity in the human
mouth, and an elixir of great complexity that evolves each second." Davids, the coffee critic, respects Illy's approach but agrees with Schomer.

"Our perception of quality is not absolute, no matter what Dr. Illy might think," he told me.

There is one aesthetic judgment on which nearly all coffee aficionados agree, however: as time goes by, it's getting tougher to find decent coffee at a Starbucks. But at this phase in the company's evolution, superior coffee isn't necessarily what it's aiming at. For Starbucks, quality has become mostly irrelevant.

Beverage Entertainment

On an international flight not long ago, I happened to sit next to a middle-aged woman from Chicago who was returning home from a trip to Venice with her two teenaged children. We chatted pleasantly for a while about Italy and kids these days, and eventually she asked what I did for a living. By then, I had learned that disclosing the fact that I was writing a book about Starbucks and the coffeehouse phenomenon was somewhat risky; many people have strong opinions about the company, and my revelation was often interpreted as an invitation to expound, at considerable length, on said opinions. But this woman's response stood out. At the first mention of the word *Starbucks*, she became almost reverent. She never drank coffee before Starbucks arrived, but now it's a "treat" she likes to buy for herself and her husband. "Oh, Starbucks has *very* good coffee — the best you can get," she said. "Doesn't it?"

Certainly, Starbucks has the best *marketing* you can find, but it's been a long time since the coffee lived up to the ads. Once, back in the company's evangelistic days, its paper bags of fresh beans included a stamped sell-by date, and its baristas possessed a near-encyclopedic knowledge of espresso arcana. The Starbucks employees of old preached relentlessly about quality, raising the consumer's expectations of what coffee could taste like in the process; essentially, they made the average American cup of coffee better. The company's early zeal so impressed Mark Prince, who now runs the popular coffee

Web site Coffeegeek.com, that he becomes emotionally stirred when remembering the first time he visited a Starbucks, in 1993. Prince requested a *ristretto* shot — a smaller, bolder espresso that requires making subtle tweaks to the equipment. Outside of Italy, very few people had even heard of it. "The barista said, 'I know exactly what you're talking about,'" Prince recalled. "He actually went and adjusted the grinder and pulled one shot he didn't like, then he pulled another. You'd *never* see this at a Starbucks past 1998. I don't want to say it was as good as the espresso I got in Italy, but it was damn close."

Providing a world-class coffee snob with such a treasured memory is quite a feat, but the company doesn't figure to repeat the accomplishment anytime soon. Over its years of expansion, Starbucks has jettisoned many of the quality-control standards that vaulted it to prominence in the first place. In the past, baristas crafted each espresso shot personally; Howard Schultz used to compare his employees to culinary artisans. Today, machines pull the shots. The company's date-stamped paper bags of coffee beans gave way to plastic packages with indecipherable codes printed on the bottom to disguise the date of roasting. "When I first started working at Starbucks, a five-pound 'bullet' bag had a one-week sell-by date," the Starbucks veteran Jana Oppenheimer, who now works for Portland's Stumptown Coffee Roasters, told me. "Now, that same bag, which hasn't advanced in technology at all, has nine months stamped on it."

So as the company's prices continue climbing toward the stratosphere, the quality of its coffee isn't keeping up. In a way, this is inevitable. "Look, when you have ten thousand stores to supply, how much quality coffee can you buy?" asked Alfred Peet. "There's not that much good coffee in the world!" According to Peet's reasoning, the vastness of the Starbucks empire makes it impossible to maintain the standards of times past. But, of course, Schultz is a firm believer in his company's ability to achieve the impossible. He claims Starbucks hasn't just maintained its quality levels but that the coffee is actually better now than ever. "I know we're buying higher-quality coffee today than we ever have," Schultz told me, offering a list of the areas where he thinks the company has improved. "The proprietary technology with which we roast the coffee in the plants, everything we do around freshness, blending, our standards, being able to age coffee now in the numbers that we are — there's no doubt that the quality of the coffee has gotten better." His marketing sense notwithstanding, Schultz likely does consider this statement absolutely true. "With Howard, I think it's a sincere belief that despite all of the growth, the quality at Starbucks hasn't gone down a bit over the years," said Kevin Knox, Schultz's former roasting expert. "They truly believe their own PR."

For years, gourmet coffee wonks have been engaged in a sort of tacit contest to see who can come up with the most acidic put-down of Starbucks's coffee-roasting expertise. "In a company as large as Starbucks, you can find whatever you're looking for," Schultz's former mentor Jerry Baldwin said, waiting a beat before adding, "except fresh coffee." Of Starbucks's drip brew, Peet said simply: "I detest it. The coffee talks to me. It says, 'I wasn't roasted too well.'" Many coffee novices have gotten in on the game too. "I accept that Starbucks coffee will taste burnt," one *Boston Herald* writer quipped, "but if I'm handed a cup that's actually on fire, I have the right to a free biscotti or a $20 bill, whichever is of greater value." This last dig about the company's beans is a common one. For as long as Starbucks has enjoyed the spotlight, people — customers included — have complained about its signature dark roast, nicknaming the company "Charbucks" and "Star-yucks."

To the coffee geeks, Starbucks's ultra-dark beans and sugary concoctions are an affront to the art of coffee roasting. So-called third-wave roasters — quality-mad independents like Stumptown Coffee Roasters in Portland and Intelligentsia Coffee in Chicago — want customers to think about their beans the way they would think of a fine wine, appreciating the coffee's subtler characteristics. The practice of burying the flavor of the beans under hazelnut syrup and whole milk disturbs them the same way that mixing a few packets of Equal into a first-rate Bordeaux would offend an oenophile.

But before we pile on the jabs, it's important to understand what Starbucks is really trying to do with its coffee. The company didn't build a forty-million-strong customer base by turning people into monocle-wearing, snifter-sipping dilettantes, nor does it aim to. Today, with its thousands of stores to supply and its forays into music and books to worry about, Starbucks wants to accomplish two coffee-related goals: keep people interested and turn out a consistent product.

Starbucks's focus on capturing the consumer's attention traces back to the midnineties, when the colossal success of the Frappuccino amazed everyone, especially Schultz. Before, Schultz assumed Americans were snapping up Starbucks's drinks because they hankered after a pure European coffee experience, but the Frappuccino's popularity was evidence otherwise. Consumers just wanted luxury-priced caffeinated fun in their cups — what the coffee consultant Tim Castle calls "beverage entertainment." Nobody cared that coffee aficionados sneered at the whipped cream and caramel they desired; people love sugar, and a beverage like the Toffee Nut Latte is a dessert they can order every morning. "You can look at Starbucks as a beverage theater, as opposed to a movie theater," Castle said. "You come in for things that entertain you." With this in mind, Starbucks unveils a slew of new drinks each season, many of them featuring flavors God surely never intended to see paired with coffee. As of a decade ago, no coffee drinker in history had ever looked down at his mug and said to himself, "You know what would make this so much better? *Banana puree and coconut flakes!*" Yet today we've witnessed not only the Banana Coconut Frappuccino, but also the Pumpkin Spice Latte, the Raspberry Mocha Chip Frappuccino, and the Eggnog Latte. Each is what Starbucks calls a "sophisticated coffee indulgence."

This widespread preference for sugary drinks raises an obvious question: if customers like sweet things, why would Starbucks deliberately produce bitter coffee? Indeed, Starbucks has made a fetish of its ultra-dark roast, even using it as a selling point. In a tour of the company's roasting plant, the Starbucks coffee specialist Major Cohen once boasted to a *Boston Herald* reporter that "the black coffee beans are seconds from incinerating into cinders," as if burning something to a carbonized crisp could only result in deliciousness. The dark roast is partly a product of tradition; Peet's, the company's spiritual forefather, still roasts quite dark as well. But some believe Starbucks has an ulterior motive in blackening its beans: the bitter coffee, they say, baits customers into buying milkier, higher-margin drinks. "I would guess they don't want to sell just coffee," explained Illy. "It's too cheap. This aroma of burned stuff, they must do it on purpose, to make more money from syrup and milk. Otherwise, why would they do it?" Many have declared that Starbucks is "in the milk business," and without a doubt, consumers are willing to pay a huge premium for hot milk — the more of it, the better. "When we at Peet's finally joined the civilized world and came out with a twenty-ounce cup, that immediately became a third of our business," Baldwin told me. "Do you know how much milk that is? I mean, one of those has more milk than I drink in a year." Plus, customers still want to taste the coffee when they order an ounce of espresso in twenty ounces of milk, and nothing punches through better than dark-roasted beans.

Consistency, Starbucks's other major coffee priority, is nothing short of essential to the company's appeal. With coffee, consumers want to know that what they're buying will be decent; a bad cup of coffee can crack the fragile shell of modern contentment, destroying one's day entirely. "People hate to gamble with this," said Ward Barbee, the *Fresh Cup* publisher. "Americans are herd driven. We like everything to be the same. We know that if we go to another part of the country — Oh look! There's a Starbucks! — you're assured of getting the same thing." Whether you're in downtown Seattle, an office building in Dubai, or an airport in Japan, Schultz wants your cappuccino to taste exactly the same. Travelers in particular appreciate this focus on reliability. To the coffee drinker in unfamiliar territory, Starbucks looms like an oasis on the horizon; it means you're assured of getting a consistent, passable cup.

And nothing is better at producing a consistent product than a machine. The company's transition from manual espresso machines to hyperefficient automatics, which pull precisely the same shot every time the barista hits a button, has been a quiet one. Understandably, Starbucks hasn't been eager to contradict its claims about the importance of its "partners" by advertising that it has completely removed them from the drink-preparation process. But surprisingly, many coffee snobs applaud the new, bionic Starbucks. Since the company couldn't possibly train every one of its 125,000 employees to pull a good shot, they say, mechanization ensures the consumer gets a steady "seven-out-of-ten" product, instead of a "nine" one day and a "three" the next. When I mentioned this assessment to Schultz, he looked pained. "I don't know if that's a good way of putting it," he said. "We have to do everything we can to try to exceed the expectations of our customers. If waiting in line became such a burden, we had to find ways to accelerate that and be more efficient. And we believe one hundred percent that efficiency has not been compromised by quality."

That was an ill-timed slip — he obviously meant to say that *quality* has not been compromised by *efficiency*, not the other way around. But really, it doesn't matter; reduced quality isn't likely to sink Starbucks one inch. As its competitors know, the company's sugary and consistent concoctions please the middlebrow, which is all that matters. "If you were to ask one hundred people in Portland at random what's their favorite coffee shop, probably not more than a few would say Starbucks," Jerome Conlon, the market research expert, told me. "But guess what?" He held up a Starbucks cup. "This is good enough."

The "Bitter Invention of Satan"

Coffee fiends might fuss over the subtleties of a Kenya AA or a Sumatra Mandheling today, but for Europe's earliest coffee drinkers, flavor and quality were beside the point; they first used coffee as a medicine — a cure-all wonder potion. A seventeenth-century Londoner, for example, would have come across an assortment of medical pamphlets claiming coffee cured everything from melancholy and measles to smallpox and the plague. And it wasn't enough to merely drink the brew. Physicians administered coffee through a variety of methods far removed from the present-day "Starbucks Experience." One technique, used to treat gastrointestinal distress, called for the patient to drink a mixture of coffee grounds, salad oil, melted butter, and honey, after which the physician would insert a yard-long whale bone called a *provang* down the victim's throat and stir it around. That might sound archaic or plain crazy, but such things still happen today. One current homeopathic coffee booster is the pop singer Janet Jackson; in 1997, Jackson revealed to *Newsweek* that she had treated her chronic depression with a "coffee enema," which she said helped "bring out the sad cells" in the liver.

Despite its early fame as a universal remedy, coffee soon acquired precisely the opposite reputation — that of a poison. (Which maybe had something to do with widespread postprovang trauma.) This idea has lingered for the past three hundred years, even as coffee drinking became universal. The most common allegation against the bean was also the most subversive: that coffee caused impotence.* A group of London women played this charge to maximum effect in 1674, when they issued a public complaint about the continuing disappearance of Englishmen into coffeehouses. The petition, credited to "several Thousands of Buxome Good-Women, Languishing in Extremity of Want," declared that coffee had turned "the *Ablest Performers* in Christendom" suddenly limp. "To our unspeakable Grief," they wrote, "we find of late a very sensible *Decay* of that true *Old English Vigour;* our *Gallants* being every way so *Frenchified,* that they are become meer Cocksparrows, fluttering things that come on *Sa sa,* with a world of Fury, but are not able to *stand* to it, and in the very first Charge fall down *flat*

---

*Calm down — it doesn't.

before us." (Since women were banned from London's coffeehouses, this protest was more likely a deliberate low blow against men, so to speak, than a legitimate complaint.)

Even scientific evidence of coffee's harmlessness failed to fully redeem the beverage in the public mind. In the late eighteenth century, for instance, King Gustav III of Sweden concocted an ingenious experiment to test the toxicity of coffee and tea. Gustav commuted the death sentences of a pair of murderous twin brothers, ruling instead that they would serve life sentences as lab rats, with one twin drinking huge amounts of coffee each day and the other drinking the same amount of tea. The twin that died first, he reasoned, would be the one who had imbibed the more poisonous brew. Unfortunately, Gustav didn't live to see the results: the tea drinker went first, at age eighty-three, followed by the coffee drinker, at eighty-eight — not bad, for the 1700s. Coffee also received a baptism of sorts, when Pope Clement VIII ignored calls from priests to ban this "bitter invention of Satan" and pronounced coffee not just acceptable for Catholic consumption, but "delicious" as well. Still, health concerns trickled down through the ages, with canny entrepreneurs taking full advantage. C. W. Post, the loony inventor of Grape-Nuts cereal, campaigned relentlessly against "coffee nerves" at the turn of the twentieth century, urging consumers to hop on the "road to Wellville" by replacing the brew with his powdered substitute, Postum. (Not that Post himself gave up the coffee habit.)

Today, however, we worry not so much about *coffee* as we do about *caffeine*, the life-giving molecule that makes the drink go. On any given day in the United States, 80 percent of the population will consume some form of the drug, most commonly in coffee and soft drinks. For most of us, caffeine is even a part of our lives in the womb; in the developed world, the majority of babies are born with small amounts of it in their bloodstreams, from their mothers' caffeine intake. In our modern, sleep-deprived world, we've come to rely on its invigorating powers for our very survival.

Given the drug's tyrannical sway over our physical and mental well-being, it should come as no surprise that many health activists regard caffeine (and by extension, coffee) as a biochemical villain that should be purged from our lives completely.* Of course, as Americans, we're required to believe everything we like is killing us, yet caffeine still receives special scrutiny. Scientists and physicians conduct hundreds, if not thousands, of studies each year on caffeine's effects, arriving at a bewildering — and often contradictory — array of conclusions: caffeine slightly decreases blood flow to the heart at high altitudes, yet it helps with endurance exercise; it boosts short-term memory, but it also causes tip-of-the-tongue moments of forgetfulness.

With the constant flow of research results, caffeine scares are bound to pop up periodically. As one toxicologist put it to *New Scientist* magazine, "Somebody has published a paper linking coffee or caffeine with just about every disease known to man." The charges generally don't stick (obviously, since we'd all be dead by now if they were true), but a few were sufficiently terrifying to cause a dip in coffee consumption. The nastiest blow came in 1980, when a Food and Drug Administration researcher claimed to have found a connection between caffeine and birth defects in laboratory rats, putting a significant dent in coffee sales. (News reports neglected to mention that researchers had force-fed the rats the caffeine equivalent of two hundred cups of coffee all at once; subsequent studies with moderate doses cleared it of the birth defect charges.) It would seem that caffeine is, at the very least, a drug we should monitor closely and not devour with reckless abandon.

The problem with this approach is that we actually have no clue how much caffeine we're consuming. Here's an illustration: next time you wander into a Starbucks, try to find out how much caffeine is in the drink you order — or *any* drink, for that matter. The baristas haven't

---

*For the purposes of this discussion, I'm assuming that the atrocity known as decaf isn't an option. Perhaps as proof that divine providence agrees with this assessment, a 2005 National Institutes of Health study found that decaf coffee — but *not* regular coffee — causes an upsurge in drinkers' levels of harmful LDL cholesterol.

a clue, and the nutrition information pamphlets (which even show the iron and vitamin A content of every possible drink) never once mention caffeine. Then the information must be on the Starbucks Web site, right? But a search for the word *caffeine* on Starbucks.com yields zero matches. To find out the facts, you'd either have to call the company's corporate headquarters or be pretty handy with search engines.

And were you to scour the Internet for answers, the results might not buck up your spirits. The company's official caffeine estimates state that each shot of espresso contains around 90 milligrams of caffeine, while a twelve-ounce drip coffee boasts 240 milligrams.* But as a research team from the University of Florida discovered in 2003, these estimates don't always line up with reality. When they tested the sixteen-ounce coffees they were served at a Gainesville Starbucks on several different dates, the caffeine numbers varied wildly: on one day, the cup contained 259 milligrams; on another, it contained more than double that — a tremendous 564 milligrams of high-grade stimulant.

Bearing in mind findings like this, as well as the persistent health debate over the drug, Starbucks's policy with regard to caffeine has been to pretend it doesn't exist. Howard Schultz seldom lets the word *caffeine* pass his lips, and he has been curt with journalists who have asked about the issue, sometimes claiming to be totally unfamiliar with the idea that coffee could be harmful. One reason for this is obvious: Schultz has spent decades building up coffee as a beverage consisting primarily of passion and romance, with a touch of the human condition. What could be less romantic than a chemical called 1,3,7-trimethylxanthine?

But the strategy is also puzzling, since caffeine's presence in coffee is no secret; for most coffee lovers, it's a major part of the drink's allure. If consumers are harming themselves, they're doing it willingly. So isn't the appeal of caffeination too obvious to deny? In a memorable quote, a Starbucks roasting plant supervisor named Tom Walters of-

---

*By the way, this revelation should finally disprove the common misconception that espresso drinks are more powerful than plain drip brew; even a double shot has less caffeine than a twelve-ounce coffee.

fered another, more graphic version of this thought to *National Geographic*. "I've been asked not to make the connection between coffee and caffeine," he said. "But we see a hell of a lot of caffeine around here. When you roast the beans, the caffeine forms a kind of fuzz on the roaster. So when we're too busy to get a coffee break, some people just run a finger down the casing of the roaster and lick it, and get their jolt that way." Put like this, the significance of caffeine is hard to ignore.

The stakes are high for Starbucks in the caffeine debate. Several former and current Starbucks executives told me that they could imagine only one thing that might bring Starbucks down: conclusive scientific evidence that caffeine is unhealthy. If that contingency were to arrive, the company would bear a heavy burden; thanks to Starbucks, we're taking in more caffeine than ever. "What's a small coffee now?" asked Roland Griffiths, a professor at the Johns Hopkins University School of Medicine who has conducted many studies on caffeine. "A few years ago, a cup of coffee was five ounces, but the 'small' at Starbucks is twelve ounces. It's more than doubled." As we've seen, Starbucks also serves the most potent brew in the coffeehouse world, which, on a strong day, packs nearly as much caffeine in a single grande cup as three maximum-strength NoDoz caplets. And since the company brought coffee back into vogue, we've become surrounded with caffeinated "energy drinks" like Red Bull, caffeinated breath mints, caffeinated vodka . . . the list goes on.

All of which leads to the inevitable question: *Is* caffeine bad for us? And what does the stuff do to our bodies, anyway?

To Drink or Not to Drink?

When we humans ingest moderate amounts of caffeine, a series of pleasant sensations runs through us like an electric current. We feel invigorated, buzz with industry, the mortal coil suddenly crackling with newfound energy. The mind races. The heart thumps faster. There's a very good reason why caffeine makes us feel so keyed up: we've just swallowed poison, and our bodies are reacting accordingly.

Specifically, caffeine is bug poison — a natural insecticide that developed in plants as a means of short-circuiting the nervous systems of any crawlers who might hazard a munch. Its scrambling effect on bug brains is truly impressive. In one study, conducted by NASA, researchers dosed common house spiders with several different psychoactive drugs — Benzedrine (a variant of amphetamine), chloral hydrate (a sedative and hypnotic), marijuana, and caffeine — to see what kind of effect each would have on their webs. The tweaked, sedated, and stoned spiders spun decent-looking facsimiles of the standard web, with the necessary hubs and concentric circles. The caffeinated spiders, on the other hand, wove the arachnid equivalent of gibberish, a fractured and haphazard mess.

Since we are neither insect nor arachnid, the drug affects us far differently, but it still takes quick and decisive command of our bodily functions. Within thirty to forty-five minutes of your first sip of coffee, caffeine molecules reach their peak concentration in the body, permeating all barriers. It slips into saliva, spinal fluid, breast milk, and even sperm, which wiggle and swim more energetically when under the influence.

The source of caffeine's power within our bodies is its resemblance to adenosine, a neurotransmitter that regulates sleep. Adenosine works in the nervous system the same way a radiator works in a car: its purpose is to keep the brain from overheating. Each time a neuron fires, adenosine is produced as a by-product, and the more it fires, the more adenosine accumulates. Over time, the adenosine finds its way to receptor sites, which then tell the brain that it's time to shut down — that is, we grow tired and fall asleep. After enough time has passed, the receptor sites reabsorb the adenosine and we wake up refreshed, ready for another day of intense neural action.

Caffeine works by disrupting this process. To the brain, caffeine and adenosine look identical, which means the caffeine molecules start snapping into the adenosine receptor sites right and left — only the fit isn't exact, so the caffeine blocks adenosine from getting in, but it doesn't order the brain to shut down. As Stephen Braun explains in his useful book, *Buzz: The Science and Lore of Alcohol and Caffeine*, the effect is "like putting a block of wood under one of the brain's primary brake pedals"; our neurons begin firing more rapidly because they have no way of slowing down. (Blocked receptor sites on the colon and kidneys also account for the laxative and diuretic properties of coffee; those organs, too, get going with enthusiasm.) The body responds to the foreign menace by sending squadrons of liver enzymes to dismantle the caffeine molecules, and after six or so hours things return to normal.

But although caffeine is technically a toxin, that doesn't necessarily mean it does us any harm. Despite the extreme scrutiny scientists have placed on the drug, no serious health charges have ever been proved. If anything, the studies have given coffee drinking a better reputation. Regular coffee consumption appears to offer significant protection against Parkinson's disease, liver disease, type 2 diabetes, and certain cancers — enough benefits to offset risks like a mild rise in blood pressure.* Taken in moderation — say, three or fewer cups of coffee a day — caffeine generally enriches our lives without serious consequence. It gives us the miraculous ability to become alert on command, improves mental quickness, enhances athletic performance, and even improves the drinker's mood. Caffeine is so good at boosting one's attitude, in fact, that researchers have discovered that a strong dose of the stuff does as much to bring up a person's spirits as cocaine or amphetamines.

Which brings us around to another problem: caffeine is uncommonly addictive. Coffee neophytes can develop physical dependence

---

*Word to the wise, though: pregnant women should cut back because babies don't develop the enzymes to properly break down caffeine until well after birth. Caffeine also intensifies symptoms of premenstrual syndrome. And it doesn't help you sober up.

on the drug in as few as three days, and once they do, they need a daily dose of it just to get their brains functioning normally. And if anything gets in the way of that fix, caffeine withdrawal symptoms will begin appearing within twelve to twenty-four hours of the addict's last cup, meaning that many of us are already suffering its initial effects when we wake up each morning. Headaches are just the beginning; other symptoms of withdrawal include depression, fatigue, lethargy, irritability, and even vomiting. Should you be crazy enough to quit entirely, it takes about a week of abstention for the body to return to normal.

The situation sounds far worse than it really is. Caffeine may be fiercely addictive, but it's no drug of abuse; nobody has ever held up a liquor store to get cash for a hit of cappuccino. You don't need to drink more coffee over time to get the same buzz, and overuse is highly unpleasant, as anyone who has had the jitters from one espresso too many will confirm. Actually, overdosing on caffeine through coffee drinking is all but physically impossible, though Gus Comstock made an inspiring attempt to do so. And what's more, the addiction probably does more good than harm: caffeine may be the only psychoactive drug on the planet that routinely *saves* lives, by making the highways safer from drowsy drivers. "With coffee, it's more a habit than an addiction," said Paul Rozin, a University of Pennsylvania psychology professor who studies our relationships with the things we eat and drink. "*Addiction* is a dirty word in this culture, and I don't like using it. Technically, it's addictive, but it's really quite benign. Something so innocuous isn't that bad to be addicted to."

This verdict on caffeine bodes well for Starbucks, but it's not a green light to indulge freely in the chain's concoctions. Black coffee on its own is virtually free of calories, but the milk-and-syrup drinks and megamuffins Starbucks serves can pack a staggering number of them. When the Center for Science in the Public Interest learned that a venti Strawberries and Crème Frappuccino with whipped cream contained an astonishing 770 calories, the organization branded the drink "food porn" and described it as "the nutritional equivalent of a Pizza Hut

Personal Pan Pepperoni Pizza that you sip through a straw." New Zealand's *Consumer* magazine also found that a Starbucks venti White Hot Chocolate with whipped cream had more calories and fat than a Big Mac and a medium Coke combined. (And let's not even go into "breve" espresso drinks, which are made with half-and-half instead of milk.)

The solution here is simple: stick with classics like French press coffee, espresso, and cappuccinos — the drinks in which the complexity and refinement of coffee shines through untainted. As Dr. Illy might ask, would you want to conceal a gorgeous woman under a full-length trench coat?

When I was speaking with Illy in his Trieste office, trying to keep up with the cavalcade of charts and equations, he interrupted the barrage for a moment and took out a small black device from his desk. It was a handheld image viewer, containing hundreds of digital photographs of coffee under powerful magnification. With the manner of a museum curator, he showed me pictures of golden *crema* foam that looked like the paintings of Gustav Klimt; video of tiny oil particles in espresso dancing in unison; images of pale blue caffeine crystals arrayed in constellations of long, slender needles. "Very beautiful, no?" he asked.

And it was.

~8~

Green-Apron Army

Let us now take a moment to reflect on the plight of the Starbucks
barista, that patient indulger of obsessive-compulsive customer requests, that tireless dispenser of forced smiles, that hapless victim of a
never-ending parade of indignities. Any brave soul who dons the green
apron must endure annoyances that would crush the rest of us — or at
least send us into a cup-throwing, syrup-spraying rage. Consider just a
few of the job's daily ordeals:

★ Dealing with precaffeinated morning customers, who often
   communicate solely through grunts and scowls.
★ Deciphering novella-length orders, like a "decaf single grande
   extra vanilla two-percent extra caramel 185-degree with
   whipped cream caramel macchiato."*
★ Watching customers reach into the tip jar to help themselves
   to change when their tab comes to $4.07.

---

*According to a barista who posted on the Starbucks Gossip Web site's message
board, a Seattle-area woman orders this exact drink every day at the height of the
morning rush.

★ Needing to conduct business transactions with people as they loudly discuss their sex lives via cell phone.

★ Wearing company-issue buttons with slogans like, "I only say yes!"

★ Having to figure out how to make a "three-quarter shot" of espresso or "chewy" foam.

★ Staring all day at ads that declare, "My drink is like a mental back rub."

I could go on, pointing out the customers who pay their bills in nickels or the constant aural assault of Starbucks's easy-listening XM Satellite Radio station, but the point is obvious enough already: working at Starbucks is a constant struggle with the forces of exasperation. And sometimes exasperation wins out. Push a barista beyond his breaking point, and you'll end up receiving the universal punishment — he'll secretly give you decaf.

For Starbucks wage earners, the torment doesn't always end in the stores; company baristas must also take part in bone-chilling extracurricular events. In one such case, first revealed by the Seattle alt-weekly the *Stranger*, Starbucks subjected an auditorium full of employees to a truly cruel and unusual display. The occasion was a 2005 awards ceremony for licensed store employees (the ones who work in airport and bookstore outlets), and baristas on the scene reported that the event was plodding along as expected until the emcee announced an unanticipated arrival — "Jefferson Starbucks!" Suddenly, a band of costumed middle managers burst onto the stage. Clad in brightly colored wigs, fishnet shirts, and leather pants, with giant prop instruments in their hands and a huge record hanging behind them, the troupe looked — in one informant's words — "like a living cake decoration." As the crowd recoiled in collective horror, the supergroup launched into a tune that has often been described as "the worst song of all time": the 1985 Jefferson Starship hit "We Built This City." But this wasn't the usual version of the song; their lip-synched adaptation included lyrical gems like, "Knee-deep in the mocha / Making coffee right / So many partners / Workin' late at night." Another verse bears reprinting in its entirety:

> *Someone's always working / DM's and inside sales*
> *We care, and service levels / Are driving better sales!*
> *We just want to build here / IMDS, does it pass?*
> *We call on development / To complete the task!*

Which culminated, naturally, with the soaring refrain, "We built this Starbucks on heart and soul!" The band members were so taken with their composition that they presented each attendee with a CD, which explains how the recording made its way onto the Internet, where it will remain for all eternity as a memento mori — a grim reminder of the hazards of working for Starbucks.

Over the years, two things have kept the baristas' spirits afloat through tribulations like these. First, there was the devotion that Howard Schultz inspired in rank-and-file Starbucks employees, making them feel as though each latte they sold represented a step toward global unity. But second, on a more material level, Starbucks has long offered one of the nation's most progressive benefits plans for retail workers. Every employee who puts in at least twenty hours a week receives access to stock options and a low-cost health-care plan (which covers dental, vision, and even hypnotherapy), plus auxiliary perks like tuition reimbursement and paid adoption fees. The company has maintained this benefits cornucopia despite astronomical increases in the cost of health care, which has led to a peculiar result: according to company spokespeople, Starbucks now pays more each year to insure its employees (over $200 million) than it pays for its raw coffee beans. This benevolence wins the company no end of praise in the business press — Starbucks is a mainstay on *Fortune*'s annual "Best Companies to Work For" list — and it helps make employees want to stick around as well. The average quick-serve eatery's annual employee turnover rate is 200 percent, yet Starbucks sees only 80 percent of its baristas leave the company each year.

Starbucks has enjoyed an employee-friendly public image for decades, but that image is now beginning to lose some of its luster. Every day, the company adds three hundred new hires to its workforce of more than 125,000, and every day, the grumblings about the indignities of modern Starbucks baristadom grow louder. Of course, baristas don't just object to the petty annoyances and the eighties cover songs. According to dissatisfied employees, the company's hourly workers must deal with wildly inconsistent hours, low wages, chronic under-staffing, and glaring workplace health hazards. The job, they say, is becoming more routinized and strictly controlled over time, making them feel like dispensable cogs in an enormous corporate machine. Many baristas are furious about these trends — no one more so than Daniel Gross, a law student at Fordham University who fancies himself the leader of the employee resistance. Since the day he was hired at Starbucks, Gross has eagerly played the role of rabble-rouser, seeking to either change the chain's policies toward wage earners or shatter its compassionate public appearance. "Starbucks, more than any other company, has successfully deceived people into believing that it's a good place to work," he told me. "That couldn't be further from the truth."

To say that Gross is a radical would be selling him short. For the past four years, he has been pressing his colleagues to join up with the Industrial Workers of the World (aka the Wobblies), a storied labor union whose ideas are so far Left that they sometimes break through into an entirely new dimension of political extremism. When Gross was explaining to me his belief that every worker deserves a chance to join a union, for instance, he added "except cops and prison guards," as if it were something about which all reasonable people agree. Why not cops and prison guards? "Because those folks have chosen to betray their class interests," he said. "The security apparatus in this country is aligned with the bosses. Whenever you see capital in distress, they're quick to intervene." Ah, yes. An articulate and surprisingly good-natured twenty-seven-year-old, Gross nevertheless has a rabid temperament when it comes to Starbucks. One press release for his nascent IWW Starbucks Workers Union claimed that "Starbucks, with its poverty wages and rampant repetitive-stress dangers, resembles a sweatshop more than it does a decent place to work." Since no barista has ever been locked into a Starbucks and forced to work a sixteen-hour shift without breaks, bathrooms, or food, the comparison may not *quite* fit.

But despite the penchant for distasteful exaggeration (or maybe because of it), Gross and his prounion colleagues have made the grievances of the Starbucks hourly workforce into a hot issue, generating scores of news stories and sparking endless debate on Internet forums. In their baristas' rights campaign, the radical Starbucks Workers Union has managed to gain the support of an unlikely ally: the National Labor Relations Board. Gross alleges that Starbucks has conducted a "vicious antiunion campaign" — threatening IWW supporters and attempting to bribe workers on the fence — and indeed, the NLRB has backed up some of his assertions. In March 2006, the company settled an NLRB claim that it had violated labor law by illegally obstructing the union — a major defeat, even though Starbucks admitted no fault in the agreement. And the worker grievances keep stacking up; the company recently paid $18 million to settle a California lawsuit filed by more than a thousand current and former store managers, who claimed that it illegally withheld overtime pay. (Similar suits are pending in other states.) The acrimony between the company and some of its employees has grown so thick that Starbucks recently suffered its first strike, in New Zealand, when over two hundred disgruntled workers from nine stores flooded onto Auckland's streets to voice their complaints.

This furor over the rights of Starbucks baristas raises a thorny issue: in a job for which almost everyone is overqualified, what can one fairly expect from an employer? After all, just as Gross and his growing band of comrades are making their union push, their jobs are becoming less and less skilled. Where the wearers of the green apron once manipulated the espresso machine with hard-won expertise, their job is now restricted to smiling, handling money, and pressing buttons on the new superautomatics. A labor union might not even make sense in a workplace where 80 percent of the workers (many of whom don't take the job that seriously) leave every year. So what does it mean to be a Starbucks barista today? Are they craftsmen or cogs? And how generous should we expect the company to be with them?

A Barista Is Born

Six hundred years ago, the birthplace of coffee — what is now Ethiopia — lay under the rule of a tribal kingdom known as Kefa. According to legend, Kefa society had a caste called the Tofaco, who were charged with a unique duty: brewing the king's coffee. This makes the Tofaco history's first baristas. (One likes to imagine them wearing polo shirts and khakis, asking their warlord if he'd like an almond biscotti with his beverage.) Long after the Kefa kingdom faded away, the idea of coffee preparation as a lifelong vocation rose again in Italy — which was somewhat necessary, since mid-twentieth-century espresso machines were about as complicated to operate as the space shuttle. The finicky, tuxedo-clad barista (Italian for "bartender") introduced humanity to coffee as a work of art, worthy of decades of devotion. Even today, the average age of a barista in Italy is thirty-eight, a far cry from the stereotypical college-age espresso jockey at Starbucks.

As coffee fever spread around the globe in the 1990s, so too did the notion that those who prepared the beverage were culinary artistes, capable of summoning drinkable masterpieces with the pull of a lever. In the twenty-first century, however, it's not enough to be just an artist. One must be a mogul, an in-your-face personality, preferably with a reality TV show and a line of branded kitchen products at Target. And actually, the world's first superstar barista may not be too far off. Thanks to the recent invention of barista competitions — flashy yet grueling exhibitions of coffee-making skill — barista celebrities do exist. They even have groupies.

The stars of the barista cosmos emerge at the World Barista Championship, an annual event that draws entrants from countries as far-flung as Estonia, Puerto Rico, and Lebanon. In fact, when I attended the 2005 contest, which was held in a spacious wing of Seattle's old public library building, the Lebanese supporters were some of the wildest, most snappily dressed people there; they all wore matching gray shirts and striped pants, with a black LEBANON embroidered down the leg. This was only the beginning of the competition's surprises. Before I arrived, I expected to walk in and find a few scattered baristas quietly fixing drinks in front of a tiny crowd of socially maladjusted coffee lovers. Instead, I entered a tempest of five hundred flag-waving, cheering barista fanatics, their attention riveted on the coffee theatrics taking place at one of the three gleaming, tanning bed–sized espresso machines. Close-ups of the action played on two huge screens. An announcer offered play-by-play. Whenever a barista poured something into a cup, and especially if he did anything involving a martini shaker, the audience burst into cheers. Picture a cooking show, mix in a dash of *American Idol*, then warp the result into a parallel dimension where crowds roar their approval every time someone steams milk, and you've got a barista competition.

The contest works as follows. Within a fifteen-minute time limit, each competitor must prepare three drinks for a panel of sensory judges: an espresso, a cappuccino, and a "signature beverage," which is a high-concept concoction of the barista's own invention. The Danish contender, for instance, served a drink called ESB (for "Enhanced Sensory Balance"), which he made by combining lavender syrup, sugar drops, and green Madagascar pepper, melting the mixture into a gel with a blowtorch before the judges' eyes, then adding the result to a shot of espresso. Another signature beverage included egg whites, New Zealand honey, mandarin rind, cream, and ground cinnamon, all blended with espresso and served on a platter of dry ice. While the four sensory judges score the barista's offerings for taste and presentation, two technical judges hover around the periphery, making sure the contender's every movement is just right: the barista must position her elbow at a ninety-degree angle when tamping the grounds; she must exhibit proper "milk-frothing technique"; and so forth. The judges also give marks based on the competitor's remarks during the proceedings and, strangely enough, her cleanup skills after it's all over.

To qualify for the WBC, each entrant must first win their home nation's barista championship, which makes the competition a sort of coffee Olympiad. Instead of a gold medal, the world's top barista receives a golden portafilter — not to mention instant D-list celebrity status. The 2003 champion, Paul Bassett, got his own line of milk and a television series in his home country of Australia; other winners have had their faces emblazoned on syrup bottles. Consequently, many barista competitors have developed a serious swagger. Sammy Piccolo, the perennial Canadian champ, likes to dazzle audiences by competing in latte art exhibitions blindfolded, creating perfect rosettas and hearts in the foam without spilling a drop. The 2004 World Barista Champion, Norway's Tim Wendelboe, carries around a custom-made, James Bond–style suitcase with slots inside for pitchers, shot glasses, filters, and every other tool he might need. "A barista wielding a tamper or whisking a clean paintbrush across the grinder burrs could be, I thought, just as sexy as a secret agent deftly slipping a roll of microfilm into a hidden compartment," he explained in *Barista* magazine.

But the raw sex appeal of the star coffee-fixers notwithstanding, it's hard to imagine a less entertaining spectator sport than a barista competition. Fundamentally, you're viewing the very same motions (grinding, tamping, steaming) you watch with disinterest any time you visit a café — except these baristas offer high-concept commentary about how their signature beverage represents "a volcano erupting under a glacier." (And since all but a handful of the competitors speak English as a second language, the malapropisms can pile up; the Japanese entrant mentioned using "whole milk of the sweetness," as well as the "everlasting gentleness of cappuccino.") The audience has no way to tell who is brewing masterfully and who is failing miserably. A shot of espresso could taste like rat poison, and unless one of the judges were to keel over, the crowd wouldn't know.

So when the time finally arrived to crown this year's World Barista Champion, each of the six finalists seemed to have an equal chance of strutting home with the golden portafilter; their presentations were nearly identical, and no one had accidentally set a judge on fire. But barista dominance belonged, as usual, to the Scandinavians. (Out of the seven years the WBC has been held, Danes have won four times and Norwegians twice.) To raucous cheers, the announcer named the blowtorch-wielding Dane, Troels Poulsen, the 2005 champion. (The American contender, Phuong Tran, of Ridgefield, Washington, placed seventh in the first round, with her signature drink "Crimson Sage," barely missing the six-person final.) As the second-place Japanese competitor bowed frantically in all directions, Poulsen — who resembled a nerdier, bearded Heath Ledger — swigged champagne from the bottle and blinked at the flurry of flash-popping cameras that suddenly engulfed him. Fans wanted autographs. Networks wanted interviews. A coffee star was born.

Notably absent from this spectacle unfolding on its own home turf was Starbucks, the company that could stock a small city with all of the baristas on its payroll. But the chain would be about as welcome at the WBC as a grease-smeared fry cook would be in the kitchen of a three-star French chef. To those who seek caffeinated glory, Starbucks represents an opposing, even hostile force. Whereas the barista competitors carry on the tradition of individuals transforming coffee beans into liquid art, Starbucks outfits its workers in identical attire, trains them to follow the same script with customers, and places them in front of automatic machines that produce a standardized product. Expert baristas dread the idea of being a mere "person behind the counter" — a drone carrying out orders — which makes Starbucks the enemy. "Most professional baristas say they wouldn't be caught dead in a Starbucks," said Tran, the U.S. champ. "But I'm not *that* much of a snob." There are even stories of professional baristas who have lost their heads in a corporate coffeehouse and insisted on getting behind the counter to give the staff a free lesson in espresso preparation.

In truth, today's Starbucks employees can't fairly be called "baristas" anymore; they're more like customer service representatives. In keeping with the company's image as equal parts coffee vendor and group therapy center, new hires learn about things like maintaining self-esteem and listening to others in their training; the concentration is on providing what Starbucks calls its "Legendary Service," not on coffee. And when it comes to individuality, the chain would rather its employees refrain from expressing it. Starbucks's *Partner Guide* focuses almost exclusively on telling workers what they *can't* do. Take the company's dress code. Employees cannot wear nail polish, use "unnatural" hair dyes, or have any visible tattoos. Earrings must be small, and they are limited to two per ear. No other piercings are allowed. A clean apron is required at all times, and if the employee damages it, he must pay the company $4.45. Pins, buttons, and other personality-expressing accoutrements are prohibited. But on the other hand, bolo ties are okay.

At times, Starbucks seems to go out of its way to remind employees of how little freedom they have in their jobs. "Absolutely no horseplay is allowed," chides the *Partner Guide*. One employee newsletter bears the ominous name "The Siren's Eye" — as if to warn workers that they're being watched. Starbucks also advises its employees that it can search their belongings at any time, without prior notice and even without them present. You are dispensable, the guide appears to be saying. Just smile, take money, and push the right buttons. Indeed, as one 2002 incident proved, becoming a Starbucks barista doesn't take much expertise. Just after five a.m. on the morning of April 30, two robbers entered a Starbucks in the town of Monroe, Washington, and held up three employees at gunpoint, demanding the money in the store's safe. After the workers turned it over, the pair pronounced the amount unsatisfactory and quickly devised a plan to raise more cash: they would lock the front doors, confine two employees in a back room, and don the green aprons themselves. For the next half hour, the criminals served coffee through the drive-up window, taking money and making change, before finally fleeing the scene. None of the customers noticed anything was amiss.

Things Get Wobbly

Within the climate-controlled confines of Starbucks Center, a fleet of white-collar workers upholds the same brand of gung-ho zeal that marked the company's early days. It's not all high fives and group hugs, of course; the place does have its unique nuisances. For one, widespread access to free espresso can be dangerous. "You're never more than twenty feet away from an espresso machine, and everyone knows how to work 'em," Jerome Conlon, the former "Big Dig" researcher, said. "People were doing like five or six shots a day. And when you're overcaffeinated, your ability to deal with stress plummets. It was like working in a soap opera." With Starbucks headquarters being the marketing-obsessed entity that it is, the halls echo with business jargon — so much so that the longtime marketing employee John Moore recalls secretly playing games of "Starbucks Marketing Meeting Bingo" with colleagues to ease the suffering. As with any Bingo contest, players marked off squares on cards as their contents were called out, but in this incarnation the cues were phrases like "think outside the box," "dimensionalize," "synergy," and the puzzling "Apollo will solve for that." Moore even claims a player once scored a blackout.

But Starbucks has largely succeeded at preserving its evangelical enthusiasm, primarily because of the motivational prowess of Howard Schultz. Employees revere him; he has a talent for making people feel that their work has meaning, that working for Starbucks is less a job than a calling from above. As Moore told me, "I really lived and truly breathed the brand. I wanted people to experience it. I thought we were changing the world." Schultz likes to talk about "leading from the heart," and his unscripted, unabashedly sentimental communication style has inspired devotion in thousands of employees, from ground-floor baristas up to the executive enclave. "I would go out on these road shows with Howard to roll out new initiatives, and it was like he was a rock star with these Starbucks people," said Paul Davis, the former president of Starbucks North America. "There were people who had read his book and almost memorized it. They could quote it chapter and verse." Most every new hire catches the pro-Starbucks fever — at least for a while — after going through the chain's training regimen. "You were brainwashed," one longtime barista said. "I know people who are *still* brainwashed. It's like those Grand Poobah meetings, except instead of elk horns, we had green aprons."*

When we spoke, Schultz told me his foremost priority today is maintaining the trust of his 125,000 "partners," and there's really no reason to doubt his sincerity in this. No one would have faulted Starbucks if it hadn't offered its part-time workers health insurance and stock options, yet it did as a matter of principle.† Schultz has always taken his employees' welfare seriously. In the early nineties, for example, he found out that Jim Kerrigan, a Chicago store manager and Starbucks veteran from the Il Giornale days, had contracted AIDS; his health was degenerating so rapidly that he couldn't work any longer. Schultz was disconsolate at the news. "At the time, there was no system at Starbucks for handling something like this," recalled Dawn Pinaud, the early Starbucks employee. "He didn't have to do it, but Howard turned human resources upside down and got everything taken care of for him." Ker-

---

*A note about sources in this chapter: Starbucks doesn't allow its baristas to speak with members of the press, but former employees were happy to speak about their experiences there.

†Although Schultz's critics point out that this generous health plan is only feasible because Starbucks's workers are predominantly young and healthy. It also helps the bottom line: Schultz himself admits that offering full benefits to lure a barista into sticking around costs only half as much as training a new hire.

rigan died within a year, but Starbucks paid all of his medical costs — a policy it continues today for any terminally ill employee.

After another tragic incident, Schultz reaffirmed the message that he would never keep a haughty managerial distance from his workforce. As three employees were closing a Washington, DC, store one evening in July 1997, a young man named Carl Cooper walked in, took out a handgun, and demanded the keys to the safe, which held more than $10,000 in cash. When the store manager refused to hand them over and attempted to run, Cooper opened fire, killing all three employees and hiding their bodies in a backroom before fleeing empty-handed. Another employee found them the next morning. Schultz was on vacation when the shootings occurred, but once he learned what had happened, he immediately chartered a jet and flew to Washington to be with the victims' families. He later announced that all future profits from the store would go to a nonprofit dedicated to preventing violence.

Given the lengths to which he has gone to show that he cares for his employees' well-being, Schultz seems to view the notion of labor unions existing within Starbucks as a personal insult, as though union advocates are saying he is an oppressive force that must be battled. Schultz makes no secret of his belief that benevolent management can render organized labor obsolete; it takes care of workers' needs, he says, without any us-versus-the-corporation acrimony. Several passages in his book reflect this idea. When Schultz bought Starbucks in 1987, two unions represented employees in the stores and in the roasting plant; in his eyes, this constituted proof that they didn't trust management. Schultz pledged to change that and to make the union appear unnecessary in the process. "I was convinced that under my leadership, employees would come to realize that I would listen to their concerns," he wrote. "If they had faith in me and my motives, they wouldn't need a union." As Schultz tells it, his display of compassion so impressed employees that they voted, unbidden, to kick both unions out of the company.

So when Daniel Gross started stoking the unionization debate anew at Starbucks No. 7356, in midtown Manhattan, Schultz immediately voiced his displeasure — to the entire company. In May 2004, Gross shocked Starbucks's executives by announcing that he had enlisted the support of more than half of the workers at his store and was formally requesting a vote on joining the IWW's new Retail Workers Union. Days later, Schultz recorded a voicemail message that went out to all company employees, in which he called the union developments "very disappointing and disturbing" and encouraged workers to share any complaints about their jobs with management. This announcement violated no labor laws, but as Gross portrays things, it was the beginning of a "relentless" and "vicious" antiunion campaign.

It's hardly surprising that Gross would paint the situation in such an angry red hue; he freely admits that he took a job at Starbucks to both pay the rent and stir up a brawl. A number of "bad jobs," notably a stint as a bookseller at Borders, had soured Gross on corporate America. "After that, I just started to realize I needed to search for a solution for the exploitative practices of multinational corporations," he said. His idea of a "solution" — joining up with the Wobblies — was an unusual one, considering that the IWW had all but disappeared from existence. Founded by a group of anarchists and socialists, the IWW gained prominence in the early 1900s, but its extreme goals always held it back. Then, as now, the Wobblies sought to overthrow the employing class, do away with the wage system, and abolish capitalism itself, which made it a frightening entity to bosses and ordinary citizens alike in its brief heyday.

Despite the IWW's ragtag radicalism, Gross attracted interest from his Starbucks colleagues because of their frustration over a number of widespread grievances. They have three main complaints. "First of all, there's the poverty wage," Gross told me. "Starbucks workers make six, seven, or eight dollars an hour. That's far from being enough to live on. The second part is the lack of guaranteed hours. Chairman Schultz degraded the hours of everyone outside of management, so not a single one of us has any guaranteed hours — we're all part-time. One week, I can get thirty-two hours of work, and the next week it might be twelve. It's incredibly difficult to budget for necessities if you have no idea how much money is coming in." Then there's the worker safety issue. Gross claims routine understaffing at Starbucks stores makes the baristas work at breakneck speed, leading to repetitive strain and carpal tunnel syndrome. "This is not a quaint European coffee shop or a nice mom and pop," he said. "This is a McDonald's-like entity that generates lines out the door every day. You have to work consistently at a very high rate, which takes its toll. You'll be working at the bar, and the manager will come up behind you and say, 'Speed of service! Go quicker! Nonnegotiable!' over and over." To those who try to counter these charges by mentioning the company's generous benefits, Gross points out that employees must put in an average of twenty hours a week over six months to qualify, and that many baristas say their hours mysteriously disappear at the end of this cycle, leaving them just short.*

Gross may appear to be just kicking up dust, but the facts show he has a point. Out of Starbucks's entire workforce (two-thirds of which is part-time), only 42 percent of employees receive health insurance from Starbucks. This rate is even lower than that of the widely condemned benefits scrooge Wal-Mart, which covers 46 percent of its employees. (Starbucks claims the comparison is unfair, since its workers are younger and may be insured by their parents or college.) And employees have cause to grumble about the company's scheduling software, called "Star Labor," which assigns each worker a skill rating and then churns out bizarre, inconsistent schedules designed to maximize productivity. Thus, a barista might find herself working four to eight p.m. one day, then five to nine the next morning. Employees have no recourse in the matter; as the *Partner Guide* warns, "There is no assur-

---

*Though it would be almost impossible to prove that Starbucks systematically cuts workers' hours to keep them from qualifying for health coverage, this is a pervasive complaint from employees.

ance or guarantee that any hourly partner will receive the hours desired, the same schedule each week, or a minimum or maximum number of hours."

Rather than address these employee complaints, Starbucks went for the union's throat instead, attempting to crush the organizers' efforts before they could gain any steam. Store No. 7356 suddenly became the recipient of what Starbucks spokeswoman Audrey Lincoff called "random acts of kindness"; the would-be Wobblies called them bribes. Managers gave baristas at the store free pizza, passes to a local gym, and tickets to Mets games. One shift supervisor told *New York* magazine that Starbucks management had instructed her to "look for red flags, like if employees hang out too much." Several union sympathizers — Alex Diaz, Anthony Polanco, and Sarah Bender — found themselves fired over what they deemed minor offenses. Regional executives showed up at the store and warned baristas that joining the union would entail losing a number of perks.

The company was overreacting. Though the IWW had attracted a modicum of support, it never went through with the union election. (Gross refuses to say how many employees had signed up, citing fears of retribution from the company. He claims at least six New York stores have a majority in favor of the IWW, plus one in Chicago.) Instead, the Starbucks Workers Union focused on wreaking havoc (and drawing media attention) through protests. Its organizers seem to enjoy nothing more than marching into a Starbucks en masse during a busy afternoon and presenting a list of demands to the bewildered manager, or dressing up as "billionaires" and handing a district manager an award for "Outstanding Unfair Labor Practices," or stopping up stores completely by having dozens of union members pay for drinks with pennies. This rabble-rousing gained a measure of vindication when Starbucks decided to settle the 2006 claim by the National Labor Relations Board that it had illegally tampered with the union's organizing efforts. The company admitted no guilt, but it did have to offer Polanco and Bender their jobs back, reverse a number of warnings given to union sympathizers, pay \$2,000 in lost wages, and pledge not to interfere with the IWW's efforts again.

But putting Starbucks's hostility to unions aside for a moment, there's a larger question waiting to be answered here: is this even the kind of job where a union makes sense?

McBaristas

In 2003, the editors at Merriam-Webster triggered a minor controversy when they decided to add one simple word to the eleventh edition of their popular collegiate dictionary. That word was *McJob*. Defined as "a low-paying job that requires little skill and provides little opportunity for advancement," the slang term had been in common use for more than a decade. But by the time the Merriam-Webster editors elected to legitimize the term, the proliferation of McJobs had become a national issue, bemoaned in bestsellers like Eric Schlosser's *Fast Food Nation*; the general contention was that they were dehumanizing, tedious, dead-end posts that did no favors to the tens of millions of people who worked them. Realizing it had to protest or risk admitting its culpability in the trend, McDonald's executives lashed out at Merriam-Webster, calling the inclusion a "slap in the face" to the nation's service workers and claiming that "a more appropriate definition of a 'McJob' might be 'teaches responsibility.'" (In the 1991 novel *Generation X*, Douglas Coupland quipped that a McJob is "frequently considered a satisfying career choice by those who have never held one.") The editors, apparently convinced that the companies that created the McJobs were the ones doing the face slapping, kept the word.

While the Starbucks baristas of times past needed considerable coffee expertise to perform their work, today's company baristas must carry out a series of tasks that are as simple and deskilled as possible; the chain emphasizes speed and efficiency above all else. "It is absolutely mindless labor," one former Starbucks employee told me. "They've made it so that anyone can do it." In other words, the position is now a textbook McJob. As if to underline this point, one source recently over-heard a disgruntled barista at a Manhattan Starbucks complaining to a coworker, "You know, we're just glorified McDonald's employees."

Calling the post a McJob in no way implies that Starbucks baristas ought to resign themselves to feeling ill-treated and disposable or that they don't deserve union protection. But one unavoidable fact makes unions at Starbucks all but impossible: as long as the work remains so unfulfilling, very few people will want to keep the job for long, no mat-ter what Schultz says to keep them inspired. Recent events bear this point out. As it turns out, the Wobblies' New York crusade actually wasn't the first time baristas moved to unionize under Schultz. In 1996, 116 Starbucks employees from ten stores in British Columbia joined the Canadian Auto Workers Union and succeeded in negotiat-ing several concessions from the company, like higher wages and more rights for long-tenured workers. While this union campaign lacked the fireworks of the IWW's raucous struggle, it is far more illuminating about what it means to organize a chain coffeehouse.

Starbucks was similarly hostile toward the Canadian union, refus-ing on several occasions to come to the bargaining table to hammer out a new contract and publicly declaring that "We don't believe we need a third party to act on behalf of our partners." Yet the organizers soon encountered problems of their own. Starbucks's 80 percent turn-over rate is low for the quick-serve industry, but it still means the vast majority of workers leave within a year — and consequently, union leaders began having trouble keeping the stores organized. As Frank Sobczak, the CAW Local 3000 representative in charge of the Star-bucks bargaining unit, told me, employees started staying for ever-shorter tenures. As more employees came to view the job as a tolerable version of fast-food work, Local 3000's future looked increasingly bleak. Finally, in April 2007, high turnover and worker apathy sunk the union for good; the CAW stores voted to decertify. As one frustrated Local 3000 worker told the *Vancouver Sun*, "For a lot of people in the service sector, their job is not a significant part of their life, so they don't really care." This is the dilemma with McJobs: you can't unionize them if no one wants to keep them.

Which complicates the case of IWW versus Starbucks somewhat; in a sense, both sides are wrong. And neither party emerges from the fray looking especially sympathetic. On one hand, Starbucks has been bafflingly tone deaf on the union issue, inundating employees with company propaganda and chafing at the notion that anyone else could take better care of its employees than it does already. After some roasting-plant employees attempted to reunionize in 1999, their representative from the Operating Engineers Local 286 told *Northwest Labor Press*, "In 30 years of working for the union, the worst employer I ever dealt with in their attitude toward the union was Starbucks." (The bid ultimately failed.) On the other hand, IWW members have shown little in the way of tact or discretion in their campaign. Besides comparing Starbucks to a sweatshop, Gross has claimed the company's baristas suffer under the yoke of "wage slavery," adding that "We are very aware of the implications of that term. We wouldn't use it if we didn't think there were inherent similarities to plantation slavery." The union has also complained that Starbucks makes its baristas gain weight — because it offers employees free drinks and leftover pastries.

To be fair, each party has its virtues. The union has won a few substantial concessions from the company, including pay raises, holiday bonuses, and some policy changes to address repetitive strain injuries. And Starbucks still offers far better benefits and wages than any other similar retail company. If you accept the job as just another menial and slightly demeaning corporate gig, not as a career, the perks can't be beat.

But beyond all of the bad taste and heavy-handedness, they're both in error. In trying to unionize a McJob, the IWW organizers are attempting the impossible. But in a way, Starbucks is guilty of making them think they *should* do this. After all, what we believe a Starbucks barista can fairly expect depends on how we view the job: is it dehumanized fast-food labor or a lifelong vocation descended from fussy

Italian craftsmen? Gross claims it's the latter, and ironically, the company has to back him up in this. Starbucks's employees obviously aren't in the same league of artistry and obsession as those who vie for perfection in barista competitions, yet the company depends on its workers to maintain its romantic aura. If customers realized that Starbucks baristas are merely pushing buttons to get lattes — almost like a glorified vending machine — would they still be willing to pay four dollars for their daily cup?

When I asked Gross whether Starbucks baristas could really expect careerlike benefits and wages from a job devolving into fast-food work, I saw that he had obviously given the matter much thought. "It's a good question," he said. "Our expectation is that in a company that is seeing record profits — one that says it values the contribution of its workers above all else — those workers should not have to live in poverty. There's a misconception that retail workers are just looking for arcade money, or beer money. That's not true. Retail workers have families, and they have rent to pay."

"But you're a bright guy," I said. "Why not just quit and move on to something better?"

"Because I think this could be a decent job," he replied.

He's right. Being a barista can be a great and fulfilling job — but probably not at Starbucks. And perhaps Gross will soon find that out for himself. In August 2006, the company fired him, allegedly for making a hostile statement to a district manager at a union rally. After conducting its own investigation into the incident, the NLRB has filed a lengthy complaint against Starbucks on Gross's behalf, claiming that the company intentionally subverted the union on dozens of occasions. Starbucks is contesting the charges. Despite it all, Gross wants his job back.

~9~

The Seattle Colonies

Le Procope, the first café ever built in Paris — and, by extension, the forefather of all the world's coffeehouses — is still open for business today, in the very same spot on the city's Left Bank where it started serving patrons over three centuries ago. In a contest of café bona fides, few can even put up a good fight against Le Procope. The size of a Parisian café's reputation corresponds to the number of famous people who have visited it, and Le Procope's guest list reads almost like a history textbook: Voltaire, Rousseau, Robespierre, and Hugo all frequented it in their time, as did Benjamin Franklin, who reportedly worked out many of the ideas for the Constitution within its scarlet walls. A young, broke Napoleon ran up such a high tab playing chess and drinking coffee here that the proprietor once made him leave his hat behind as collateral. The establishment has changed considerably over the years — it's now a pricey, lobster-serving restaurant — but its collection of antique brewing devices still lines the walls, reminding visitors of Le Procope's prominence in the formidable French café tradition.

If you walk out Le Procope's back entrance into the quiet cobblestone alley, take a right turn, then go about thirty paces, you'll hit the bustling Boulevard Saint-Germain, home of the famed next-door rival cafés, Les Deux Magots and Café de Flore. (Both lay claim to the loyal patronage of Jean-Paul Sartre and Simone de Beauvoir; both award their own literary prizes; and both are outrageously expensive tourist traps.) Directly to your left, you will see the French translation of a Tex-Mex restaurant, which offers American culinary classics like "Indiana Fried Chicken," "U.S. Fries," and a "Burger" made with a chicken breast, a sunny-side-up egg, and a dollop of Thousand Island dressing. Just south of where you're standing, families will be strolling across the palatial grounds of the Luxembourg Gardens, where a hard-up Ernest Hemingway used to catch pigeons for dinner. And right in front of you, sandwiched between a Bureau de Change and a lingerie store called "Women'secret," you will find a new kind of Parisian café, one that has been appearing all over the city as of late: a Starbucks.

To step inside this Starbucks is to enter a twilight-zone version of the traditional Parisian café, where all of its defining attributes are twisted and inverted. Instead of the clanking of dishes and the din of conversation, the sounds of Creedence Clearwater Revival and The Lovin' Spoonful dominate the air. Instead of tiny porcelain cups of strong, high-priced coffee (what the French call an "express"), it serves huge paper cups of strong, high-priced coffee. Instead of immaculately dressed waiters who have perfected dozens of inventive ways to communicate disdain for your order, it employs polo shirt–wearing teenage baristas who field your requests courteously and with a smi — actually, the French are still working on the whole customer service thing. Parisian cafés are relaxed and radiate authenticity, whereas Starbucks is efficient and feels sterile. In short, one is quintessentially French, while the other is quintessentially American.

Which is fine, except this isn't America; it's France, one of the proudest and most culturally distinct nations on the globe, a country so concerned with preserving its national identity that it has enacted laws to stop people from using English words and phrases. Here, one can become a national hero by destroying a symbol of American cultural imperialism, as we learned after the farmer-turned-activist Joseph Bové bulldozed a partially built McDonald's in the southern town of Millau in 1999, winning widespread praise. Obviously, France has no interest in assimilating money-hungry American corporations into its strong, vibrant culture.

At least that's what you'd think. But that's not the reality of things. Paradoxically, France is one of McDonald's' most profitable markets — so much so, in fact, that the company's French operations helped keep its American restaurants afloat when McDonald's entered a slump in the early 2000s. All over Paris, one spies French people shopping for jeans at the Gap, devouring sandwiches at Subway, and nibbling cones of Chunky Monkey at Ben & Jerry's. It's not abnormal to see a UPS truck pull up behind a Ford coupe, right in front of a building with a Century 21 for-sale sign out front. And every day, those infamous white-and-green cups become more pervasive.

Starbucks made its French debut in January 2004, near the peak of U.S.-French tension over the Iraq war. Howard Schultz tried to reduce the friction by portraying his company as a sort of liquid bridge between the two nations, announcing that Starbucks had come "to share our interpretation of coffee." "When we opened in Paris, the editorial coverage leading up to the opening was brutal," he told me. "But people were lined up from day one. CNN covered it live. We've never looked back in Paris." Just as it did in every major American market, Starbucks has blanketed Paris with stores. Within two and a half years, the company opened twenty-three of them in the region, and more are in the works. There's a Starbucks near the national library, just across the street from a new office tower with a ground-floor Accenture office, the whole tableau looking like a patch of Southern California that has been transported as is across the Atlantic. There's one down the street from the stately Palais Garnier opera house, situated among a few sex shops that advertise "Japan system video," "librairie X," and, frighteningly, "zapping." As one might expect, there's a Starbucks inside the

Forum des Halles, a bewildering, labyrinthine underground shopping mall that feels as though it were designed by hyperactive children. (Seriously — you almost need to scatter breadcrumbs along your path in order to find your way out.)

The French appear to be embracing Starbucks, even as they make a show of despising it. (When I asked a manager at the Café de Flore what he thought of the new Starbucks down the street, for example, he replied by issuing a dismissive snort.) Starbucks stores in Paris contain the expected American visitors talking on mobile phones and working on spreadsheets, but they also attract a surprising number of locals, generally young Parisians who seem quite comfortable with American brands. In one Starbucks, I spotted a young Frenchman wearing blue Converse sneakers, baggy Levi's jeans, and a red T-shirt with a giant ABERCROMBIE & FITCH logo splashed across the front. As I watched him wash down his cheesecake with gulps of venti hot chocolate, I had to wonder: can't they revoke your French citizenship for this sort of thing? When I pointed out to Schultz that his best customers in Paris were predominantly young, he responded, "Young people, but *French* people." That is to say, who cares what the older people are doing? The future of France is going to Starbucks.

In coming years, this story of clashing cultures will become a familiar one as Starbucks greatly expands its global presence. Schultz wants to hit a total of forty thousand stores, and with the U.S. market moving closer to saturation, most of that growth will happen abroad. Already, you can find the chain in thirty-seven countries, including unexpected locales like Oman, Qatar, Chile, and Cyprus. Seoul, South Korea, is home to a two-hundred-seat megastore that spans five full stories — the largest Starbucks in the world. Many of these places have no coffee-drinking tradition whatsoever, yet they take to Starbucks as a status symbol or as a place to just hang out. Often, it's a simple matter of convenience. For instance, Starbucks has obvious appeal to the French: in a conventional Parisian café, one cannot get coffee (a) to go, (b) in under twenty minutes, or (c) for less than six dollars. (I realize how perverse it is to think of Starbucks coffee as a bargain, but such is the magic of Paris.) And according to Schultz, Starbucks will soon come full circle, colonizing the country where he first received his vision for the company a quarter-century ago: Italy.*

What are we to think of this aggressive expansion of the Starbucks empire? Should we chafe at the very idea of the company selling its Americanized espresso drinks to the same gastronomically obsessed Italians who created the beverage in the first place? Indeed, many of us feel an instinctive sense of revulsion at the thought of Starbucks in a place like Paris; the fear is that the company will displace the city's centuries-old sidewalk cafés and its leisurely croissant-and-coffee breakfasts — the very cultural traditions that make Paris charming and unique. This collective worry is at the heart of what the British sociologist Jeremy Tunstall has called the "cultural imperialism thesis," which claims that "authentic, traditional, and local culture in many parts of the world is being battered out of existence by the indiscriminate dumping of large quantities of slick commercial and media products, mainly from the United States."

When Tunstall first wrote those words, back in 1977, cultural imperialism posed a much smaller threat to the world than it does today. Thirty years ago, Hollywood movies and products like Coke were America's major anxiety-causing exports. But today, there are Wal-Mart stores in Argentina, McDonald's restaurants in Pakistan, Gap outlets in Japan — all of them changing the local culture in subtle ways. Just as McDonald's has transformed eating habits around the world by offering quick, cheap, and unhealthy meals, Starbucks tends to make permanent cultural alterations as well. "I was just in Vienna, and there were people all over carrying Starbucks cups on the street," said Michael Coles, the Caribou Coffee CEO. "Before Starbucks arrived, people didn't carry around food or drinks in public — it just

---

*For years, Schultz has had an ideal location picked out for his first Italian store — which he refuses to reveal — but he has yet to announce anything concrete about his company's entrance into the country.

wasn't done. But Starbucks changed that." If you fly all the way to, say, Malaysia, then immediately spot a Starbucks, the sight makes you grimace a bit. It's as if you never left home at all, as if all the unique traditions of the world are slowly blending into one homogenous, Americanized monoculture — what the political scientist Benjamin Barber calls "one big New Jersey." Surely no one wants *that*.

Yet at the same time, it's not for us to decide what other cultures can and cannot accept. International customers are saying they want Starbucks — though not always, as we'll see — and it's impossible to explain to a Frappuccino-craving Kuwaiti why he shouldn't want this without sounding hopelessly meddlesome and elitist. How can something like Starbucks be okay for us but not for them? Wouldn't we feel a bit odd if someone claimed Americans were debased as a people by the insidious spread of Hyundai cars, Nokia phones, and Sony televisions? What's more, the coffee in many of the markets Starbucks enters is unspeakably vile. (Even in Paris: "France has some of the worst godawful coffee anywhere," the early Starbucks employee Dawn Pinaud, among others, opined. "They should stick to other food.") On a certain level, denying these people better coffee just seems cruel.

It's a complicated question, and one that grows increasingly important as more American corporations seek profits on foreign shores: when a company refuses to place restrictions on its global growth, should we draw a line somewhere for what is morally acceptable? Certainly, concerns about cultural imperialism will never stop Starbucks from placing stores wherever there's money to be made. At the 2006 shareholders meeting, Schultz placated one particularly rabid investor, who thought Starbucks ought to expand faster than it already is, by telling him, "There are going to be very few countries in the course of time that we are not going to be in. Be patient." It's safe to say that this notion provides comfort to far fewer people than Schultz thinks. Yet everyone who goes to Starbucks is implicitly sponsoring his globe-spanning vision; we cluck our tongues at a new Starbucks in Paris, yet we fund its construction with our mochas and cappuccinos.

As a recent report from the market research firm Mintel wryly put it, Starbucks has just one "main competitor" these days: "the ire sometimes caused by its global presence, which sends some potential customers out of their way to support local shops." But will this ire ever catch up with Starbucks?

Resistance Is Futile

Starbucks's foray into global coffee domination began in the late 1990s, with its swift occupation of two of the world's preeminent tea-drinking countries. The two cases illustrate very different sides of the debate over the company's corporate colonialism.

In 1996, Starbucks unveiled its first Japanese outlet, in Tokyo's posh Ginza district, with a performance that would have made any Broadway producer proud. At an opening ceremony, Shinto priests blessed the new store and prayed for harmony between Starbucks and the forces of nature, while Schultz, Howard Behar, and other executives sipped sake and washed their hands in spring water. When Schultz and Behar saw a line of one hundred excited Japanese coffee fanatics waiting for their first taste of Starbucks, the two cried together. From that moment on, Starbucks enjoyed massive success in Japan; astoundingly, the company's Japanese stores (of which there are now more than six hundred) became twice as profitable as its already-lucrative American stores. The lines at the cafés were endless, and thus customers greeted each new Starbucks with elation. (A bit of serendipity may have helped the company's chances as well: according to Japanese fable, anyone who eats the flesh of a mermaid gains eternal life.) Flush with victory, Schultz told the *Financial Times* four years later that his company had "transformed the culture" in Japan.

To be sure, Japanese consumers have long adored American brands, but the company's success there was far from preordained. In fact, when Starbucks was still mulling its Japanese debut, a consulting firm advised it not to go in at all. Although the Japanese were already drinking impressive quantities of coffee by the midnineties — both from the cramped *kissaten* shops that had long dotted the urban landscape and from the pervasive canned-coffee vending machines — the consultants believed Starbucks would clash with social norms. The chain's no-smoking rule would alienate young people, they thought, and the etiquette-obsessed Japanese would never be seen drinking coffee in public. Despite this, Starbucks made just a few slight changes to its formula, like concocting a green tea Frappuccino and offering smaller drinks and pastries to conform with Japanese preferences. Then it began the deluge of stores. And here's the crucial part: the Japanese bent to accommodate Starbucks, not the other way around. The company still opens more than one hundred stores a year there.

Yet if the Japanese welcomed Starbucks with enthusiasm, the British greeted it with something like paranoid shock. In the spring of 1998, over sixty Starbucks stores appeared in the United Kingdom at once, essentially without warning. This was the company's idea of "breaking through the noise": it acquired a sixty-five-store chain called Seattle Coffee Company and immediately converted its locations into Starbucks stores. In a way, the takeover was fitting. SCC was founded in 1995 by Scott and Ally Svenson, an expatriate Seattleite couple who had first opened a café mostly to relieve their longing for the espresso concoctions of their hometown. "You wouldn't believe all of the things you had to go through to get any kind of decent coffee in London," Scott Svenson told me.* "At the time, about ninety-six percent of all coffee consumed in the UK was instant coffee. It was so bad that my wife actually called Howard Behar and said, 'We live here, the coffee is terrible, and you should do something about it.' He said, 'Listen, we get calls like this all the time. We'll get there eventually.'" But the Svensons couldn't wait any longer; they soon started their own coffee bar,

---

*A demonstration of Svenson's point: for a time, members of an outfit calling itself the "Coffee Police" would show up at British cafés in full police dress and reprimand the owners for their awful coffee.

intending to run it as a hobby. Sales rocketed upward, however, and the Svensons kept expanding their business until Starbucks realized it had to buy them out or risk losing the British market.

The sudden appearance of these sixty-five Starbucks stores alarmed many Brits, and the sentiment only intensified as the company inundated the country with outlets. London — which, as of 1998, had no coffee culture to speak of — zipped past the two-hundred-Starbucks mark in just seven years, and it now has more stores than New York City. This invasion didn't do wonders for the company's public relations or for sales. Between 1998 and 2002, Starbucks lost £50 million (about $90 million) in the UK, because of a mixture of consumer resistance and naïveté about the London real estate market. "I don't want to give too many of my own impressions on Starbucks's public image in the UK, because I've obviously got some conflicts," said Scott Svenson, who briefly took an executive position with Starbucks after the sale. "They probably rushed too quickly in establishing a presence. They weren't localized enough. When you grow like that, I think you lose . . ." — he hesitated — "things."

Edward Bramah epitomizes the typical old-fashioned Londoner who has become angry over the decline of these "things" in his city. A tall, bushy-eyebrowed veteran of the tea and coffee industries, Bramah is the founder, head tour guide, author-in-residence, receptionist, and occasional disgruntled barista at the Bramah Muscum of Tea and Coffee, in south London. He's also a bit of an eccentric. When I first walked into the museum and said hello, he shot me a cockeyed smile and, with the kind of mischievous glint in his eye that one sees in small children wandering into traffic, asked me, "Are you happy?" I gave an uncomfortable chuckle and asked why I should be happy. "Because *everyone should be happy*," he said. And then he turned around and walked off — something he would go on to do a dozen more times over the course of our conversation.

But behavioral quirks aside, Bramah is a passionate authority on the traditional coffee-drinking methods of antiquity. "Coffee is a superb drink," he told me. "I cannot begin to tell you how one can wax lyrical about the delectable delights of delicious coffee." His ramshackle museum bursts with caffeinated arcana: Portuguese gas-heated brass urns, hydrostatic percolators, bulbous glass vacuum pots, silver-plated Victorian-era siphoning systems, egg-shaped reversible drip pots, brewing contraptions designed to look like locomotives. There was even a small diorama that depicted Gabriel de Clieu watering his prized coffee plant aboard *Le Dromedaire*. When Bramah's eye falls on his exhibits of early espresso machines, though, his demeanor sours. "The coffee served in these new cafés isn't *coffee*," he spat. "All that bloody *milk*. These people know damn well they're selling milk." For Bramah, the recent influx of espresso bars in his country represents a perversion of the civilized tea- and coffee-drinking rituals of the past — a point he underscored by pulling me a foul shot of espresso and prodding me to admit that, yes, it tasted terrible. "I'm going to cut this espresso machine off as soon as I can," he said, sneering in its direction. "It really just produces something that needs milk and sugar."

Of course, Bramah may just be resistant to change — there's a fine line between preserving cultural traditions and clinging to a romanticized past. But he has good reason to worry that espresso will overrun the customs of old. Despite its early image as ruthless corporate conquistador, Starbucks has sparked a massive shift in British tastes. Over the last five years, UK tea sales have plunged while coffee sales have soared, which has brought about a stunning result: Britons now spend more on coffee each year (£738 million) than they spend on tea (£623 million). Particularly in London, coffeehouse saturation has reached epidemic levels; one can't walk ten blocks on a commercial street without passing two or three Starbucks stores, plus a handful of its main competitors, Caffè Nero, Costa Coffee, and Coffee Republic. The tea industry has attempted to regain lost ground with espresso machine–esque contraptions like Lipton's "T-Bird," but to little effect. With the help of a major charm campaign — and more than five hundred UK stores — Starbucks is overcoming local resistance and establishing a firm grip on the wallets of Britain's proliferating coffee drinkers.

The moral of these two stories is this: in Japan and Great Britain, the initial receptions were different, but the ultimate result was the same. Starbucks typically comes in, ignoring any local outcry, and people eventually disregard their reservations and start patronizing the chain. Sometimes the company fundamentally alters its operations for a new market — as it did in Saudi Arabia, where all stores are segregated into "men-only" and "family" sections, each with their own sales counters, in accordance with the country's rigid separation of the sexes in public. (After a warning from the Saudi religious police, the Muttawa, Starbucks also removed the scandalous siren from its logo and replaced her with a simple crown; the Muttawa later had a change of heart, and the company reinstated the original logo.) But mostly, the changes are minor, like offering more savory foods in Asian markets, or croissants — if you could call them that without defaming the entire world of pastries — in France.

The company can get away with this for a reason that might upset opponents of globalization: international customers crave the full American Starbucks treatment, caramel syrup and all. "The local consumer in all these countries wants the authentic Starbucks Experience," Schultz told me. "They don't want it watered down for Mexico or watered down for China. They want Starbucks." Plus, international customers often take a liking to Starbucks for the very same reasons Americans did. In Mexico City, Starbucks stores attract the young, the beautiful, and the affluent. Consumers in Jakarta proclaim their pride in being able to drink the same cup of coffee as the country's wealthiest people, even though a Frappuccino costs more there than the average Indonesian factory worker earns in a day. Kuwaitis like the dating scene, especially since the sexes almost never get to intermingle in public otherwise. The only major difference is that 85 percent of international customers stay and drink their cappuccinos and espressos inside the store, while the majority of Americans rush out with their to-go orders.

"It's incredible," said Pinaud. "The coffee concept works anywhere." It has even taken off in war-torn Afghanistan, where a knock-off "Starbucks" in Kandahar is a community hub and a financial success, selling five hundred cups of coffee a day. "You have no idea how happy I feel here," Saifullah Habibi, one of the café's regulars, told the BBC. "By late evening, I find myself dreading the moment it will close for the night." And fittingly, there's another faux Starbucks in the northeast of that country — at the U.S. Air Force Base in Bagram, where a California National Guardsman set one up inside a metal shipping container to help boost troop morale. After all, it's tough to find a good latte in the high desert of Afghanistan.

Forbidden Desire

For five hundred years, Beijing's Forbidden City served as the political and cultural heart of imperial China. The 9,999-room palace is so vital to the country's sense of identity that an illustration of its main entrance — called Tiananmen, or "Gate of Heavenly Peace" — still adorns the official seal of the People's Republic of China. Constructed in the early fifteenth century, the walled and fortified complex housed emperors from China's final two dynasties, the Ming and Qing, up until the collapse of imperial power in 1912. Now, almost a century later, it became the home of a different empire.

In the autumn of 2000, Starbucks planted a tiny, six-seat store on the grounds of the Forbidden City, in the corner of a gold-roofed building known as Jiuqinfang — ironically, "place of many sleepers." Neither Starbucks nor the palace's administrators expected what followed: a torrential outpouring of indignation. "Not the Forbidden City!" blared the *China Consumer Journal*, which went on to proclaim, "This is no different from slapping China's 1.2 billion people and 5,000-year traditional culture in the face." In one Internet poll, 70 percent of respondents claimed they opposed the new coffeehouse that had slipped into their country's cultural hub. (Not everyone was displeased, however. "We like them here," a neighboring shopkeeper told the *Washington Post*. "It means more foreigners come. And foreigners have lots of money.") Local outcry had already doomed a KFC in the vicinity and a McDonald's in nearby Tiananmen Square, so the store's future looked grim. Palace officials, rushing to stem the public relations nightmare, ordered the company to take down two signs and stated that the only appropriate course of action would be to kick the Starbucks out of the Forbidden City.

Oddly enough, the country where Starbucks has endured some of its worst criticism as an insensitive cultural imperialist is now the company's primary target for growth. Though the rapidly industrializing nation is still predominantly poor, China's middle class and upper class number some 250 million people; Schultz believes they need lattes, even if the country has no native coffee tradition and barely uses milk at all. Starbucks hopes to ensnare China's "little emperors" — the millions who were raised as only children because of the country's one-child policy and are thus used to being spoiled. These young people are far more sympathetic with American-style individuality than their parents, and the company expects this will lead them to embrace its customizable drinks. So far, this theory has proved correct: bourgeois Chinese consumers have welcomed Starbucks, flaunting their branded white cups in the same conspicuous manner as their counterparts the world over. Imitators have sprouted up as well, such as USABucks and Shanghai Xingbake (*xing* meaning "star," and *bake* being as phonetically close to "bucks" as one can get in Mandarin).* Starbucks now operates 250 Chinese outlets, and Schultz claims the country will one day be second only to the United States in number of stores.

---

*Other international Starbucks doppelgängers include Starlight Coffee in Santiago, Chile; Starblack in Ho Chi Minh City; Star Café in Prague; and Starbutts, a gentlemen's bar in Seoul.

Schultz's strategy for minimizing future surges of anti-Starbucks sentiment is quite straightforward: he wants Chinese people to think of Starbucks as a Chinese company. "For us to succeed in China, we have to be Chinese, not American," he said. "We're in a very fortunate position. Unlike almost any Western retailer I can think of, we've established something that by and large no longer has attachment to something Western or American. It is as relevant in all of these countries as it is in the U.S. And we're not wrapping ourselves in the American flag." To achieve this goal of blending in to new cultures, Starbucks uses some of the same tactics it employs in American neighborhoods, like donating to a local charity. "We tailored our entry into China to mirror the benevolence of the company in the U.S.," Schultz told me. "Before we made a dollar of profit there, we established a five-million-dollar education fund for young girls in rural China who would never have access to an education. And we didn't do that to create a marketing event or a press release."

Which is precisely why Starbucks recruited the *Crouching Tiger, Hidden Dragon* actress Zhang Ziyi, one of Asia's biggest celebrities, to talk about the company's generosity at a press conference announcing the gift — to avoid any kind of media coverage. As we saw in Europe and Japan, there's really not much tailoring going on for each new country, just the same marketing finesse. Schultz implicitly admits as much. For every time he talks about being "locally sensitive" or coming into a new country "hat in hand," he also points out with apparent relish how all the overseas Starbucks stores are "mirror images" of those in the United States. "I was in China when we opened in Shanghai," he told London's *Guardian* in 2000, "and you would have thought we were in New York."

In regions of the world where the American flag elicits scowls and creatively worded profanities instead of admiration, this resemblance has posed a significant problem. Starbucks routinely ranks high on lists of American companies that foreign consumers want to avoid, along with old stalwarts like McDonald's and Marlboro; one 2004 survey of people in the industrialized G8 nations revealed that consumers characterize Schultz's company as "arrogant, intrusive, and self-centered." Many countries that particularly opposed the post-9/11 foreign policies of the Bush administration have also opposed the Starbucks invasion. Germany, for one, has frustrated the chain since its debut there in 2002. Starbucks planned to have two hundred German stores by 2006, yet it had just sixty at the end of that year. (A complicating factor: in the early 1970s, a Left Wing guerilla named Holger Meins terrorized Germany with bombings, eventually dying in prison after a long hunger strike; his code name was "Starbuck.")

As one might expect, Starbucks has suffered most from anti-American sentiment in the Middle East, but the animosity there was partially Schultz's own doing. In 2002, Schultz (who is Jewish) delivered a series of speeches at various pro-Israel events, issuing dire warnings about what he perceived as growing anti-Semitism. "There are people in this world who want to eliminate [us] from the face of this earth," he proclaimed at the Temple De Hirsch in Seattle. "Ladies and gentlemen, the 1930s are back, and we can't ignore it any longer." Schultz's comments also implied that the Palestinians had done little to curb terrorism, and thus the whole ensemble — duly publicized via Internet and the media — infuriated several Arab groups. Boycotts ensued across the Muslim world. Schultz offered a halfhearted apology over his comments being "misinterpreted as anti-Palestinian," yet the furor refused to die. Rumors emerged that Schultz financially supported the Israeli army. Because of the persistent uproar over his remarks, Starbucks decided in 2003 to close its six stores in Israel out of fear that they would become terrorist targets. Schultz, who had traveled frequently to the country, took the retreat hard and vowed to return. Israel remains the only country in which Starbucks has failed.

But do these anti-Starbucks outbursts abroad actually mean anything? Not necessarily. Europeans might declare their intent to avoid U.S. companies like McDonald's and Starbucks, but as the *Slate* writer Daniel Gross (no relation to the unionizer) has pointed out, *so do*

Americans — and then they go buy Big Macs and Frappuccinos anyway. It's a perplexing fact of modern consumerist life: our claims of loathing for companies and products often don't line up with our actual behavior. Lynn Kahle, a marketing professor at the University of Oregon and past president of the Society for Consumer Psychology, offers a fitting illustration of this idea. "If you just read the paper here in Eugene, you'd think everybody in the world hates Wal-Mart," he told me. "The letters to the editor are probably fifty to one against it. But drive by it, and the parking lot is always full of cars." It's the same with television; we bemoan its awfulness and its destructive effect on our minds more loudly each year, yet viewership continues to ascend nonetheless. And so it goes with Starbucks. The average consumer likely shudders at the thought of Starbucks peddling vanilla lattes amid the ancient splendor of the Forbidden City, but if she's stuck in an airport, worn-out, and needing to kill time, is she *really* going to forgo that comforting double cappuccino just to make a point?

The Forbidden City Starbucks managed to survive for seven years before a star Chinese news anchor roused enough popular indignation to force its closure, in July 2007. Yet at the rate the company expands, even the most vigilant cultural guardians could never keep up; while they're busy rallying public support, Starbucks just opens fifty more outlets. So it is not surprising that when the company built a new store in 2005 at a Great Wall of China site in Badaling — reportedly the ten thousandth Starbucks in the world — Chinese consumers barely made a peep. And why would they? Zhang Ziyi, the actress, was at the grand opening.

To Infinity and Beyond

Jim Donald, the current Starbucks CEO, likes to sum up his company's current growth philosophy in six words: "Lines mean we need more stores." That is, if a Starbucks becomes too popular and people are forced to suffer the anguish of standing in line for more than three minutes, this means Starbucks is "not convenient enough," so it must open another outlet as nearby as possible, ideally on the same block. This is what makes Starbucks remarkable and unique: it's the only company on the planet that can pull this off. Humankind has never seen a business capable of saturating a city — or a country, or the world — with so many stores.

But what happens when we take this mindset to its logical extreme, as Starbucks, left unfettered, surely will? Schultz says he plans to push his company to forty thousand stores (half of them in the United States, half of them abroad), yet he's not going to pull the emergency brake once the scoreboard at company headquarters hits that magic number. At Starbucks, there are no brakes; slowing down has never been part of the business plan. The chain will ride this wave as far as it can. And consider this: if McDonald's was able to pass the thirty-thousand-outlet mark with a few dozen restaurants in any given city, what might the limit be for a company that can plant them across the street from each other? Sixty thousand? Even more? "I think Starbucks's prediction about how many stores they can have is actually very conservative," said Coles, the Caribou Coffee CEO. "Who knows how many we'll accept? I mean, who'd have ever thought that Starbucks could open two hundred coffeehouses in *London?*"

America is a country that prizes entrepreneurialism, yet most of us find the idea of Starbucks popping up anywhere it can make a buck at least slightly distasteful. "My son was in China a few years back and saw that Starbucks in the Forbidden City," said Jean Mach, the early Starbucks employee. "I mean, why even bother to send your child to China? You can just take him to a Starbucks here." Some, like the anti-globalization advocate Bill Talen — who conducts choreographed in-store "retail interventions" as the "Reverend Billy" — have made the company a prime target in their crusade against the "Shopocalypse." (These performances tend toward the esoteric. For instance, in one Starbucks-specific set piece, a man masquerading as a stockbroker and a woman playing a flower child enter a store separately and begin arguing loudly about what the Starbucks logo means to them; the act culminates with the woman pretending to be birthed as a way of reclaiming the mermaid symbol, yelling "What am I? I am becoming! I am the mermaid frozen in the logo! And I want my nipples back!" She then pretends to swim away.) The overarching idea is that Starbucks has gone too far. As J'Amy Owens, a Seattle consultant who has worked with Starbucks, put it, "The brand has grown beyond what is appropriate, past whatever it should have been. It's like disco." If there is indeed an ethical boundary on how much a chain should grow, globalization opponents say, Starbucks stepped over it long ago — it's now just another contributor to the strip-malling of the planet.

On the rare occasion when an interviewer levels the charge that Starbucks causes cultural homogeneity, Schultz adopts a harmless, somewhat goofy smile and laughs it off. Take this exchange with the 60 *Minutes* reporter Scott Pelley, broadcast in 2006:

Pelley: *There is a criticism, and you've heard it —*
Schultz: *Yeah.*
Pelley: *— that Starbucks is homogenizing the world* [Schultz chuckles], *that you're taking the culture out of places, in China, in Japan, and Americanizing them.*
Schultz: *I've heard that.*
Pelley: *And it irritates you.*
Schultz: *It's not that it irritates me. It's just, you know, off base.*
Pelley: *And when people say you're an evil empire bent on world domination, you say?*
Schultz: *I hate that. I hate that. But I realize you're always going to have critics.*

End of debate. Proceed to footage of Schultz having a sentimental moment in the halls of the Brooklyn housing project where he grew up. Obviously, Schultz wouldn't gain much from addressing the question at length, but if he were so inclined, he might ask us this: Is Starbucks homogenizing the world, or is an already-homogenized world just clamoring for our product? After all, the company isn't forcing anyone to visit its stores; if it weren't giving consumers something they wanted, no one would stop in. So are critics simply scapegoating Starbucks for the habits and desires of its customers?

Of course, Starbucks didn't blaze this path of culinary cultural conformity. That honor belongs to McDonald's, and, perhaps fittingly, the two companies come to resemble each other a little more every day. Recognizing that its only real competition is other quick-serve megachains, Starbucks has not only introduced hot breakfast sandwiches (à la the Egg McMuffin); it has committed itself to doing what was once unthinkable: building a fleet of drive-through stores. Donald — who came to Starbucks from Wal-Mart, where he was the last executive Sam Walton ever hired — has said that half of Starbucks's future U.S. stores will be drive-throughs, another "convenience-based" policy that threatens to undermine the very tenets that first sparked the company's success. As Schultz well knows, waiting in a cramped driver's seat behind eight other exhaust-spewing cars is no pleasant "third place" experience. "When we first started opening drive-throughs, Howard was going out of his mind," said Engle Saez, the former Starbucks marketing executive. "For him, a drive-through was too much like fast food. How can you give someone a full coffee experience in their car?" You can't. But the extra cash is too good to pass up — the drive-through stores bring in $300,000 more per year than their automotive-inaccessible counterparts — so Donald and Schultz just try to dismiss the unsavory comparisons. "We are not the McDonald's of anything," Donald told the Associated Press in 2005.

These days, Starbucks seems almost constitutionally incapable of passing up opportunities to increase revenue. Whereas Schultz once bristled at the very suggestion of adding syrup or nonfat milk to the chain's handmade drinks, his company will soon unveil a new branded vending machine, which the development executive Gerry Lopez has cutely called "the smallest Starbucks store you ever saw." Again, these hardly provide a gourmet experience; the machines just heat up and dispense nine-ounce steel cans that contain a chemically stabilized latte, mocha, coffee, or hot chocolate. And while newspaper articles used to trumpet the quality of the company's coffee, readers today only see stories about its various entertainment ventures. Starbucks stores now sell a selection of books and CDs, and Schultz has even converted his cafés into billboards for a movie, *Akeelah and the Bee.* (With his company's marketing power behind it, Schultz expected *Akeelah* to be a hit, but the film fizzled at the box office; still, the company is considering making feature films of its own.) Meanwhile, in its March 2007 issue, *Consumer Reports* declared Starbucks's drip coffee "burnt and bitter enough to make your eyes water instead of open" — and in a twist that must have given company executives chills, the magazine claimed that *McDonald's* brewed a far superior cup.

Even an amateur business analyst would call this development an unambiguous sign that Starbucks should slow down and refocus on the things it excelled at for so long: making good coffee and providing a haven for its customers. Generally, Schultz ignores this sort of outside guidance; in the past, any suggestion that Starbucks's course needed correcting would have only increased Schultz's conviction that he was headed in the right direction. This inclination has steered him well before. Few would have predicted in 1987 that a housewares salesman from Brooklyn could hook America on four-dollar Italian espresso drinks and build a handful of oddball coffeehouses into a global empire, yet he did.

But while Schultz has publicly stated nothing but certainty about his company's current direction, an internal memo leaked to Jim Romenesko's Starbucks Gossip Web site in February 2007 tells a different story. In the message, titled "The Commoditization of the Starbucks Experience" and addressed to a dozen high-ranking company executives, Schultz bluntly assesses his chain's fading cachet. "Over the past ten years," he writes, "in order to achieve the growth, development, and scale necessary to go from less than 1,000 stores to 13,000 stores and beyond, we have had to make a series of decisions that, in retrospect, have lead [sic] to the watering down of the Starbucks experience." Among his many criticisms, Schultz laments the loss of "romance and theater" with the new superautomatic espresso machines and complains that Starbucks stores "no longer have the soul of the past," admitting that they seem "sterile" and "cookie cutter."

The antidote for these ailments, Schultz says in the memo, is a return to "the true Starbucks experience" — something he still believes in with the same passion of twenty years ago. "What people fail to understand is that we do not sell just a cup of coffee," he told me in his Seattle office, eyes smiling. "As technology has evolved, and it has become both a tool and a burden on our individual and collective lives, I believe that we as people have lost a level of closeness and sensitivity around human connection and human contact. And we all long for that. I'm not trying to say in any way that we are the cure for all that ails humanity, but every single day, Starbucks brings people together."

And if this vision ever falters, Schultz can take solace in the prognostications of his onetime real estate czar, Arthur Rubinfeld. "Look," Rubinfeld said. "Starbucks does have two of the four legal vices left in this country, if there's liquor, sugar, tobacco, and caffeine." So if all else fails — if droves of customers decide their local café makes better coffee, or if they finally get tired of seeing the chain's outlets everywhere they look — Starbucks can always hit all four by introducing the Tequila Nicotine Chip Frappuccino.

With or without Starbucks, the coffeehouse phenomenon will continue to plow forward, at least until something better comes along to replace it. But the coffeehouse is a hard act to top. "This is more than just a caffeine thing," said Tom O'Keefe, the Tully's chief. "If it was a caffeine thing, you could just pull into 7-Eleven and get a jolt. You could drink robusta, with three times the caffeine. But you don't." No other place but the coffeehouse provides a safe urban harbor where one can spend hours reading, refueling, conversing, studying, or doing nothing whatsoever, all for the price of a mug of coffee. No other place allows one to connect with the community without having to, you know, actually *interact* with anyone. And pending the legalization of cocaine, no other place is going to supply the energy lift we need in order to confront the day. Regardless of what our personal opinions about the company might be, Starbucks saw that these things were lacking in people's lives, and its rise paved the way for an entire industry dedicated, in a sense, to making daily life better. "Starbucks, I think, was the first to recognize that coffee really is the fuel of human life," said Robert Thompson, the popular-culture professor at Syracuse University. "If the world runs on a thick, dark substance called petroleum, we run on a dark liquid called coffee.

"I've actually never developed a taste for it," he added. "Sure, I've had a couple of sips of it, but I didn't like either of them. The interesting thing is, as a pop-culture person, you really have to be up on coffee and Starbucks. Coffee is really important to people, I've found."

EPILOGUE

The Last Drop

grew up in a small Oregon town called Ashland, which sits a few miles north of the California border, on a grassy valley floor in the Siskiyou Mountains. It's the kind of open-minded, outdoorsy community where people don fleece vests whenever possible, and where clerks at the co-op market talk earnestly about the healing power of crystals as they scan your groceries. Subaru station wagons roam the city streets in packs, their bumpers broadcasting an assortment of faded liberal slogans dating back to the Reagan administration. To the extent that Ashland is known at all outside Oregon, it is as a summer destination for theater-loving tourists; the town is home to the popular Oregon Shakespeare Festival, which puts on about a dozen different plays a year. Recently, Ashland has become a trendy locale for wealthy Californians, who have built scores of McMansions out in the foothills. Still, it's a nice place.

For years, the local government protected Ashland's appeal by keeping chain stores out of the town's core, forcing them to open on the outskirts. This nonconformist ethic was part of the city's collective identity. When the McDonald's outlet down by the highway on-ramp went out of business, the entire town seemed to rejoice, as though this was proof of the community's inherent goodness.

In 1996, a familiar controversy arrived: Starbucks announced plans to put a store in the heart of downtown Ashland, a quaint area that aspired, however pathetically, to radiate a Victorian England vibe. The whole community appeared to oppose the new store. Locals led protests. Students at the high school handed out "Friends don't let friends go to Starbucks" bumper stickers. Didn't we have enough coffeehouses already, they asked, what with Evo's, the Rogue Valley Roasting Company, the Beanery, the Key of C, and so on? These were excellent hangouts — places where we would all get together, indulge in a stimulant we could buy legally, and impress each other with our knowledge of Michel Foucault and Jacques Derrida. (Their existence and nomenclature were basically the extent of our teenage expertise, however.) My girlfriend at the time, whose pronouncements I heeded with great zeal, swore she would never set foot in the new Starbucks.

Yet a few months after the store opened, she and I were meeting there for coffee all the time. (Need I mention that it was her decision?) This was the magic of Starbucks at work. The formula Schultz and company established back in Seattle turned the locals from hostile Starbucks bashers to furtive users to full-blown addicts in what seemed like a matter of months. Everyone, even those who held out, had to admit that the company knew what it was doing. When we went back to a coffeehouse like the Beanery, we'd suddenly find ourselves asking, "Was this place always so tacky, or did they cover it in linoleum and add fluorescent lights since the last time we were here?"

Today, there are three Starbucks in Ashland, a town of twenty thousand people. One of them is in a building that once housed Leo's Campus Drive-In, a burger joint I used to frequent as a kid — it had both the best fries in town and an awesome poster showing a fleet of Ferraris parked near an ocean cliff. The new Starbucks has no awesome Ferrari posters. After I graduated from college, I waited tables for a summer at a tourist restaurant downtown to save money. Something that happened at that restaurant quite often used to set my teeth on edge: tourists would ask me if there was a Starbucks nearby. Not a *coffeehouse*, of which Ashland had plenty, but a *Starbucks*. If I recommended a locally owned café, their hesitation was palpable. "But that place is strange and alien," their demeanor said. "I'd rather stick with the familiar." The reluctance to veer from routine was only natural, but weren't they here to do things they couldn't do at home? As I watched them walk off toward the Starbucks, it always struck me that they were missing out on something, and that the chain, by inundating the nation with stores, was partially responsible for making their lives that much blander.

This is where my uneasiness with Starbucks began. By the time I saw the town's third outlet on a visit home years later, my apprehension was firm. I mean, there weren't three of *anything* in Ashland — not even *two* of anything. Uniqueness was supposed to be the community's strong suit, yet here were three troublingly identical corporate coffeehouses. For a while, I had to wonder if I was just uncomfortable with change in my hometown, if I somewhat irrationally wanted everything to stay just as it was when I was seventeen. What, exactly, are those stores hurting? It's tough to put a finger on it. Many Ashlanders obviously want them, or they wouldn't flock there in such numbers. And the Starbucks stores haven't put any mom-and-pop coffeehouses out of business; amazingly, the local cafés are all still there, almost scientifically preserved. So what's the harm in having a few indistinguishable Starbucks stores? The chain's viral growth couldn't possibly be a sign of the "end of the universe," as the comic Lewis Black says, only half jokingly. It's just a coffee company, right?

But still, the unease about these three stores lingered, and I could never quite express why until I came across a passage by the French anthropologist Claude Lévi-Strauss. In his 1955 book *Tristes Tropiques*, a memoir of his fieldwork in South America, Lévi-Strauss reflects on the differences between societies that have industrialized and those that have retained their old traditions. Specifically, he's interested in rum;

puzzlingly, the more modern and efficient a culture is, Lévi-Strauss says, the worse its rum tastes. When the liquor comes from factories packed with gleaming, uniform steel tanks, the result is undrinkable, yet rum stored in "ancient vats thickly encrusted with waste matter" comes out "mellow and scented" — much better, despite its "archaic method of production." In this comparison, Lévi-Strauss sees what he calls the "paradox of civilization": "Its charms are due essentially to the various residues it carries along with it." That is to say, the things we like about society are most often the things that modernization eliminates; despite their virtues, efficiency and standardization have produced a worse-tasting rum. Taking this a step further, Lévi-Strauss concludes that since the prevailing trend of today's civilizations is toward streamlined corporations and homogeneity, then "Social life consists in destroying that which gives it its savor." By embracing modernity and sameness at the expense of cultural integrity, we strip the richness and zest from our own lives.

Starbucks diminishes the world's diversity every time it builds a new café, and I can't help but feel troubled by this. For me, Ashland's three Starbucks stores — so plainly reminiscent of their thirteen thousand clones around the world — take something irreplaceable away from the character of the community. Fundamentally, the town's distinctive culture is all it has; this is equally true of well-loved neighborhoods from Seattle to London to Beijing. The company, by its very nature, endangers cultural uniqueness, and this is why I am not a Starbucks customer.

But if I'm stuck at an airport, well . . .

ACKNOWLEDGMENTS

In a sense, this book is the product of a dumb joke. One autumn evening a few years back, as I was sitting with friends outside a neighborhood café in Northwest Portland, our conversation turned to the incredible profusion of coffeehouses in that area of the city; just from where we sat, a Tully's and — of course — a Starbucks were visible on the same tree-lined block. From out of nowhere, I found myself wondering out loud how far one could possibly get from the nearest Starbucks store while still staying within the city limits. I pledged to find the answer. My friends, showing naive but touching faith in my sanity, thought I was kidding and laughed accordingly.

When I suggested to my editor at *Willamette Week* — the alt-weekly paper where I was a staff writer — that this investigation could yield an entertaining news story, he laughed too. Then he changed the subject. But I was persistent (by which I mean "extraordinarily annoying"), and soon I was conducting highly scientific research into Starbucks's local saturation. My tools were pushpins and a large city map; I used the pins to indicate on the map where there were Starbucks stores and then found the spot in the city that looked farthest away from one. To my surprise, the resulting article failed to electrify Portland as much as I'd hoped. But, undaunted, I later prevailed on my editors to let me write a cover story examining whether Starbucks was as awful as its detractors claimed. (My entreaties got a boost from the fact that someone

Acknowledgments

had just tried to set a new local Starbucks on fire; see page 148.) For whatever reason, I kept thinking there was something inherently interesting and culturally relevant about the whole coffee phenomenon and the ubiquitous, consumer-friendly business megahit at its center. The feature I wrote attracted enough interest — both in Portland and elsewhere — that I decided to try to expand the story into the book you now hold in your hands. (Or maybe it's in your lap; I don't know how you prefer to read.)

This endeavor would have gone down in flames more or less immediately without the help of a number of incredible people — first and foremost my literary agent, Melissa Flashman, who patiently walked me through the whole bookmaking process and who is, as far as I'm concerned, a living saint. I feel preposterously lucky to have ended up with an agent as spectacular as Mel.

My editor, Liz Nagle, was hugely helpful and a fantastic champion of this book, for which I'll always be grateful. Whenever I would call in some state of anguish or panic, Liz's advice was invaluable. Also at Little, Brown, I'd like to thank Geoff Shandler, Marie Salter, Jason Bartholomew, and Heather Fain.

A number of friends commented on early drafts of the book and offered very useful counsel, without which I may have quite literally gone crazy. Thank you to Wilson Vediner, Zach Dundas, Nigel Jaquiss, Carissa Wodehouse, Francesca Monga, and Anne Adams.

In no particular order, I also want to thank Sarah and Jonny Betts, for putting me up ever so kindly in London; Alex Morris; Mark Zusman; John Schrag; Gary Mailman; Michael Rubenstein; Michael Pilon, for the map work; Julie Beals; Chris Lydgate; Rewrite; Ashley Shelby, for planting the book proposal seed in my mind; Elsbeth Allanketner, for a lot of free coffee; Jenny Lee; Janette Fletcher; Christy Salcido at Starbucks; *In These Times*, the magazine wherein I first encountered the word *Starbucked*; Don Schoenholt, Jake Batsell, Dawn Pinaud, and Harry Roberts, who were especially helpful in my reporting; and the barista staffs at Crema, Fresh Pot, Stumptown, Blend, and

Acknowledgments

Sound Grounds — the great Portland coffeehouses where much of the writing of this book was done.

Finally, my most heartfelt appreciation goes out to my mom, my dad, Gina, Lauren, and Laurel — the most loving and supportive family a guy could ever hope to have.

NOTES

In addition to my firsthand reporting and the interviews I conducted with more than a hundred sources, this book is the product of countless hours of research into the work of other writers. I would love to be able to list my source for every fact in this book, but space constraints prevent this. Hence, I've confined these notes to resources I found particularly helpful, leaned on particularly hard, or quoted from directly. In the text, I've done my best to cite sources for as many important facts and statistics as I could without disrupting the story. Unless otherwise noted, all quotations come from my interviews with the speaker.

Introduction: The Experiment

Page 4.

My account of the Robson Street story comes primarily from my interviews with the sources involved, but also Brad Stone, "Grande Plans," *Newsweek*, December 27, 2004; and Ian Edwards, "Marketing in Vancouver: Starbucks the Star of the Coffee Craze," *Strategy*, May 15, 1995.

Page 6.

The Lewis Black quotation is from his book *Nothing's Sacred* (New York: Simon Spotlight Entertainment, 2005).

Page 7.

Two useful sources for my discussion of caffeine seeping into bodies of water were Tom Mashberg, "Starbucks for Starfish: Harbor Waters Yield Caffeine," *Boston Herald*, May 30, 1998; and Chris Bowman, "Medicines, Chemicals Taint Water: Contaminants Pass Through Sewage Plants," *Sacramento Bee*, March 28, 2000.

Page 8.

Ashley Fantz, "Church's Coffee Campaign Is Stirring Up New Interest," *Miami Herald*, April 17, 2006.

Page 9.

The Orin Smith quotation is from Cora Daniels, "Mr. Coffee: The Man Behind the $4.75 Frappuccino Makes the 500," *Fortune*, April 14, 2003.

Most of the general specialty coffeehouse statistics I've used in this book come from three institutional sources: the Specialty Coffee Association of America (http://www.scaa.org), the International Coffee Organization (http://www.ico.org), and the international market research firm Mintel (http://www.mintel.com).

Page 10.

The Laurier and Philo report can be found at http://web.ges.gla.ac.uk/ ~elaurier/cafesite/index1.html.

Page 12, footnote.

Karen Palmer and Peter Edwards, "Man Who Had Penis Pinched 'Embarrassed,'" *Toronto Star*, December 1, 1999.

PART ONE: THE RISE OF THE MERMAID
Chapter 1: Life Before Lattes

Page 17.

For the story of Samuel Cate Prescott, I relied primarily on two sources: Larry Owens, "Engineering the Perfect Cup of Coffee," *Technology and Culture*, October 2004; and Maurice Holland, "A $30,000 Cup of Coffee," in *Industrial Explorers* (New York: Harper & Brothers, 1928).

Page 20.

I drew the John Adams quotation from Antony Wild, *Coffee: A Dark History* (New York: W.W. Norton, 2005). The Daniel Webster quotation is in Minna Morse and Regis Lefebure, "Across the Country, It's All Happening at the Coffeehouse," *Smithsonian*, September 1996. And the Abigail Adams quotation comes from William H. Ukers, *All About Coffee* (New York: The Tea and Coffee Trade Journal Company, 1935).

Page 21.

The information for my whirlwind tour of coffee history comes from the dozens of useful books that have been published on the topic, among them: Stewart Lee Allen, *The Devil's Cup: A History of the World According to Coffee* (New York: Ballantine Books, 1999); Mark Pendergrast, *Uncommon Grounds: The History of Coffee and How It Transformed Our World* (New York: Basic Books, 1999); Ukers, *All About Coffee*; Bennett Alan Weinberg and Bonnie K.

Bealer, *The World of Caffeine: The Science and Culture of the World's Most Popular Drug* (New York: Routledge, 2002); Tom Standage, *A History of the World in 6 Glasses* (New York: Walker & Co., 2005); Wolfgang Schivelbusch, *Tastes of Paradise: A Social History of Spices, Stimulants, and Intoxicants* (New York: Pantheon, 1992); Roger Schmidt, "Caffeine and the Coming of the Enlightenment," *Raritan*, Summer 2003; and Wild, *Coffee: A Dark History.*
Page 22.
   The Muhammad quotation comes from Pendergrast, *Uncommon Grounds.*
Page 25.
   The beer soup recipe is from Schivelbusch, *Tastes of Paradise.*
   I drew the Frederick the Great quotation from Ukers, *All About Coffee.*
Page 26.
   I got the Balzac quotation, which originally appeared in his 1839 "Treatise on Modern Stimulants," from Weinberg and Bealer, *The World of Caffeine.*
Page 30.
   The *Consumers' Research Bulletin* quotation can be found in Pendergrast, *Uncommon Grounds.*
Page 32.
   On the beginnings of specialty coffee and Starbucks, see Howard Schultz and Dori Jones Yang, *Pour Your Heart into It: How Starbucks Built a Company One Cup at a Time* (New York: Hyperion, 1997); and Pendergrast, *Uncommon Grounds.*
Page 39.
   The Gordon Bowker quotation originally appeared in Terry McDermott, "Cash Crop," *Seattle Times*, November 28, 1993.
Page 41, second footnote.
   At least one instance of Schultz claiming this occurred on the November 22, 1997, episode of CNN's *Larry King Live.*

Chapter 2: A Caffeinated Craze

Page 52.
   On Howard Schultz and the early days of Starbucks, see Howard Schultz and Dori Jones Yang, *Pour Your Heart into It: How Starbucks Built a Company One Cup at a Time* (New York: Hyperion, 1997); Hugo Kugiya, "Seattle's Coffee King," *Seattle Times*, December 15, 1996; Kathryn Robinson, "Bean Town: How Starbucks Created a Coffee-Crazy Seattle — and a Horde of Competitors," *Seattle Weekly*, August 2, 1989; Jennifer Reese, "The High Church of Starbucks," *Salon*, November 24, 1997; Oliver Burkeman, "Howard's Way,"

Guardian, October 20, 2000; Andrew Davidson, "The Man with Grounds for Global Success," *Sunday Times* (London), September 14, 2003; and "The Success of Starbucks Coffee," *Larry King Live* transcript, CNN, November 22, 1997.

Page 53.

Howard Schultz: Profile, BBC Four documentary, June 8, 2002.

Page 54.

Alex Witchel, "Coffee Talk With: Howard Schultz; By Way of Canarsie, One Large Hot Cup of Business Strategy," *New York Times*, December 14, 1994.

Page 58.

Nelson D. Schwartz, "Still Perking After All These Years," *Fortune*, May 24, 1999.

Page 61.

Schultz's 1986 quotation is in Rick Anderson, "Starbucks: Just Getting Started," *Seattle Weekly*, April 30, 2003.

Business Unusual transcript, CNN, May 23, 1998.

Page 67.

Robinson, "Bean Town."

Page 68.

Leah Harrison, "Starbucks' Caffeine Rush," *Seattle Times*, June 18, 1993.

Page 72.

Kathie Jenkins, "America's Best: Brews with Attitude," *Los Angeles Times*, November 1, 1990.

Page 73.

Zena Burns, "Celeb Assistants Tell All," *Teen People*, May 2005.

Hudson Morgan, "Any Grounds to the Ben/Jen Java Story?" *New York Daily News*, November 29, 2005.

Page 74.

My discussion of recent U.S. social trends and the changing American consumer owes much to Michael Silverstein and Neil Fiske, *Trading Up: The New American Luxury* (New York: Portfolio, 2003); John de Graaf, David Wann, and Thomas H. Naylor, *Affluenza: The All-Consuming Epidemic* (San Francisco: Berrett-Koehler, 2005); Robert D. Putnam, *Bowling Alone: The Collapse and Revival of American Community* (New York: Simon & Schuster, 2000); David Brooks, *Bobos in Paradise: The New Upper Class and How They Got There* (New York: Simon & Schuster, 2000); Juliet B. Schor, *The Overspent American: Why We Want What We Don't Need* (New York: HarperPerennial, 1998); and Ray Oldenburg, *The Great Good Place: Cafés, Coffee*

Shops, Bookstores, Bars, Hair Salons, and Other Hangouts at the Heart of a Community (New York: Marlowe, 1999).

Page 75.

The Staffan Linder information comes from de Graaf, Wann, and Naylor, *Affluenza: The All-Consuming Epidemic.*

Page 76.

Terry Lefton, "Schultz's Caffeinated Crusade," *Brandweek*, July 5, 1999.

Page 77.

My source for the oft-repeated Polgar quotation was Paul Hofmann, "Savoring the World, Cup by Cup," *New York Times*, January 29, 1995.

Page 78, footnote.

Robinson, "Bean Town."

Page 84.

Julia Sommerfeld, "Coffee Cool — The 'Other' Teen Drinking Scene," *Seattle Times*, October 26, 2003.

Steven Gray, "More Than Caffeine: For Southern Maryland, the First Starbucks Means Modern Suburbia," *Washington Post*, March 10, 2002.

Sylvia Wieland Nogaki, "Starbucks' New Splash," *Seattle Times*, May 18, 1992.

Chapter 3: The Siren's Song

Page 86.

The story of Hsing-Hsing the brand-loyal panda comes from Michael Kernan, "Animal Old Folks," *Smithsonian*, December 1999; and James V. Grimaldi, "Ill Panda Needs Starbucks," *Seattle Times*, July 22, 1999.

Page 88.

Michael J. McCarthy, "The Caffeine Count in Your Morning Fix," *Wall Street Journal*, April 13, 2004.

Page 89.

Mike Hofman, "Upstarts: Dry Cleaning," *Inc.*, January 2001.

Page 90.

For more on Starbucks's marketing and the story of the "Big Dig," see Scott Bedbury and Stephen Fenichell, *A New Brand World: 8 Principles for Achieving Brand Leadership in the 21st Century* (New York: Viking, 2002); and Kim Murphy, "More Than Coffee, a Way of Life," *Los Angeles Times*, September 22, 1996.

Page 92.

The story of Starbucks hypnotizing "hip young people" comes from Ruth

Shalit, "Hypnotizing Slackers for Starbucks, and Other Visionary Acts of Marketing Research," Salon.com, September 28, 1999.
Page 93.
Naomi Klein, *No Logo* (New York: Picador, 2002).
David Brooks, *Bobos in Paradise: The New Upper Class and How They Got There* (New York: Simon & Schuster, 2000).
Page 94.
Howard Schultz and Dori Jones Yang, *Pour Your Heart into It: How Starbucks Built a Company One Cup at a Time* (New York: Hyperion, 1997).
Page 96.
David Shields, "The Capitalist Communitarian," *New York Times Magazine*, March 24, 2002.
Page 97.
Oliver Burkeman, "Howard's Way," *Guardian*, October 20, 2000.
Page 98.
Dave Barry, "A Tall Order, Grammatically," *Miami Herald*, October 10, 2004.
Page 100.
On design at Starbucks, two particularly useful sources were Virginia Postrel, *The Substance of Style: How the Rise of Aesthetic Value Is Remaking Commerce, Culture, and Consciousness* (New York: HarperCollins, 2003); and Arthur Rubinfeld and Collins Hemingway, *Built for Growth: Expanding Your Business Around the Corner or Across the Globe* (Upper Saddle River, NJ: Wharton School Publishing, 2005).
Page 106.
On efficiency and changes to the Starbucks retail formula, see Paco Underhill, *Why We Buy: The Science of Shopping* (New York: Simon & Schuster, 1999); Steven Gray, "Coffee on the Double," *Wall Street Journal*, April 12, 2005; Christina Ianzito, "At the Coffee Shop, It's Always a Tall Order," *Washington Post*, August 7, 2002; and Paul J. Lim, "The Starbucks Challenge — Specialty-Coffee Maker Hopes New Products Won't Dilute Its High-Class Reputation," *Seattle Times*, June 19, 1995.

Chapter 4: Leviathan

Page 112.
Frederic Biddle, "Coffee Connection on the Defensive as Starbucks Comes to Town," *Boston Globe*, January 2, 1994.

Page 113.

The Bloomberg quotation comes from Gersh Kuntzman, "Subverting Starbucks," *Newsweek*, October 28, 2002.

Page 115.

The two exceedingly pessimistic pronouncements on Starbucks's future come from Joshua Levine, "The Java News," *Forbes*, May 22, 1995; and Margaret Webb Pressler, "Finding Grounds for a Consolidation," *Washington Post*, August 1, 1995.

Page 116.

For more on the Starbucks real estate strategy, see Arthur Rubinfeld and Collins Hemingway, *Built for Growth: Expanding Your Business Around the Corner or Across the Globe* (Upper Saddle River, NJ: Wharton School Publishing, 2005); and Dina ElBoghdady, "Pouring It In: The Starbucks Strategy? Locations, Locations, Locations," *Washington Post*, August 25, 2002.

Page 122.

Anne Krueger, "Residents Welcome Starbucks with Arms Wide Open," *San Diego Union-Tribune*, March 15, 2003.

Joel Achenbach, "One Tall Cappuccino Conundrum, To Go: At Starbucks, Jitters Precede the Caffeine," *Washington Post*, August 11, 2003.

Page 123.

For more information on Nancy McGuckin's gridlock-causing "Starbucks Effect," go to http://www.travelbehavior.us/the_starbucks_effect.htm.

Page 124.

On other coffee chains, see Monica Soto Ouchi, "Tully's Coffee: A Brand that Belies Its Size," *Seattle Times*, February 20, 2005; John Reinan, "Ready to Lock Horns: No. 2 Caribou Coffee Is Setting Its Sights on Market Leader Starbucks," *Minneapolis Star Tribune*, January 26, 2004; Mya Frazier, "Starbucks It Isn't — and Purposely So," *Advertising Age*, March 14, 2005; Eric A. Taub, "Rival Moving Beyond Roots Entwined with Starbucks," *New York Times*, June 4, 2005; Justin Doebele, "The Brew to Be No. 2," *Forbes Global*, May 12, 2003; Linda Tischler, "It's Not About the Doughnuts," *Fast Company*, December 2004; and Jean Halliday and Kate MacArthur, "BK, McD's Wake Up to Premium Coffee," *Advertising Age*, April 11, 2005.

Page 129.

Kim Murphy, "More Than Coffee, a Way of Life," *Los Angeles Times*, September 22, 1996.

Page 130.

Timothy Gower, "Starbucks Nation: A Caffeinated Juggernaut Gives Competitors the Jitters," *Seattle Weekly*, August 10, 1994.

Stanley Holmes, "Planet Starbucks," *Business Week*, September 9, 2002.

Nathan Cobb, "The Bean Stalk: Deal Leaves Coffee Mavens Uneasy," *Boston Globe*, March 31, 1994.

Page 134.

You can find the *Forbes* list of the four hundred richest Americans at http://www.forbes.com/lists/2006/54/biz_06rich400_The-400-Richest-Americans_land.html. As of September 2006, Howard Schultz was ranked 354th.

Page 135.

Percy Allen, "Schultz: Sonics May Leave Without Cash," *Seattle Times*, February 2, 2006.

Page 138.

Howard Schultz and Dori Jones Yang, *Pour Your Heart into It: How Starbucks Built a Company One Cup at a Time* (New York: Hyperion, 1997).

PART TWO: GETTING STEAMED
Chapter 5: Storm Brewing

Page 144.

In formulating my summary of charges against Starbucks, one source that helped shape my early thinking was Kim Fellner, "The Starbucks Paradox," *Colorlines*, Spring 2004.

Page 147.

Stanley Holmes, "Planet Starbucks," *Business Week*, September 9, 2002.

Page 148.

For more on the Hosford-Abernethy firebombing story, see Joseph Rose and Stephen Beaven, "Firebomb Hits New Starbucks," *Oregonian*, May 6, 2004.

Page 149.

Two useful books for understanding the opposition to large chains are Naomi Klein, *No Logo* (New York: Picador, 2002); and Stacy Mitchell, *Big-Box Swindle: The True Cost of Mega-Retailers and the Fight for America's Independent Business* (Boston: Beacon Press, 2006).

For a very thorough discussion of gentrification, see Maureen Kennedy and Paul Leonard, *Dealing with Neighborhood Change: A Primer on Gentrification and Policy Choices*, April 2001, which is available at the Brookings Institution Web site: http://www.brookings.edu.

Page 150.

J. K. Dineen, "Starbucks Sparks Battle in Japantown," *San Francisco Examiner*, May 17, 2005.

Page 150, footnote.

Patricia Sellers, "Starbucks: The Next Generation," *Fortune*, April 4, 2005.

Page 151.

Scott Bedbury and Stephen Fenichell, *A New Brand World: 8 Principles for Achieving Brand Leadership in the 21st Century* (New York: Viking, 2002).

Page 152.

The Civic Economics Andersonville study is available at http://www.andersonvillestudy.com.

Page 153.

Matt Viser, "Seeking Starbucks Status: Towns Line Up to Lure Company with Its Desirable Demographics," *Boston Globe*, July 15, 2004.

Tamara Lush, "Palm Beach Thinks Starbucks is a Café Without Any Cachet," *St. Petersburg Times*, October 1, 2006.

Page 154.

Louis Aguilar, "Hey, Starbucks: What's Wrong with Detroit?" *Detroit News*, May 16, 2006.

Page 155.

On small towns luring in Starbucks, see Viser, "Seeking Starbucks Status"; and "Developers Will Pay for Financial Boost, Prestige of Starbucks," Associated Press, March 31, 1999.

Page 158.

On Starbucks as predator, see Timothy Gower, "Starbucks Nation: A Caffeinated Juggernaut Gives Competitors the Jitters," *Seattle Weekly*, August 10, 1994; and the piece where I first saw the term that I've used as the title of this book (though it has also been used to great effect by Jeremy Dorosin, whose antichain Web site is http://www.starbucked.com), Nicole Nolan, "Starbucked!" *In These Times*, November 11, 1996.

Page 159.

Arthur Rubinfeld and Collins Hemingway, *Built for Growth: Expanding Your Business Around the Corner or Across the Globe* (Upper Saddle River, NJ: Wharton School Publishing, 2005).

Page 162.

John Simons, "A Case of the Shakes," *US News and World Report*, July 6, 1997.

For more on Starbucks not actually succeeding as a predator, see Kevin Helliker and Shirley Leung, "Despite Starbucks Jitters, Most Coffeehouses Thrive," *Wall Street Journal*, September 24, 2002; and David Schomer, "How to Compete with Starbucks," http://www.espressovivace.com/archives/lucidcafe/LC28.pdf, October 16, 2001.

Notes

Page 166.

Kim Roberts, "Surviving Starbucks," *Omaha World-Herald*, October 27, 2003.

Page 167.

Gower, "Starbucks Nation."

Chapter 6: A Fair Trade?

Page 170.

On the current coffee crisis, see Nicholas Stein and Doris Burke, "Crisis in a Coffee Cup," *Fortune*, December 9, 2002; Joshua Kurlantzick, "Coffee Snobs Unite!" *Washington Monthly*, July/August 2003; Peter Fritsch, "Bitter Brew: An Oversupply of Coffee Beans Deepens Latin America's Woes," *Wall Street Journal*, July 8, 2002; Roger Downey, "The $8 Latte," *Seattle Weekly*, March 27, 2002; and Jake Batsell's excellent three-part series on coffee farming conditions for the *Seattle Times*, which ran September 19–21, 2004.

Page 171.

Antony Wild, *Coffee: A Dark History* (New York: W.W. Norton, 2005).

Page 174.

My telling of the Gabriel de Clieu story is drawn from Bennett Alan Weinberg and Bonnie K. Bealer, *The World of Caffeine: The Science and Culture of the World's Most Popular Drug* (New York: Routledge, 2002); William H. Ukers, *All About Coffee* (New York: The Tea and Coffee Trade Journal Company, 1935); and Stewart Lee Allen, *The Devil's Cup: A History of the World According to Coffee* (New York: Ballantine Books, 1999).

Page 177.

Three useful sources for general information on coffee farming through history are William Gervase Clarence-Smith and Stephen Topik, eds., *The Global Coffee Economy in Africa, Asia, and Latin America, 1500–1989* (Cambridge: Cambridge University Press, 2003); John M. Talbot, *Grounds for Agreement: The Political Economy of the Coffee Commodity Chain* (Lanham, MD: Roman & Littlefield, 2004); and Terry McDermott, "Cash Crop," *Seattle Times*, November 28, 1993.

Page 178.

My source for the "Brazil is coffee, and coffee is the negro" quotation was Mark Pendergrast, *Uncommon Grounds: The History of Coffee and How It Transformed Our World* (New York: Basic Books, 1999).

Page 187.

For more on Fair Trade coffee, see Laure Waridel, *Coffee with Pleasure: Just Java and World Trade* (Montreal: Black Rose Books, 2002); Steve Stecklow and Erin White, "What Price Virtue?" *Wall Street Journal,* June 8, 2004; Jennifer Alsever, "Fair Prices for Farmers: Simple Idea, Complex Reality," *New York Times,* March 19, 2006; and Kerry Howley, "Absolution in Your Cup: The Real Meaning of Fair Trade Coffee," *Reason,* March 2006.

Page 189.

William McAlpin, "Coffee and the Socially Concerned," *World Coffee and Tea,* July 1994.

Page 195.

Mark D. Fefer, "A Hill of Beans?" *Seattle Weekly,* March 31, 1999.

Chapter 7: What's in Your Cup

Page 199.

The story of Gus Comstock comes from two unbylined *New York Times* stories: "Issues Coffee Challenge," January 7, 1927; and "Drinks 85 Cups of Coffee and Regains Championship," January 12, 1927.

Page 204.

For more on the science of coffee, see Andrea Illy and Rinantonio Viani, eds., *Espresso Coffee: The Science of Quality* (London: Elsevier Academic Press, 2005); "In Search of a Perfect Cup — Espresso Coffee," *Economist,* December 22, 2001; and Ernesto Illy, "The Complexity of Coffee," *Scientific American,* June 2002.

Page 212.

On general coffee quality, see Corby Kummer, *The Joy of Coffee: The Essential Guide to Buying, Brewing, and Enjoying* (Boston: Houghton Mifflin, 1997).

Page 213.

Beth Teitell, "Evil Empire: Starbucks' Cup Overflows with Attitude," *Boston Herald,* June 5, 1999.

Page 214.

Kerry J. Byrne, "Starbucks HQ the Place to Be If You Know Beans About Coffee," *Boston Herald,* April 27, 2005.

Page 216.

My discussion of caffeine and its health effects is particularly indebted to Stephen Braun, *Buzz: The Science and Lore of Alcohol and Caffeine* (New York: Oxford University Press, 1996); T. R. Reid, "Caffeine," *National Geographic,* January 2006; Richard Lovett, "Demon Drink," *New Scientist,* September 24, 2005; and Roland R. Griffiths and Laura M. Juliano, "Caffeine," in Joyce H. Lowinson, Pedro Ruiz, Robert B. Millman, John G. Langrod, eds., *Substance Abuse: A Comprehensive Textbook* (Baltimore: Lippincott Williams & Wilkins, 2005).

Page 217.

The provang information comes from Kenneth Davids, *Coffee: A Guide to Buying, Brewing, and Enjoying* (New York: St. Martin's Press, 2001).

More of Janet Jackson's beliefs on the treatment of depression can be found in Allison Samuels, "Rhythm and the Blues," *Newsweek*, November 17, 1997.

The full text of the London women's petition against coffee is at http://homepage.univie.ac.at/thomas.gloning/tx/wom-pet.htm.

Page 218.

For more on C. W. Post's entertaining war on coffee, see Mark Pendergrast, *Uncommon Grounds: The History of Coffee and How It Transformed Our World* (New York: Basic Books, 1999).

Page 219.

Lovett, "Demon Drink."

Page 219, footnote.

Learn more about the perfidy of decaf at http://news.bbc.co.uk/2/hi/health/4444908.stm.

Page 220.

For the entire University of Florida study, go to http://news.ufl.edu/2003/10/22/caffeinecontent/.

Reid, "Caffeine."

Page 222.

A great image of the various webs spun by NASA's drugged spiders can be found at http://www.newscientist.com/data/images/archive/1975/19750501.jpg.

Page 224.

The CSPI's pronouncement on the 770-calorie Frappuccino, along with nine other "foods you should never eat," is at http://www.cspinet.org/nah/10foodSept06.pdf.

Page 225.

For more on *Consumer* magazine's study of the nutritional value of coffeehouse fare, see Nicola Boyes, "Coffee Beats Big Mac in the Fat Stakes," *New Zealand Herald*, November 12, 2005.

Chapter 8: Green-Apron Army

Page 227.

The "We Built This Starbucks" story first appeared in David Schmader, "Last Days: The Week in Review," *Stranger*, March 3, 2005.

Page 228.

For more general information on working at Starbucks, see Jennifer Reese, "Starbucks: Inside the Coffee Cult," *Fortune*, December 9, 1996; Lynn Van Matre, "The Espresso Express," *Chicago Tribune*, January 24, 1994; and Gretchen Weber, "Preserving the Counter Culture," *Workforce Management*, February 2005.

Page 229.

One great source for details on the Starbucks unionization push is Anya Kamenetz, "Baristas of the World, Unite!" *New York*, May 30, 2005.

Page 233.

Tim Wendelboe, "Inside the Toolbox," *Barista*, April–May 2005.

Page 235.

Candace Heckman and David Fisher, "Starbucks Robbers Serve Up Coffee in Holdup," *Seattle Post-Intelligencer*, May 1, 2002.

Page 236.

The full "Starbucks Marketing Meeting Bingo" board can be found at http://brandautopsy.typepad.com/brandautopsy/2004/12/starbucks_marke .html. It's definitely worth a look.

Page 238.

Howard Schultz and Dori Jones Yang, *Pour Your Heart into It: How Starbucks Built a Company One Cup at a Time* (New York: Hyperion, 1997).

Page 240.

The information on the "Star Labor" scheduling program comes from Naomi Klein, *No Logo* (New York: Picador, 2002).

Page 241.

Kamenetz, "Baristas of the World, Unite!"

Page 242.

For a more thorough discussion of McJobs, see George Ritzer, *The Mc-Donaldization Thesis: Explorations and Extensions* (Thousand Oaks, CA: Sage Publications, 1998).

Douglas Coupland, *Generation X: Tales for an Accelerated Culture* (New York: St. Martin's Press, 1991).

Page 243.

Bruce Constantineau, "Last B.C. Starbucks Outlets Cut Ties to Union," *Vancouver Sun*, April 28, 2007.

Page 244.

Don McIntosh, "Union Label Rare at Starbucks," *Northwest Labor Press*, June 4, 2004.

Chapter 9: The Seattle Colonies

Page 249.

A good, though very academic primer on the issue of cultural imperialism is John Tomlinson, *Cultural Imperialism: A Critical Introduction* (Baltimore, MD: Johns Hopkins University Press, 1991).

Jeremy Tunstall, *The Media Are American* (New York: Columbia University Press, 1977).

Page 250.

For more on Starbucks's international expansion and the charges of cultural imperialism, see Jackson Kuhl, "Tempest in a Coffeepot," *Reason*, January 2003; and Stanley Holmes, "Planet Starbucks," *Business Week*, September 9, 2002.

Page 252.

On Starbucks Japan, see John Simmons, *My Sister's a Barista: How They Made Starbucks a Home Away from Home* (London: Cyan Books, 2005); David A. Kaplan, "Trouble Brewing," *Newsweek*, July 19, 1999; and Nicola Wasson, "Tokyo Savors New Starbucks," *USA Today*, August 9, 1996.

Paul Betts and John Thornhill, "Starbucks Steams into Italy," *Financial Times* (London), October 21, 2000. (The headline was a bit premature; despite a decade of speculation about it, Starbucks still hasn't opened a store in Italy.)

Page 253.

On Starbucks UK, see Deborah Ball, "Starbucks Lures Brits from Tea to Coffee," *Wall Street Journal*, October 20, 2005; John Arlidge, "War of the Coffee Kings," *Evening Standard*, January 14, 2005; Joanna Blythman, "Spilling the Beans," *Guardian*, August 4, 2001; and Sarah Robertson, "Starbucks Fights 'Arrogant' Jibes," *PR Week*, January 21, 2005.

Page 257.

On Starbucks China and the Forbidden City uproar, see Keith Bradsher, "Starbucks Aims to Alter China's Taste in Caffeine," *New York Times*, May 21, 2005; Janet Adamy, "Different Brew: Eyeing a Billion Coffee Drinkers, Starbucks Pours It On in China," *Wall Street Journal*, November 29, 2006; John Pomfret, "Tempest Brews Over Coffee Shop: U.S. Chain Stirs Ire in Beijing's Forbidden City," *Washington Post*, November 23, 2000; and Martin Fackler, "The Forbidden City Gets a Starbucks," Associated Press, November 28, 2000.

Page 259.

Oliver Burkeman, "Howard's Way," *Guardian*, October 20, 2000.

Page 260.

Mark D. Fefer, "Flappuccino: Arabs Boycott Starbucks," *Seattle Weekly*, June 26, 2002.

Daniel Gross's *Slate* piece, "Don't Buy American," can be found at http://www.slate.com/id/2112272/.

Page 261.

For a good look at the future of Starbucks, see Barbara Kiviat, "The Big Gulp at Starbucks," *Time*, December 10, 2006; Elizabeth M. Gillespie, "Customers in Driver's Seat at Starbucks," Associated Press, December 24, 2005; and Steven Gray, "Fill 'er Up — With Latte," *Wall Street Journal*, January 6, 2006.

Page 263.

Scott Pelley, "Howard Schultz: The Star of Starbucks," *60 Minutes*, CBS, April 23, 2006.

Page 264.

Gillespie, "Customers in Driver's Seat at Starbucks."

Page 265.

"Starbucks Wars," *Consumer Reports*, March 2007.

The full Schultz memo is at http://starbucksgossip.typepad.com/_/2007/02/starbucks_chair_2.html.

Epilogue: The Last Drop

Page 270.

Claude Lévi-Strauss, *Tristes Tropiques* (New York: Penguin, 1992).

INDEX

Index

ABOUT THE AUTHOR

Taylor Clark grew up in Ashland, Oregon, and attended Dartmouth College. After college, he began working for the Portland, Oregon, alt-weekly *Willamette Week* as a freelancer and then a news staff writer. Clark lives in Portland and his tastes in coffee run toward a good Ethiopian Yirgacheffe. This is his first book.